ELVIS MEMORIES

Also by Michael Freedland

Al Jolson (later and in the US, *Jolson*)
Irving Berlin (later, *Salute to Irving Berlin*)
James Cagney (in the US, *Cagney*)
Fred Astaire
Sophie: The Story of Sophie Tucker
Jerome Kern
Errol Flynn (in the US, *The Two Lives of Errol Flynn*)
Gregory Peck
Maurice Chevalier
Peter O'Toole
The Warner Brothers
So Let's Hear the Applause: The Story of the Jewish Entertainer
Katharine Hepburn
The Goldwyn Touch
The Secret Life of Danny Kaye
Dustin
Leonard Bernstein
Kenneth Williams
Sean Connery
André Previn
Music Man
Bob Hope
Bing Crosby
All The Way: A Biography of Frank Sinatra
Michael Caine
Doris Day
Some Like It Cool: The Charmed Life of Jack Lemmon
Liza with a 'Z': The Traumas and Triumphs of Liza Minnelli
Witch Hunt in Hollywood
The Men Who Made Hollywood
Judy Garland: The Other Side of the Rainbow

With Morecambe and Wise
There's No Answer To That

With Walter Scharf
Composed and Conducted by Walter Scharf

Memoirs
Confessions of a Serial Biographer

ELVIS MEMORIES

THE REAL PRESLEY - BY THOSE WHO KNEW HIM

MICHAEL FREEDLAND

The Robson Press

First published in Great Britain in 2013 by
The Robson Press (an imprint of Biteback Publishing Ltd)
Westminster Tower
3 Albert Embankment
London SE1 7SP
Copyright © Michael Freedland 2013

ISBN 978-1-84954-358-3

10 9 8 7 6 5 4 3 2 1

A CIP catalogue record for this book is available from the British Library.

Set in Sabon and Edition

Printed and bound in Great Britain by
CPI Group (UK) Ltd, Croydon CR0 4YY

In adored memory

My Sarala – you were lovely. Everybody said so.

CONTENTS

THE FRIENDS' STORY

Everyone knows Elvis. At least, that's what you might think. You don't need a surname. Yes, there's another popular and highly successful singer who adopted that name, which was very clever of him. But the Elvis who comes to mind – and this is a challenge not to be ignored – is the fellow with the long shiny black hair who appeared to sneer as he swivelled his white jumpsuit-clad hips and answered to the appellation Presley.

Yes, everyone knows Elvis. But this is a book about people who *really* knew Elvis. Men and women who knew him in poverty in Tupelo, Mississippi; who travelled with the Presley family to Memphis, in neighbouring Tennessee; the ones who saw his burgeoning success there and who stayed with him in the mansion home he called Graceland, and those who travelled with him to Hollywood and the place where he established his virtual fiefdom called Las Vegas. They were among the throng who also witnessed the power he had in the music business in Nashville. We go into the army with him to Germany, experience his peccadillos, watch with his intimates the food fetishes which many say killed him, and the relationships with women which others could testify kept him alive.

We note the man's generosity and his concerns. In many ways, this poor boy whose family were dismissed as white trash grew to be a true Southern gentleman.

That is the kind of book this is. It is not another conventional Elvis Presley biography. You won't read any reviews of films or records – in fact, it has been a struggle to avoid mentioning any of his movies and/or his songs, but I have tried. There came the obvious moments when I found it inevitable. You won't hear from any big stars either. This is a book about Elvis and his friends, as told by his friends. The ones who really knew Elvis.

We'll meet the hairdresser who changed his life, the girls who fell in love with him, the nurse who set up home in Graceland because that was how he wanted it – in case he had a heart attack or cut his little finger. He gave her a car to make travelling to and from her own home a little easier. There's the black maid who created the infamous hamburgers, the peanut butter sandwiches – and who saw how the girls were lined up night after night to suit the master's pleasure. He gave her a car, too.

Then there are the guys who shared the same apartment block where Elvis lived as a teenager and went on raves with him, the 'coloured' boy – the term used by the more polite white folks from the other side of the Memphis tracks – who went to the movies with him, sneaking past the race laws as he did the black-only barriers; and also the man in the shop that was probably more essential to the Elvis Presley story than any other institution – because it was there that he was bought his first guitar. And talking of shops, I won't be forgetting the one the young – the very young – Elvis used to stand outside, his nose pressed against the window until he was invited to come in and buy his first stage outfit – on what they called in those parts the instalment plan. There, today, more than half a century later, the big speciality is their own version of a pair of blue suede shoes. (See what has happened? Hardly past the first page and I've already given you a Presley song title.)

This all started on a BBC Radio Two series called *The Elvis Trail*. What you will 'hear' in this book are so many of the things that could never be included in a five-part, thirty-minute (complete with music) radio programme.

So, conventional biography or not, this is the real Elvis story. It is about the real man; neither the one that the publicity machine – and what the infamous (and phoney) 'Colonel' Parker dreamed up – nor the kiss and tell stories that have appeared since his death all those years ago.

THE BIRTHPLACE

The signs are everywhere – to 'Elvis's birthplace' they declare. Well, yes and no. The house is the one in which he was born. The church is the one in which he prayed and where he sang his first gospel songs. But they are not where they were originally, on the wrong side of the railroad tracks. Brick by brick, log by log they have been moved to either end of a landscaped grassy mound. Appropriately, the two buildings – if that is not glorifying a shack and a chapel whose structures were originally put up by local artisans who knew a hammer and shovel much better than any architect's blueprint – have been arranged alongside the statue of a local boy made good. The house itself (and its painfully primitive furniture) was built in 1934, just before the star's birth, by Elvis's father Vernon and 'daddy's' (remember, this is the Deep South we are talking about, where they use the term well beyond childhood) brother Vester working with their own father, Jesse Presley.

It's all appropriate because without the blessing of that local boy in working man's dungarees, the one with the tousled hair and the guitar that he first saw on a rack in the nearby hardware store, Tupelo would be just another Mississippi town,

its 45,000-strong population like any other from that part of
the world, driving down Main Street, seeing rail tracks that
have both good and bad sides, overhead power cables, some
greenery and lots of Confederate flags flying around the place.
For this is as deep as the Deep South gets. As much part of
the fabric as a dish of grits and gravy. The accents, the words
they speak, betray the origins of the few septuagenarians who
really do remember the Presley family and their boy Elvis.

The people of Tupelo claim him as their own. Susie Dent,
who goes around Tupelo stressing the work of the North
East Mississippi Historical and Genealogical Society – with
great effect, it has to be said – plainly needs to stress the Elvis
Connection whenever she can. She emphasises that not only
was Tupelo influenced by him, but he was influenced by Tupelo.

As she said: 'He had a Christian upbringing. The old-style
fundamentalist churches had loads of music and he got a lot
of soul from that music. He went from rags to riches, but a lot of
people thought his magic would rub off on them.' But did it?
'He was pretty good at giving away his wealth.' We shall see
that as the story moves on. And then, said Susie, 'his musical
riches stayed around.'

What becomes clear is that it took a long time for Tupelo
really to appreciate him. 'When I first came here in 1970,' Susie
said, 'most people had never even been to his birthplace, but
now with the influx of people from all over the world, people
have more respect for him.'

So there is more to this place than those locals. The signs are
the big giveaway. For this is, above all, a place of pilgrimage
and, in truth, many of the pilgrims make this a combination
of Graceland and Lourdes – in the belief that Elvis couldn't

possibly have died without leaving behind some mystical powers. They think and possibly really do believe that they know more about the young Presley to whom they owe so much than those who can actually recall the time when he carried a few poor quality groceries home for his mother, Gladys, in what they describe, round and about, as his 'wagon' – in effect, a combination of wooden box and old pram wheels.

The day I was there, a couple, Sheri and Lois Hathaway had travelled 500 miles to pay their annual visit to the 'house', two tiny rooms in which the young Elvis, his mother Gladys and his father, newly released from jail, slept and a living room-cum-kitchen and – somewhat grandly, I thought – 'laundry room', where they did everything else.

Was this perhaps really some religious rite for the visitors? 'Well,' said Sheri, 'it makes you feel closer to Elvis Presley. It started for us when we became fans forty years ago.'

Tupelo is the sort of place where people tend to know everyone else's business. There are those who knew the Presley story before he became famous, and no one more so than the local genealogists, like Julien Riley. He told me how the family stemmed from both Scottish and Native American roots. But, although as this story moves on you will hear people who make statements to the contrary, suggestions that he had Jewish blood are denied by this source at least.

'There's not a sliver of evidence of that. It's just a myth.' A myth perpetuated by the fact that he sometimes wore a Star of David around his neck – along with his famous 'Taking Care of Business' badge.

Riley is convinced that the family came from Itawamba County, whose Native American name accounts for the

ancestry of which he was always proud. A certain Dunnan
Presley, who was born in Tennessee and had been a soldier
in the Texas Revolution against the Mexicans – which included
the famous Battle of the Alamo of 1836, the history of which
makes no mention of an Elvis ancestor – was a bigamist and
perhaps even a 'trigamist'. He married Martha Jane Wesson,
who had two daughters, Rosella and Rosalinda – two young
ladies who never married but had thirteen children between
them (showing perhaps a proclivity for one of the joys of life
taken up with alacrity by their descendant), all with different
surnames, but who eventually took the name Presley – which
Riley says proves Elvis was not a Presley after all. In fact, he
told me, he should have been known as Elvis Wallace, the true
name of his great-grandfather, John, who was a Scottish fiddle
player. 'Had his great-grandmother married, there wouldn't
have been any Presleys at all.'

I wondered if the emotional impact of Elvis's death on
16 August 1977 was as traumatic for the Hathaways as it
was for seemingly millions of others. Did Sheri, for instance,
cry when he died? 'Oh yes,' she said. She didn't have to say
anything else. Like those other pilgrims, she knew, almost
literally, every movement of Elvis's life. Me, I couldn't imagine
there was anything more to find out. But no. The journey had
only just started.

'We see all the museums,' Sheri said. In fact, there was one
just the other side of what is now very much a public park
– perhaps the fact that they had the pink Cadillac that once
belonged to the man people like to call 'the King' had something to do with it. Actually, the town and the people who have
taken it upon themselves to preserve the Elvis legacy didn't

like the idea of this place cashing in on what they consider to be their own bailiwick and, before long, it closed.

But while it was there, the museum formed part of the pilgrimage for a couple who stay five days and never fail to visit the place they and everyone else calls 'the mansion', but which the rest of the world knows as Graceland. It's a sort of refresher course for two people who wouldn't dream of letting a day pass without listening to some Elvis song or other. 'We are always listening to Sirius Radio', a station which special-ises in the King's music.

And at the end of their five-day stay, they take on a job for themselves. As Lois told me: 'As soon as we leave, we plan our trip for next year.'

It's a familiar story for the custodian of the birthplace, Dick Guyton, a man who could claim to know more about Elvis and his early days than anyone else. It is as if he himself had sat in a classroom and heard the kid who, in fact, lived a mile or so away, singing his favourite Southern ditty, 'Old Shep', all about the love of a boy for his dog – 'When I was a lad and Old Shep was a pup, over hills and meadows we'd stray ...'

Certainly, he knows the visitors. 'We had people here from twenty-one countries this year,' he told me. 'There was a lady from the UK who came here and kissed the floor.' But not all the people who come to what is officially known as 'the Birthplace' are dyed-in-the-wool fans. 'No,' said Guyton 'some are just interested.' Which is, perhaps, an understatement.

Plainly, it isn't just the Elvis legacy that benefits from all this attention. Economically, it has great impact on Tupelo. Seventy-five thousand people visit annually. But more than that, there is the honour of saying the king of rock'n'roll was

born here, where he learnt about the music of the time. You
can't live here and not know about Elvis Presley. Or know
about his impact on local religious life.

'You are welcome' reads a sign outside the white clapboard
First Assembly of God church. And it's a good bet, to use a
probably inappropriate term, that you'd find more than one
person inside the extraordinarily rudimentary building willing to talk about Master Presley. Willing? They *rush* to talk
about him, the pride in their relationship fairly bursting out of
their pores. And relationships there were aplenty. Real blood
relationships.

Like Sybil Presley, his second cousin (or perhaps that should
be, for the more pedantic among us, first cousin, once removed;
to remove any doubt, it's enough to say that their paternal
grandfathers were brothers). We had first met on the porch
outside the birthplace house. I asked Sybil what the name
Presley meant in those parts. She dismissed any suggestion of
either trading on the name or, even if it had meant anything,
of anyone giving any favours. 'We're just simple country folk,'
she insisted. I liked that.

I asked about memories. 'Oh, Elvis was shy, kind and
generous.' But they didn't stay close. 'We were a close-knit
family, but the money separated us. Then the drugs, the fame,
the fortune.'

It's well known that the most important person in the world
for Elvis Presley was his mother. But the fame and fortune threat-
ened to cause trouble for Gladys, too. As Sybil remembered:
'My most vivid memory is of Gladys coming back here after
Elvis got famous ... Gladys crying, wanting to be back in Tupelo.
Graceland was an isolation for her.' If you took Sybil's word for

it, you could come to the conclusion that, all those years later, Graceland was to be an isolation for Elvis himself, too.

'He had an old brown Dodge and Elvis used to sneak back. Then one day [Tupelo] girls started screaming for him, so he couldn't come so often.'

She puts the blame for his leaving his roots down to the ubiquitous Col. Parker, Elvis's manager and some would say the evil spirit in his life. 'We don't have a good opinion of "Colonel" Parker,' she told me. 'He fed Elvis Presley drugs, overworked him.' That made me wonder – how could a strong person like Elvis, a man to whom no one ever said no, allow that to happen? 'I never saw Elvis as a strong person. He was nurturing, reaching out; the strong personality at the end was not him normally. True, he came alive on stage. Wasn't he gorgeous? Some people say he was the perfect man.' And Sybil demonstrated that fact by saying, that to her mind, his loyalty to Tupelo said it all.

'He got offended at people misusing funds. [When he came back to Tupelo] in 1956 and 1957 at the fairs, he used the funds to buy all this back – the swimming pool, ball park, a youth centre.' But things didn't always go his way. 'He wanted to have a guitar-shaped swimming pool built here, but the funds were misappropriated.'

Those were amazing days all the same – and everyone who was around at the time, or who had even a vicarious interest in it or, let it be said, liked to convince people that he or she was there, no matter whether they were or not, had their own story to tell. Not least Robert Norris, the policeman detailed to supervise the event and who ended up dragging kids off the stage.

'They brought him to the fairground at ten o'clock that morning with wailing sirens. The kids stormed his Cadillac and there was no show that morning. So they brought him back at 2 p.m. and we had to come back that night.'

Norris was twenty-four years old at the time. 'My chief was in his fifties and didn't know what sort of crowd Elvis Presley would attract and I tried to tell him. I told him we needed a fire hose, but he said we didn't need that.' He seems to have anticipated the situation early on. 'I was on the night shift and the phone rang at eleven and we were told we were needed at 1 a.m. sharp at the fairground.'

He was one of fourteen policemen on site. The youngsters spent the night waiting for the local lad who was by now established as their idol. The noise that greeted those cops was overwhelming. 'I've never heard such screaming. They crowded in there. When it came to the afternoon show, it became clear that fourteen policemen were not going to be enough. So Governor J. R. Coleman got in the National Guard.' That alone was an indication of precisely how difficult the task was going to be. So difficult that the Guard, used to quelling political demonstrations and race riots, couldn't stop Julie Hopper who, the then young cop maintains, was shoved to such an extent that she ended up on the stage, an event that hit the national headlines as much as the National Guard did.

'She didn't even touch him.' Elvis spoke to her, however. But it was one of those intimate whispers he loved to have with pretty girls and Norris maintains nobody heard what it was he did say.

Elvis was already a local fixture – as much with the local policemen as any of Tupelo's farm workers. Robert Norris was wearing overalls when we met – just like Elvis did in those old pictures and sculptures. But, as I put to him, Presley would have been even happier swapping with the local cop. He would have dearly loved to wear a police uniform. 'He was obsessed with the police,' he told me. Why? 'I don't really know. He had a thing about policemen and he was made an honorary deputy.' But that was in years ahead.

Yet even then, in his early twenties, Elvis had a reputation for generosity. 'But Presley people are proud people. They wouldn't accept handouts.'

All that is jumping a few years.

The First Assembly of God church glorifies the boy Elvis. Or at least the one he was reputed to be. But what comes so clear is that those old-timers who knew the boy Presley saw the man to be in the kid in the dungarees. Sure, there could be an element of 20/20 hindsight, yet the stories read true – all have an element of being able to place the big star in the life of a tiny Mississippi town all those years ago. They are all as redolent of the age as Elvis was himself. Like his own, their names speak of the Old South. None more so than the delightfully named Azalia Smith Moore, a psychologist who proudly talks about growing up with Elvis.

Azalia also remembers him, as do most Tupelo residents of a certain age, as a kind, warm youngster. However, unlike Sybil Presley she remembers his generosity to people who don't appear to have been in his inner circle. As she told me, he was famous round and about for giving gifts to local people.

I found it fascinating that people who were aggressive to him as classmates were more recipients than those who were in his cadre of buddies. He didn't try to buy them off, but I think there was a sort of – like the biblical [passage] – 'Be kind to those who despitefully use you ...' We grew up with a respect for seniors, administrators, our preachers, then our teachers, our parents, the neighbourhood parents. And what I think happened to Elvis is that he was psychologically manoeuvred into that kind of a dependency syndrome with 'Colonel' Parker and other people who were in his control system. He would have said, 'Yes, sir, thank you.' That was the way we were brought up.

As for Azalia herself: 'We stayed friends whilst we were growing up. My family is distantly related to Elvis Presley's. We were a gang. We played together. We swapped comic books.'

But even then his reading habits went beyond the books filled with primitive drawings and conversations recorded in bubbles.

Azalia remembers the times when even the less than modest 'birthplace' was too expensive to keep up. 'Vernon was in the penitentiary, so Gladys lived in little similar shacks. One of them was in one of my dad's houses. He owned two rental houses – this prevented homelessness and brought in income. They were just tiny houses.'

They were always going to have problems, Gladys and Vernon. She because keeping a house together and looking after her only child – Elvis, of course, was one of twins: his brother died at birth, but would always be remembered as a long-lost, loved relative – he because of his brushes with the law.

Vernon had trouble. He was later a lovable old fellow, as was his brother Vester. Their father Jesse was not. But Vernon was. He was a playboy. He got into trouble because he was not responsible with money. When the wolf is at the door, the owner may be forced to do things he might not otherwise do. He was never abusive. He had a twinkle in his eye and there was a lot of devotion to each other. The destruction of their relationship occurred when he took charge of the household.

Plainly, the love and in many ways domination of her son by Gladys in his early years has had psychologists like Azalia pondering so much about them. Was Gladys, I asked her, a stage mother in all that that name applied?

I'll give you a two-level answer. Gladys wanted him to have every opportunity. She kept him in school when others picked cotton. She provided the best clothes she could afford. She was made into a stage mother as he became a protégé of Parker. She wept every time she came back here. She didn't hunger for the lavish world she lived in at Graceland.

Ms Smith Moore sees the troubles of Elvis's early home life as the root of what would eventually kill him. 'Vernon's departure for the penitentiary came at the worst time. Separation, anxiety ...' Both were difficult for a child and his mother. 'The need to provide better things for his mother is a need we'd all share. We were highly maternal in our closeness in the family. [If] the father was away, the mother became a central force. Gladys needed to belong, but she didn't get that at Graceland.'
    Elvis undoubtedly comes out of it all as the hero for the

people of Tupelo. And there is no getting away from those sad parts of the story. What's more, there was always more to come. 'Elvis and Gladys were put out of the house, because they couldn't keep up the payments.' Round those parts, those properties were known as 'shotgun houses'.

Her memories of her school friend are kinder. 'He was sweet, kind, bashful. He started in the first grade, then he left the town in the second grade because his dad moved for a naval job. Then he returned and stayed until the fifth grade.'

At the church I met the man who was responsible for refurbishing the building and putting on a 'Cinerama'-style film show – one recalling the boy Elvis leading the service, guitar in hand, voice ready for his favourite gospel songs. Guy Thomas Harris says that Elvis called him his 'little brother'. He proudly showed me the pictures of his pal along with a group of other young citizens from seventy years before. As if there were proof needed of what small-town American life was like, Harris reels off the names of the other kids in the photo. 'There's James Farrell, Laverne, Bobby Spencer and Odell Clarke.' He is sure that if Elvis were around today, he'd remember the gang, too.

They played with everyone of their own age. The highway divided the town as much as did the railroad tracks – the poor and the almost but not quite so poor. It was difficult to know which was which. As Harris said: 'Well, we were all poor. You'd have a hard job trying to raise $100. Those who had a job didn't actually make money. They were all trying to raise money to buy a house. Most people raised [just enough] for all that they could eat.'

It was a town of broken dreams – and broken marriages. 'There was a time when Vernon wasn't there and Elvis [in effect] was the victim of a broken marriage, as was I. I was raised by my mother and my aunt ... two mothers ...'

Some in Tupelo think that the one-parent family made the children independent. No one can be sure it made Elvis that. In fact, most of the evidence is that he was very much a mommy's boy. But Harris says that he was one of the boys who bonded with each other.

> It was because all our parents worked, so we had to be with each other. We were in our own little world. We were wishful shoppers in the hardware store. We were like one big family. If we didn't have cornmeal we'd go from one house to another to get it. We were close-knit.

The games Elvis played with those close-knit friends were unconventional – and cheap.

'We played, when we were eleven, telephone men, stringing telephone wire from one house to another – until a woman told us off.'

Such was fun in the Tupelo of the 1940s. 'The closeness of the association imprints good happy memories,' Azalia maintained to me.

Tupelo wasn't quite the place that other books have made it. As Azalia said:

> We call this 'country', but it's farm country, hill country and there's a difference. The bottom land is where the cotton and corn are grown. But here [in Elvis country, where we were talking] is red-clay hills. We rode up and down them, playing hide and seek, and swinging on ropes. But it's not rural America.

Our parents had come from really agrarian backgrounds in Alabama.

And that reflected in Gladys's life, for sure. It certainly reflected in the food she cooked on her old black stove. The stories of her menus are repeated time and time again. 'I can imagine Gladys's routine,' said Azalia. 'We lived on collard greens, polk salad. She was known as Miss Gladys.'

They need no help in placing where Elvis was part of their lives. Said Guy Thomas Harris: 'The last seat that Elvis sat in this school was right there. A friend called Hoyt Richie and his brother Bobby sat there first and then Elvis came in.' All that, Azalia believes, confirms to her that 'attention to detail' is a contributory factor to those happy memories.

Tupelo has had Elvis Presley associations all Harris's life. It was, he said, because

> my ma and Gladys were best friends and I was born three and a half years later than Elvis and Ma said we grew up together. I was like the little brother he didn't have. We played together daily in the creek, in the woods. We had pickled polk salads [together]. We picked up scrap iron to sell. All the kids in East Tupelo were close.

And – this appears to be common among Presley friends of the era – they stayed friends for years, if not close forever. 'In 1970, Elvis Presley and Priscilla came to visit. In the 1950s, my brother and I stayed at Graceland a lot.' But it was not to last. 'It ended in 1958 when I got married. He had other friends.'

There was another crowd at another school, the Milam Elementary School, who could remember the ever so young

Elvis. Jimmy Gault was there when I called, playing his mouth organ. He recalled being in Miss Miller's class with Elvis in the seventh grade, when they were about seven.

'He was a brilliant student in his own way. He was gifted in music. When he came back to Tupelo he was popular and stood out, a jolly person. A one-on-one person. A one-to-one person.'

'Not many people,' said Roy Turner, the town's historian,

realise that Tupelo was divided into two white communities. There was Tupelo proper and East Tupelo, where I grew up and so did Elvis. That was for the factory worker, the less educated, whereas Tupelo proper was for the professionals, teachers and doctors, store owners and so on, while the black community there has the same division between the community that was called 'The Hill' and the community that was called 'Across the Tracks'. It is interesting that both the [working-class] communities were called 'Across the Tracks'.

It was then that another name came into conversation, Shakerag – the black area of this race-divided town. But Shakerag was the term used only by the residents of Shakerag. It was disrespectful if outsiders referred to it as Shakerag.

Billy Welch lived close by Elvis, across the tracks in East Tupelo. Like the others, Welch has only pleasant memories of the young Elvis. 'He asked me to call him "Tex" sometimes', which could have given an impression of a youngster with big ideas of his own importance – or perhaps high hopes.

He was fun. One day, we decided to pick cotton to make some money. It was hard work and we made one dollar each. We had what we called a home room programme in the classroom. He'd play the guitar and we'd sing together. He played well, but we never thought he'd go as far as he would.

I asked James Ausborn, who also went to this school, if he really did think of Elvis Presley when he sat in this room and looked around him. 'Yes,' he said in that Deep Southern drawl so common in Tupelo. 'It brings back memories. We'd play football with a girl – he always liked to tackle her.' He didn't, however, go further in describing that incident. Elvis was happier about going with an unnamed black boy to listen to black music on Green Street. 'We loved it together. He brought his guitar and my brother Mississippi Slim helped him.'

There's more to come about Mississippi Slim, a name spoken with some respect by the country music fans in this part of the state. Ausborn remembers an Elvis who thought a lot about girls – which makes him pretty normal; unless, that is, he was tackling one in a football game.

> We talked a lot about girls. They seemed to be attracted to him, which was also a look into the future. We loved to read Enid Blyton books. He once said he had a parrot. I found that when I went to his home, it was a plaster of Paris parrot. He laughed.

One can almost think of a kind of sibling rivalry when talking to these veterans of the days when the name 'Elvis Presley' just meant a boy in overalls and a pal from the other side of the tracks.

It wasn't all roses for Elvis Presley while he was at that school. 'He got into a fight at school,' recalled Jimmy Gault, going back in time as though he were telling me about something that had happened on the very morning we were talking and they were both sitting in the same classroom, listening to the same teacher, pointing to the same blackboard. 'The teacher came in and took him and the other boy into the office. People outside heard the head asking who was going to go first?'

The words unuttered were that they were both going to get a good hiding – and what they also heard were a few cries from both boys.

But most of the fun took place outside the school. Jimmy Gault remembers:

I'd ride up to his house and I'd have my saxophone on my bike and I'd go to see him and stay Friday night. Elvis's dad had a grocery round and I went with him a few times, to a place below Verona, to a gas station. We took the groceries round the back and Elvis is here and he told me to get on to the tailgate. Vernon told me to pitch up a case of cabbages which he thought would go off if they hit the floor.

Such are the stories that make up memories.

Billy Welch had ideas for a business for them both. 'We thought we'd make money by picking plums. But we ate all the plums before we got round to selling them in the street.'

There were hidden talents in the Elvis household. Gault remembered staying with him in the shack. 'Gladys was a good cook. Also a ghost-story teller.' He was convinced it was that which led to one of them turning into a sleepwalker. To this day, he can't be sure if it was him or Elvis. Whoever it was, he himself didn't exactly sleepwalk into fortunes.

It was a good time, then – and resulted in prosperous times later on. Elvis wasn't the only success, Jimmy maintains. 'There were seven millionaires and a billionaire out of a class of 120.' Which is not bad going for the children who sometimes didn't have more than one shirt to their backs. Gault says that most of his contemporaries were 'regular factory workers on regular wages'. But he added: 'It was the businessmen who got the cash. Many made their successes, like Elvis, without their parents' help. One student became wealthy by setting up a shirt factory and then buying a furniture factory. Elvis and I weren't part of the wealthy clique. We were the lowriders.' He himself, he says, had 'one pair of shoes and two pairs of pants'. The people who knew Elvis at this time kept insisting to me that everyone was just the same, 'poor without knowing it'. It was echoed by so many of the people to whom I spoke on the trail, they could have rehearsed the line over and over again. Like Charlene Presley, Elvis's cousin, who, talking about the Presley family, put it like this: 'They were so poor, it was pathetic.'

Others depended for their work on such establishments as the Millam manufacturing company, the Daybright Company and a cottonseed mill – featured by *Life* magazine in a feature on Tupelo: 'They wanted to make it seem rural, so they put a cotton cart on the front page, but we were very forward thinking,' says Gault – and that was why they built a handsome new hospital in 1935, one which has since grown to be the pride of the town.

It they weren't all poor as children, the Great Depression shaved a lot of the comforts from many of their parents, a Depression which still had echoes when Elvis and his friends were at school. A great tornado in 1936 had only made things worse.

Billy Welch, son of a truck driver, became a psychiatrist. He is proud of his father to this day. So are the others. 'My mother was a nurse,' says Jimmy Gault. 'My father,' Jimmy Ausborn adds, 'worked in a sawmill. Then he was in a peddling truck, then a candy car, then a Standard Oil truck, then he worked in a grocery store.'

So was he, like the rest of Tupelo, proud of their local boy? By all accounts, they were like brothers. But, seeing what happened afterwards, did that also imply jealousy?

None of his real friends, if you believe them, were themselves jealous. As Guy Thomas Harris told me: 'If there was jealousy, I haven't seen it yet. I'm not saying they in Tupelo all like his music a hundred per cent, but he was one of the best gospel singers ever.'

'No,' said Billy Welch, making it sound very emphatic indeed. 'I recall no jealousy. We were all thrilled to death when he made it.'

And, surprisingly, there really doesn't seem to be any envy at all – so unlike, for instance, the story of the young Frank Sinatra, who was virtually disowned by his contemporaries at Hoboken, New Jersey. They thought Sinatra was arrogant. He thought the boys with whom he went to school, and later with whom he sang, had wide green stripes down their backs.

For all the way that Azalia and others believed they knew that the character of Presley didn't change, no one claims they had a foretaste of the Elvis who later dominated the world of entertainment. There was, says the now ageing Azalia, no inkling of his later talent. 'He sang a lot, but that was natural because we were all immersed in gospel music. Gospel music was the entertainment alongside some Grand Ole Opry kind of music. On Sundays, we would go from house to house and sing.'

And that led to talking about the most formative thing about his life in Tupelo, although no one realised it at the time. His guitar. 'He really wanted a wagon and he got that. But it got destroyed and the man who destroyed it paid him out and he used the money to go on something else. He wanted a rifle, but Mom wouldn't let him have that, so he had a guitar.'

The story was taken up at the Tupelo Hardware Store. There, an emporium stacked floor to ceiling with the sort of things people in small towns couldn't do without, a place where people still buy their screwdrivers, hammers and a dozen boxes of nails, an establishment where the smells are as redolent of its stock as the things they have to sell, we find another kind of Elvis memorial. It was at the hardware store that the manager, Howard Hite, recalled the big event in the story of this veritable Aladdin's cave. Hite looked around the building, founded in 1926 by a man still remembered in local folklore as 'Poppa'. 'It was 1945 and Elvis came with his mother to buy a bike. He and his mother came in through that same front door over there and spotted a rifle. But he was ten years old and Gladys wouldn't let him have it. So he started crying.'

History was made that day, thanks to the man who tried to serve the Presley couple. His name was Forrest Bobo. 'Forrest pulled out a guitar and handed it to Elvis Presley. Elvis took it and started to play it. "Yes, Ma'am," he said, "I'll take it." Music history started here.'

So Elvis played and the first people who heard him strumming a guitar were the ones who happened to be shopping at the Tupelo Hardware Store that day, just a week or so before his eleventh birthday.

Naturally, the store is another place of pilgrimage, a site at which Howard Hite is the leader. Those who come simply because of the Elvis connection are known as 'Howard's people', but he warns them that they are open to a particular danger. 'Prince Albert of Monaco came here one day and I told him it was dangerous to remain where he stood – because [it is likely] your lip curls and your leg shakes.' He has something else which qualifies him to greet those pilgrims: 'The UK visitors say I am the first one they've met who had seen Elvis Presley in concert. I saw him three times.'

Azalia Smith Moore was in full flow the next time we met. We got to talking about the woman who was really responsible for Elvis taking up the guitar that, along with the curled lips and leg shakes, was undoubtedly his trademark. Gladys would always be the biggest influence in her son's life. 'Gladys was kind, generous, loving, but also fierce,' she recalled.

> Perhaps [it was because] she had to be living in the dire poverty that went hand in hand with life the wrong side of the tracks in Tupelo. The black stove [in the birthplace], it was used for cooking and heating. It was very cold here, especially in winter. She'd put on a pot of beans the night before for soaking, then greens, then hot corn bread ... fatback [bacon] in the morning, few eggs. Her life was filled with a sort of makeshiftness we don't know today. But it was a good life.

That was a difficult one to swallow. A meal of beans and greens? No money to the extent that she and her son lose their home?

Her answer was: 'We had faith and no demarcation between faiths, church and community.'

And what about black people? This was, after all, Dixie.

Over the road from a Civil War memorial – for the fallen soldiers just of the South, of course – is the Lyric Theater, built for live performances although, apart from special events like beauty pageants and talent shows, it only ever showed movies. But it was at one of those talent shows that Elvis made his first appearance on a stage in Tupelo. Azalia Smith Moore remembers it like she recalls her first arithmetic marks.

To her, he was a 'shy, gentle soul. It's strange when you see him on stage. When you see the [much earlier] talent show [which he entered] pictures, you see the real Elvis Presley, you see him with glasses and home-made clothes.'

The show was a big event in Tupelo life. It was sponsored by the Baker Company, a furniture firm. Elvis won two tickets for the show and, when it was all over, waited for the results, decided by audience response.

Historian Roy Turner – and a fascinating fact of life is that every small town in America seems to boast its own tame historian – talks about that important date in the Mississippi history books. 'Elvis sang a cappella,' he told me.

He didn't have his guitar at that point and he had to climb on to a stool to reach the mike. He'd actually asked [the promoter] Charlie Borne whether he could be in the show and Charlie said, 'Yes, just as long as you don't sing "Old Shep".' So what does Elvis do? He sings 'Old Shep'.

Hardly surprisingly, Turner is happy to boast about being

'a native Tupelan ... just like Elvis. We had the same teachers.'
And then adds for good measure, 'my father worked with his
father'. Which you have to accept is another indication of the
almost incestuous relationship that Tupelo had with its citizens.
But does the town of the twenty-first century truly understand
what Elvis did for it? 'He put us on the map,' Turner says,
which might strike you as stating nothing less than the obvious.
'But the average man knows very little [about the stamp Elvis
made on the town] or understands his impact. Eighty thousand people come here every year. There's money coming in.
I've proposed a class in the local college to educate people
in Elvis Presley.' When we spoke, it hadn't yet happened. On
the other hand, he doesn't doubt that Elvis himself came to
appreciate the connection.

It was Roy Turner who recalled the 1956 visit that Elvis
paid to Tupelo.

He said that he was going to perform to home folks. He got
extremely nervous when he was performing to the home
folks. He knew he had to be at his best and that, while this
was happening, other stuff was going on – [people said] that
rock'n'roll was going to be the ruination of our youth and
preachers were declaring that Elvis music was bad. He certainly
never wanted to do anything to make his home town ashamed
of him. That was part of his upbringing that was burned into
him by Gladys. For them to come back, the toast of the town,
and be treated like royalty, I just sensed that Elvis felt he was
giving them a tremendous gift. It was important that he not
disappoint the mother whom he adored or Vernon, who was an
ex-con, parents who had lived on the wrong side of the tracks

to the people from Tupelo proper – a perception that still exists today to a certain extent.

Turner says that people who were at that concert remember him being particularly nervous simply because of the fact that he was playing to those home folks, the ones who had remembered the kid in glasses and home-sewn dungarees.

But it was the talent contests that helped shape him. He entered a show at the Lyric when he was eight years old and won – two tickets for the theatre. That was in 1941. Four years later, there was another contest at the Alabama Dairy Fair, held at the Tupelo fairgrounds. He came third. Or perhaps it was fifth. Nobody can give a definitive answer, except, of course, they stick to their own memories and they don't dispute that the winner was a local girl now called Shirley Gilentine.

This is a town where everyone knows the name of everyone else, or at least knows who they were. Turner knows who came second on that night. 'It was Nubbin Payne. She was twelve years old, a cowgirl in full regalia. She was already known around town.' And if Elvis did have to settle for fifth place – and the evidence seems to point to that – there was a third runner-up who seems to have disappeared from the records, and Hugh Jeffries, who later became an optometrist. 'When I interviewed him,' Turner recalled, 'Jeffries said he never knew that it was Elvis whom he beat.'

But their musical paths did cross again. 'In the 1950s, there was a place called the Eagle's Nest in Memphis, a hot place. Elvis Presley and some friends played there whilst Dr Jeffries's band took a rest.'

Not only that, this cinema played a big part in the much

earlier life of Elvis Presley, too. It was also important for his friend Sam Bell. His friend? That will surprise some people – because Sam is black. Yet for a time they did everything together, fired their BB guns, air rifles made specifically for shooting at birds. 'Real BBs. If you fire a shotgun, all the BBs come out and spread – shot by compressed air.'

Together, they went to play at Shakerag. The Bells lived on 'The Hill', the other side of the tracks which divided what he called 'the two cities', the poor area and the one that was not quite so poor, which on 'The Hill' was. But it was a place for 'respectable' black families. The Presleys were, to some people, white trash. 'Even so, there were still white families living in black neighbourhoods and vice versa. I grew up in East Tupelo, across the tracks, like Elvis.'

Sam Bell recalled, with the joy of memories dancing through his brain: 'We were little boys and we played together.' And went together to see the movies at the Lyric. 'We'd come down here and he'd crawl over to my bit, the part reserved for the blacks. We'd sit in the aisle.' It was strictly against the law, but there were no complaints unless some white racist in the auditorium took it upon himself to point to the 'Coloreds only' sign. 'The owner was a nice guy, a white guy but nice,' said Sam. How they did it has become part of local folklore. 'We got inside to see the movie. There were girls in front and behind. Elvis said, "Let's sit here." Then two big gopher rats jumped up and the girls came on to us.'

Both Sam Bell and Ray Turner are convinced that westerns were Elvis's favourite movies. Did he behave himself – aside, that is, from frightening girls? Children watching cowboy films are used to shouting and screaming. 'Well,' he said, 'he hollered.'

There doesn't seem to have been much hollering about Elvis's friendship with Sam Bell, who doesn't look back on those times as being particularly hard for members of his own community. A terrible time? I suggested. 'Yes, but you don't think about it. It was a way of life. The relationship between black and white here in Tupelo wasn't bad. It got to be a problem later on. There were black and white signs. But if you needed water, you'd [still] go into a white bathroom.'

They even went to the same drug stores: 'black and white; we were too young for bars'.

I asked if Sam took his pal to places where he wouldn't otherwise have gone. 'I wouldn't say "take". We just went. We went around together.'

That, of course, extended to talking about church and church music. Together, they would go, he said, to a black church which used to be a theatre, just to listen to the music. There was no doubt that the gospel songs were, says his friend, very much black music, a strand of rhythm that was to remain always Elvis's principal love and inspiration. 'Yeh, it was black music. He wanted to be a gospel singer. Long back, he'd sing to a broom, pretending it was a guitar. We thought he was crazy.' But, he then added: 'Man, he played that broom all the way to the top.'

There would be some places where a white man singing black music would be considered an appropriation of another people's heritage, almost a burglary of their lives. But not in Tupelo. 'There were no worries because he was a homeboy,' said Sam Bell. 'Blacks played guitar with him, taught him things.' That, despite the racial regulations, seemed the natural way of life in the town. But not quite. 'No, the only time it was different was when we went to school. We had segregated schools. But there was no separation in football teams, or the swimming pool. Everyone went.' Then he thought about it. Yes, most places were restricted. 'But we had the fairground – and the Lyric.'

It didn't stay that way. 'After I went away, there were riots, but we never had that trouble [at that time].' Neither was there any indication that there would be trouble. Elvis was a welcome guest in Sam's home. 'He came in and used the fridge, whatever. Poppa called him "that boy".'

The fridge was the centre of attraction at another black boy's home on 'The Hill'. Elvis used to go there with Sam and his friends, all of whom made a beeline for that fridge, which was always filled with the goodies. But not Elvis, said Sam. No, the family who lived in that house also had a piano and the young Presley was more interested in thumping out what he believed were notes on the instrument than eating. He couldn't play then, but he thought he was making music.

The Lyric Theater was very much a meeting place for the youngsters of Tupelo. James Ausborn says that – and his relationship with Elvis there was, as we have seen, vividly etched on his memory. 'I used to cycle here and Elvis would sit on my handlebars. We loved the same kind of cowboy films.'

Sam Bell remembered the westerns, too. And once again the Presley–Bell firearms came into use.

When we got home, we used to enact what we'd seen – only the BB guns were used instead of pistols. The BBs were in shotgun shells. But just single BBs. You could kill a bird, but you wouldn't hurt anyone. And you weren't allowed to aim at people, just [shoot at] things, like rocks. It was dangerous. We had a guy called Harold. Humpty Harold, we called him. Elvis and Harold didn't get along. Elvis had a pump gun. We had cock guns. Elvis shot Humpty Harold. I remember he shot a blackbird and said, 'I guess I'll go home now.' If you put enough compressed air in it, you could keep on shooting, like an automatic. Harold wanted to go on fighting, but Elvis said, 'I've shot one blackbird, but no more.' Everyone had a gun. We all wanted a BB gun – and a bike. And we had [toy] metal aeroplanes.

That might, of course, explain how the Elvis of Tupelo became the Elvis we knew. But, before that, there was a lot of action, as they say in those parts. A lot of it concerning music.

Elvis was keen, although it could never be said that he spent all his time thinking about his guitar or of one day using it for his living. Ausborn remembers what served as good fun in old Tupelo. 'If we had a little money we'd go up to Johnny's Drive-In, just on the corner over yonder. He wanted a dough burger – a burger with meat mixed with dough, you know, biscuit dough.'

A lot of it occurred at Johnny's Drive-In, which still stands on the highway leading into town, the place where, as Ausborn confirms, the Presley enthusiasm for foods not recommended in the better cookery books had its roots (and we're not talking about root vegetables). But it's the place itself that Ausborn remembers even more than the food, which is still the speciality of the house. 'There's more traffic now,' he said. Plainly. There wouldn't be anywhere for Elvis to park his bike outside these days. There is a plaque outside, commemorating the visits of the place's most famous former customer. It doesn't put any emphasis on what should be its main position in the Elvis Presley story – the fact that it was, indeed, here that he discovered, fostered and satisfied his devotion to those hamburgers which many consider were his silent killers, but which were, supposedly, according to Presley, the best in the South. As Ausborn told me: 'This really was a good place to eat. We'd have burgers, sit and think about what we were going to do. Go to a movie, ride around on a bike.'

Another day I met Mr Ausborn when we were talking with a bunch of other former pupils – students, as they were called there – at the Milam High School, which is still standing, along with its pictures of Elvis and the plaque that states 'Rock with responsibility, roll with respect, shake up good attitudes, swing into excellence'. Elvis was at the elementary school in another building, but the two schools shared more than just a name – Elvis. The plaque, among so many other things, seems to sum up 'the Elvis Effect'. Not many junior schools celebrate rock'n'roll. But, then, Presley epitomises achievement.

At the school, with those old former fellow students now showing signs of ageing in a way that Elvis himself never did, the stories multiplied of that sense of achievement coming from a lad who never showed it when he sat at a desk at that locally honoured educational establishment. Don Winders still betrays signs of astonishment at the fact that Elvis became an international star of such magnitude. 'He was a good kid but shy, quiet. I was outside, running, playing ball while he was inside. Not outgoing.' But he did like singing. 'I remember [him singing] "Old Shep" – till I was tired of it. But I liked his recording of it.'

Azalia jumped to Elvis's aid, although she was not necessarily saying that his rendition of the boy and a dog song was the best thing he ever did. 'Don remembers him being inside because he himself was academically smart.'

Gladys Presley was well aware just how smart her boy was. She was always hoping he could carry on his education without having to worry too much about money. That was never on the cards. The parents were always broke. Gladys didn't want any other anxieties, which is why she escorted him to school every day. There was an ever-present fear that some car or truck would run him down while he was humming one of the hit songs of the day, which he did incessantly.

Said Don: 'Gladys would walk with him to the school. The highways were always busy, partly with military traffic. And other traffic – factory traffic in the morning; momma traffic in the afternoon.'

Some children went home for lunch. Elvis didn't. He had a bowl of hot vegetable soup in the cafeteria. Nobody knows for sure if his meal was free, but the general consensus is that he was one of the poor boys who had a free lunch.

What is surprising is that there were always presents for Elvis. As if to challenge the inevitable, the Presleys went without the seeming necessities of life – like having enough food to eat – to give Elvis treats and gifts. The guitar from the hardware store was just one of these. Don brought up again the story of the 'wagon' that he had before the guitar entered his life and the man who accidentally destroyed it.

'Christmas was a time for sacrifice for all our parents. Elvis was given the wagon as a sort of functional gift. It was something he could use to collect things from the grocery store, to carry coals, wood etc.'

That was until a certain Pete Gamble, driving a truck

collecting scrap iron, backed into it and broke the wagon. 'Gamble,' Don recalled, 'was so distraught, he paid for the broken wagon.'

Elvis would not have been normal had he not shed a tear or two over his destroyed pride and joy. Azalia, the psychologist, thought he was very disciplined, a factor, she believes, he carried over into adulthood. 'He would be under control but the pressure cooker would sometimes explode.'

And she added, to back up her theories:

> I've known him since we both were toddlers together. He cried. His mother helped my mother [to do cleaning] when Vernon was in prison. We had an old pipe organ which neither of us could play. He would sing 'I'll Fly Away'. But he never gave any indication that that was what he would want to do.

As she said: 'He was not a temper-ridden child at all.'

In fact, give Elvis a guitar and a dog he was a happy little fellow. Maybe that was why he used to sing about 'Old Shep'. 'Elvis loved my old white English bulldog when we were kids. He would fall asleep on the bulldog.'

But even dogs would take second place to his music. 'Elvis's uncle drove a yellow school bus full of black kids from the churches and we sang on the bus.' She put it all down to what she described as 'the spirit of man's need for rhythmic activity', which, in this case, was singing and without sexual connotations. And that led to other memories. 'It was common on Green Street, going up to where Elvis lived, for people to sing on front porches.' That was certainly an influence on him. So was a trumpet player well known in those parts, a certain Mr Bayhou.

He had a girlfriend named Elois Sandifer. 'She was sweet,' Azalia recalled for me. 'She had freckles. I remember her father was a plumber.' It was a romance that lasted through the first grade.

'Oh, he was fickle,' she laughed. 'He passed her a note one day, saying he was leaving her for a girl called Magdalene Morgan. She always wished she had kept that note.' Wished it a lot more in later years than she would have done at that time.

Boyfriends and girlfriends make special relationships here in Tupelo, perhaps more than in others. Kisses would be exchanged ... they were caring relationships. Teachers would make sure we all had our special relationships. It was encouraged. Kids today don't have that. We developed comfort zones and we, on the whole, stayed together a long time. It would have been quite a thing for Elvis to have dumped Elois.

He was, however, a romantic – more so than most boys at the school. He never joined a violent gang. As Don put it: 'He never played games. He was a quiet boy, except for playing music. He was shy.'

I was tempted to ask a strictly non-PC question. I didn't resist the temptation. 'Was he,' I asked, 'seen as something of a cissy?' 'Possibly,' Don ventured, 'but we never thought that about him. He was a nice kid. He was never involved in anything. I was – I was involved in everything – including fights. But those fights weren't acts of violence.' Not easy to understand that. How could a fight ever be non-violent? But Don was adamant.

So Elvis was just a goody-goody? Azalia counters that

thought. 'He was not a cissy. He did boy things, like slipping off to go swimming, hunting.'

I wondered what there was about Elvis that kept him away from those supposedly non-violent fights? It was simply, Azalia believes, a case of his being introverted and, she said, 'little has been said about his introversion'. Until now, that is.

The best schools are often remembered because of outstanding teachers. When I asked if there was one who stood out as their – including Elvis's – mentor, as if speaking from the same script the old students called out in unison one name – 'Miss Grimes'. She was Elvis's teacher in the fifth grade at the East Tupelo Consolidated School, and used to live a hundred yards from the Presley home. 'She would help all the pupils,' they all said. And then Azalia let slip a contradiction to her statement that Elvis was academically smart. It came with another reference to Miss Grimes.

'Elvis and the other dumber ones stayed near their teacher, i.e. Miss Grimes. She would have been drilling them at any time of the day, you'd get her drilling them in the shade, after class after recess, with multiplication tables.'

'I didn't realise that,' Don Winder joined in. Ms Smith Moore, proving that she was no more one of the 'dumber ones' now any more than she had been in those far-off days, answered: 'That was because you didn't have to, hon, you got it the first time.'

None of these old students seemed to doubt the influence of the school on themselves and their parents. As Azalia said:

If the school were in a contest today to be the most effective, we would be very close to first – for three reasons: our parents knew education was an avenue to be personally responsible and financially secure; we were all religious kids, we were obedient and the teachers all knew us, knew our parents. If I misbehaved Mr Morgan would tell my parents before I got home. Mr Morgan was the principal, but Miss Grimes was the big wheel. Everybody followed her model of caring, pushing and challenging. I remember Elvis loved poetry and loved learning classical elements – from 'Sunset and Evening Star' to 'Little Orphan Annie', elements that impacted on the children. We have – and Elvis had – immense East Tupelo school loyalty.

Certainly, Elvis did his bit at school, not that he had much choice. Whatever his teachers told him to do, he did it. Including taking part in school plays. Plainly, he made an impact. She remembers to this day the one line he had to recite – 'My name is Fear. People tremble and shake when I am near.'

No one then knew just how he himself would shake – or that the first appearance of Elvis Presley was not exactly with a rock'n'roll beat.

Don illustrated the unusual influence of Elvis's and their own teacher with a story that indicates just how small this small Mississippi town was, a place where once more I realised that everyone knew everyone else and when you mentioned a name, no one was in doubt who it was referring to. By doing so, he also proved another aspect of Miss Grimes and her influence. 'She was a very smart lady,' said Winder. 'One day I was in class and I kept jumping because Wayne Stevenson was punching me with a pencil. She left the room but she watched. I beat the devil out of Wayne and she let me do it.' The rest of the class cheered – Elvis included.

Another one there that day at the school was Elvis's talent show rival, Shirley Gilentine – or Shirley Jones as Elvis would have known her, a woman who still lives in Tupelo.

'We sang a lot,' Shirley recalled for me. 'He sang "Old Shep" a lot. We also went to the fair and we sang in that contest.' The failure he suffered that day was to prove a decisive moment in the Elvis Presley career.

'There's a picture of Elvis at the time with a look of disgust on his face, which seems to say, "I can't believe I didn't win this thing".'

Again, the same images cropped up. 'I sang in the chapel with Elvis,' Shirley remembered. And once more … 'He sang "Old Shep".' Once more, groans were heard all around. But what was he like to sing with? 'Oh, he was very shy – except when he was singing.' So with her, too, it was a surprise when he became the most successful child Tupelo ever had.

'I used to smile a lot when I heard about it and I thought of the little boy singing in the chapel. A lot of people wouldn't believe that I was a friend of Elvis. But then I had a picture of us together to prove it.' Whether Miss Grimes ever felt the need to prove that Elvis was one of her students – or even if she were alive when he hit the headlines – is not on record. But her achievements are there in the memories of those who learnt the multiplication tables at her feet. James Ausborn certainly agrees with the thought that Elvis epitomised the sense of achievement that the school imposed.

I knew Elvis Presley for about three and a half years. My
brother, Mississippi Slim, was on the radio in a tent show and
went to Nashville to sing with Hank Williams. Elvis [wanted to
go] on Slim's radio show. I asked him to do it. Slim said, 'Yes,
if he's good.' Elvis sang 'Old Shep' and 'God Bless My Daddy'.
Slim said he needed more practice. 'Then, I'll let you be on.'

Ausborn took him to the radio station – riding on his handlebars again. Later, his friend did go on to the show.

And Elvis sang in the Assembly of God church and my brothers
would show him chords on the guitar. My brother said that
Elvis had a good voice but couldn't carry a tune. When I got
back from the [Korean] war, Elvis Presley was on his way up
and Slim apologised to him. Elvis fell over the couch laughing.

Jimmy Gault is another who remembers talking music with
Presley. Without laughing. More than that, he recalls an
Elvis song that nobody else knows about. 'He wrote it – a
four-line song that he wrote in our class.' He began to sing
it, demonstrating the fact that Elvis was always more likely
to make money from performing music than he ever would
writing his own songs. And yet it has a poignancy which possibly demonstrates the way of Tupelo life. It's a song that has
never been published, never recorded, never mentioned, a song
that goes:

'City girl. She lives in a fine brick home / Poor girl, she do
the same / But my girl, she lives in Tupelo County Jail / But it's
a brick house all the same.'

Elvis brought his guitar to school with him, but he was only allowed to play once a week. Miss Grimes probably heard him as he strummed the instrument.

Azalia departed briefly from her more scholarly approach to her Elvis memories.

'He was very generous as he always was. Vernon's uncle, Noah Presley, was a prime image, known as a generous person. Noah would put in two-penny suckers in a sack for a penny.'

As Azalia indicated, in later years when Elvis returned to Tupelo he didn't forget those who had been kind to him – and not *just* those. 'You know, we all had a tremendous respect for our elders in Tupelo.' And that was where the psychologist in Azalia came into its own. 'I think that might be the way he felt towards Col. Parker.' Before very long, the name comes up in conversation after conversation.

No, the people of Tupelo have no love for the memory of the phoney colonel who, as we shall discover, also had a phoney name. But when I visited Tupelo, there was another feature of the Elvis memory psychology business that rankled with some, an issue over which the local citizens were happy to take sides. The cause of the trouble was plainly in view from the mound on which the birthplace stood as well as from the chapel and the boy statue – a modernistic building called the Elvis Museum. Bill Kynard, who established the place, was talking about the civic fathers wanting to drive him out of town. In a way, you got the picture instantly: the other Presley institutions and the people to whom I had talked had a kind of seal of approval to them. They were all official – almost as if they didn't have it, there was no licence to talk. Mr Kynard certainly didn't have that seal.

'No, sir,' he said. 'We're not [popular]. When we got here, a man offered us $2 million to get out. My wife said "No". He then said he'd run us out with dogs, chainsaws and shotguns. My wife said, "Bring it on. I'm from Kentucky. We'll be needing our cemetery sooner or later."' In other words, she was ready to fire the first shot and make use of the burial ground she and her husband were also planning for Elvis fans, all part of their own plans for a commercial enterprise undoubtedly cashing in on the Presley connection. Kynard was quite vituperative about the problems of the cemetery as well as of the museum. 'We didn't get started till 2003. Then we had a setback, the City of Tupelo stole our dirt. They used it to build foundations [of another building]. We sued them and we got $125,000. It cost us $200,000 to do repairs.' But they did manage to put up a granite wall containing the names of past Elvis fans. It resembled a kind of miniature version of the Washington, DC, Vietnam memorial. As if they were fighting for civil rights, they all but sang 'We Shall Not Be Moved'. But before long, the Kynards did pack their bags and locked the museum's doors.

In its way, the memorial summed up small-town attachment to an idol. Local names are established here, some in death as in life. Bill Kynard went through the names as though they were neighbours they would call on for a cup of sugar, or perhaps a hash of grits.

Fans paid $100 for names to be 'sandblasted on to the wall'. Some people gave a present of such an inscription. 'We have J. D. Sumner's name paid for by a fan. And then over there is Joyce Logan ...' Who's she? 'Oh,' says Kynard, 'she wanted to see her name here, but not on a gravestone. And over there, is Rosemary Reynolds ... she's English. And Bill Williams, mayor of Saltillo. And there's Mary Jenkins; she was Elvis's cook.

Also, Patsy Anderson, who worked at Graceland for twenty-two years.' For those names, and for Bill's parents, who are on the wall and on gravestones – this is not just vanity, but, as they see it, a kind of place in the Presley pantheon, a final testament to their idol, one of the righteous men in their lives to whom their last testament is a way of being a final reckoning of where they stood for him.

There was more optimism for the future of the cemetery than for the museum itself. The struggle with getting the building accepted seemed to represent to Kynard his own one-man (or, rather, one-couple – for his wife, Linda was in it, too) war. But one they thought was unnecessary. Yes, they surrendered, the war was lost. But they tried their damnedest.

The place was being advertised. Yet even that wasn't easy. 'We had problems getting our ads placed in time. There was someone blocking us financially. We couldn't borrow a dollar in Lee County.'

When I was there, it seemed to be struggling to fill up with enough Presley memorabilia. It was a vast hall, but the hopes were there. And so was something very special – one of Elvis's own famous pink Cadillacs.

Other items were not so easy to come by. They had a microphone in prime position. 'Not the actual one [the mike featured in a life-size cut-out by the side of the entrance],' said Kynard, 'but similar.'

Meanwhile, Linda was in no doubt about the reasoning behind the museum. It was something of a shrine. 'I loved him. I loved his songs and he was a giving, loving person. He bought groceries for people. Medicines. He did many kind deeds. His songs will sound in my ears until the day I die.'

Perhaps that was what separated Elvis from other perform-ers who have millions of fans during their short periods of fame. The Elvis Presley legacy is that sort of love, but much more. Very much more. And to folks (the term they would use in Mississippi) thereabout there was always, but *always*, that other thing about him – religion. If Elvis seems still to be a god to his worshippers – who would not be at all surprised to discover a resurrection before very long – to them the connec-tion with a higher force is certainly there. Even so, Bill Kynard puts them right: 'This is not a cult. Elvis said there was only one king: Jesus.'

As he sat in that museum, the memories flooded back for an elderly man who recalled the time when he had what was plainly the scoop of his life as a radio broadcaster – when he interviewed not just Elvis, but his ma and pa, too. Now living in Jasper, Alabama, Charlie Watts was in those days working with radio station WTUP. That was when Elvis came back home to Tupelo in the 1950s. 'It was a real stroke of luck because he was a great person even then, already known by his first name.' That was a point that, strangely, other people had been slow to pick up on. It put him instantly in the same league as Bing and Ella. Conversely, Sinatra and Jolson only needed surnames to get the instant recognition that the one word brought to them.

It seems that Mrs (or perhaps that should be Miss, as they say in that part of the world) Presley dominated the conversa-tion. No one was allowed to think of her as a stage mother, but in front of Mr Watts's microphone that's what she was. All pride and enthusiasm. 'I asked them [Gladys and Vernon] about the adulation around their famous son, almost worship.

They were very proud of him. They'd had a parade through Tupelo that day. They had every reason to be proud'.

Also on the programme was Julie Hopper, then a young girl who had had her fifteen minutes of fame at that time. When Elvis was singing, she forced a way on to the platform on which he was appearing at the local fair ground. 'I asked her why she did it. She said she wanted to get Elvis.' That phrase, 'get Elvis', was never properly explained. But she was happy that day. 'They promised to take her backstage and they did.'

The interview was later issued on an LP by RCA – who, to Watts's disgust, took his voice out of the recording that was released and failed even to mention his name. No way to treat a scoop. He got a copy of the record – 'which I had to pay for'. He is sure that Elvis, whom he admired greatly, would never have allowed that. Knowing the star's later reputation, he could have been right. 'It was a great interview with him. He answered quickly and politely. He was very humble. Yes, a great interview.'

Humility is rarely associated with that group of people who go under the name 'superstar', but it crops up regularly in the conversation of Elvis's pals. And in strange, out of character ways. The man who was in the public eye was not above going out in disguise – but not in a face-mask kind of disguise. His assumed likenesses had to mean something. So when Elvis, more used in those parts to being seen wearing dungarees, made his trips back to Tupelo, he put on ... a police uniform. Complete with gun. As we have already seen, he loved guns the way he loved guitars – a fact which, later in life, would prove how fortunate he was to be born Elvis Presley.

It was in the Tupelo Elvis Presley museum that Robert

Norris, the retired policeman who was to control the crowds at the first coming-home concerts, told me how he had to try to convince a sceptical boss that, when local girls screamed for the kid already known as The Pelvis, they weren't in some kind of mass panic.

Elvis not only had the crowds shouting, but also the inhabitants of the local police station – when he walked in, dressed from cap to shiny boots in all the cop clothes he could find.

'Elvis was obsessed with the police and would come in at night. So we made him an honorary deputy.' He had a thing about being a policeman.'

Did he ever make an arrest? 'Don't know,' said Norris, whose brother was in the same class at school as Elvis. Which might strike some people as strange. Had it actually happened, you could imagine old lags not exactly forgetting the moment they were thrown into the jug by Elvis Presley.

If they were, one man who would have heard about it quickly was Steve Holland, a local assembly man for twenty-seven years – and, although Elvis had been dead for eight years when he first joined the Mississippi legislature, representing Tupelo, he already knew everything there was to know about life in his home town. At least, that is what he believes. Others, even now, will say no one knew everything about anyone – particularly a star as complex as Mr Presley. But, then, Mr Holland is privy to a lot of local secrets and had been so, even before becoming a legislator. As the local undertaker, he has discovered more about people than most.

After fifty-five years living in Tupelo, for Holland the magic of Elvis's voice remains as strong as ever. When Presley sang 'Dixie', his heart was speaking along with his voice. 'Yes, I think so,' he agreed. But like most people, he would have wanted a lot more. 'He was proud of his birthright. Had he lived longer, he might have had more opportunity, more of a mainstream area.'

But now I discovered there was also evidence of a different side to the way Tupelo looks on its favourite son. It may be a place for memories, but there's also a cause for resentment. Don't think, the legislator declaims, that it's a place that didn't exist before Mr Elvis Aaron Presley came on the scene. He is determined about that. As he said, forcibly, 'We were one of the first towns to mix agriculture with industry and we are prosperous here now.'

But ... and there is quite a 'but' in his statement ... even Steve Holland has to admit that Tupelo would be a different place without the Elvis legacy. 'We wouldn't get the traffic we get here,' he said. And that should be just the start. 'We want people to spend more time here, the same as they spend in Graceland.'

The people he blames above all for tourists not swarming into Tupelo in Memphis-style droves are his fellow members of the state authority. 'The State of Mississippi has never put a dime in here,' he maintains. Given the money, he says, he has ambitions for Tupelo. 'I want to buy the whole Elvis Presley thing and make it an Elvis Presley village,' he told me.

It would be a project rather more attractive to him than embalming corpses. But, no, he is speaking from his heart, the way Elvis always did.

And talking as a musician himself – in addition to his other work Holland plays the organ at local civic (and Elvis) functions – he went back to his crystal ball. 'I don't know what [had he lived] Elvis would have become, musically. But he would have implanted the culture of Elvis Presley here and it would have gone round the world.' That was not to say Elvis hadn't gone sufficiently around the world as things were. So he felt it necessary to explain. No, he believed he would have scored in other directions. 'He would have become the South's greatest spokesman.' Yes, the Representative and others saw something that had happened to other people in related worlds – 'like Ronald Reagan in the White House, Sonny Bono in Congress – Elvis having a political role'.

And he had history to back him up. 'I've studied the Presleys all my life. They were very interesting people, eclectic people. They took chances and didn't just stand by. They had thorns amongst them. Had he stayed, he would have made the South a better place.' I think I understood what he meant.

Oh yes, they love talking about Elvis – to the extent that one wonders whether, by now, all those years after, a live Elvis would have fared anything like as well as the dead one. But there are plenty around to make that an unnecessary exercise in contemplation. Steve Holland is not the only representative of civic life in Tupelo rejoicing in the Elvis connection – to say nothing of the number of 'firsts' connected with the town.

Linda Eliff is sales director at the Tupelo Convention and Visitors' Bureau. She and I were standing outside the local courthouse, which had a certain piquancy, I thought. Elvis didn't appear before the local justices any more than he arrested anyone who did, but as far as his link with Tupelo was concerned, this place was more than merely important. It was there that a day inscribed on Tupelo's heart – and also on a plaque – entered the local history books. Taking full advantage of the manicured lawns surrounding the building, it was the scene of one of those regular Saturday jamborees where Elvis finally made the locals realise he was more than just a kid in overalls.

Linda set the scene. 'There was Mississippi Slim waving his hat and introducing acts whom he knew would make some people happy, but not enough pizzazz to take away the spotlight from himself.' In a way it was like Jack Benny's famous radio shows which everyone was listening to on Saturday nights – he knew that no matter who he had on the programme, he was the one the audience was waiting for.

Mississippi Slim wasn't all that broken-hearted when he introduced Mrs Presley's boy. But Elvis was. He worshipped Slim, Linda maintains, and, after the youngster became famous, the man who took his state's name for his own would claim to have discovered him. But he got quite a kick out of the fact that when he first told the good people of Tupelo that this youngster was about to appear, the boy chickened out and decided to leave the nerves to other people. But then he had second thoughts on another day. That was when he said he would come – and come he did. Mississippi Slim was eclipsed and that's how it stayed.

The site was perfect, said Linda. Looking around, she said: 'It was a real centre, with big lawns and a square.' Of course it didn't then boast what is today its main feature – that plaque embossed with the Elvis image, the thirteen-year-old boy in overalls, potentially rich in talent but poor in monetary wealth.

That was just before he and the Presley family packed up and left Tupelo, crossing the state line to Memphis, Tennessee. But, in a way, that's a part of the history that the Mississippi town seems to want to forget ever happened. To them, anything he did outside Tupelo was merely incidental. Certainly, that's the impression the locals like to give.

There's another civic place that for Linda is redolent of Elvis. It recalls another return visit to his home town. It was here, in 1956 and again the following year, that he appeared once more at the Mississippi and Alabama Fair and Dairy Show. Not, then, to sing 'Old Shep' at any talent show. This was when Robert Norris wanted fire hoses to control the crowds and the governor brought in the National Guard. That was not at all the way the people at the fair usually behaved. Imagine the scene from the old movie *State Fair* – girls in flowing dirndl skirts, boys in check shirts beneath their overalls, daring to steal kisses while various bands played; cows mooed while they produced what their owners proclaimed to be the best milk ever given in the state, let alone the ice cream that was the part of every all-American home. Meanwhile, there were fairground rides and carefully groomed horses that were put through their paces. At the same time, kids seemingly smothered their faces in pink cotton candy (candy floss to those foreigners in Britain) as they listened to the young man in black pants and gold lamé jacket swivelling his hips and shaking his legs. 'Oh, he was gorgeous,' Linda recalled.

Gorgeous and caring about his roots in Tupelo, too.

And the ones that did not bring smiles and songs. I went with Charlene Presley, Elvis's cousin, to the Priceville Memorial Garden and it was there that I discovered the existence of another kind of Presley pilgrimage. This time, not one to see Elvis and the places closely associated with him. This was a pilgrimage in reverse, one made by Elvis himself. It was where first the young and then the triumphant Elvis would go in the dark of night – to visit the spot where he believed his stillborn twin Jesse lay buried, the child whom Gladys never stopped mourning, even though he never breathed, the one whose immediate coming out and going in (to his tiny coffin), made her all the more caring of Elvis. For his family, Jesse had always seemed like a living person, a member of the family. Elvis was no exception. It is clear that he never stopped thinking about the one he considered his other half. But where was he buried? Elvis – if he ever knew – never revealed the site of what has always been an unmarked grave. Some think he lies at the foot of his great-uncle Noah's resting place. 'There are lots [of unmarked graves] here,' said Charlene, looking around the so-bleak cemetery. If ever there were proof that this was an area gripped by poverty, the fact that so many people could not afford the price of a piece of granite is damning evidence.

But the way most of Tupelo thinks about their favourite son is of the life Elvis always evinced and the rejuvenation of the town that he brought about.

Susie Dent, of the North East Mississippi Historical and Genealogical Society in Tupelo, summed up the relationship between Elvis and the town perfectly. 'When Elvis left here he took some of Tupelo with him. Things stick in your heart and soul.'

The gorgeous boy was on his way to superstardom and, as far as Tupelo was concerned, he was its favourite son.

MEMPHIS

It was a place that has come to symbolise rock'n'roll – real rock'n'roll, that is, not the kind played in clubs or in certain films by people who really didn't know what they were doing. Memphis would go on to do it with an intensity and originality of the sort that made New Orleans famous for jazz or even Vienna for the waltz – to say nothing of Liverpool for the Beatles.

Elvis never regretted being part of Memphis and Memphis has never stopped thanking Elvis's God for bringing his family there. You drive down Elvis Presley Boulevard and know who the highway is dedicated to. You stop your car in a parking lot near the iconic Heartbreak Hotel and a loudspeaker not only plays Elvis music, but interviews with him, too. It's a broadcast on 'Elvis Radio' in which a fan declares, 'Just don't remember Elvis. We never forget. The first concert I went to ... chills go down my spine. That was all those years ago.' They'll be playing that sort of music and that sort of comment when someone talks about going to a concert seventy years ago.

In truth, Memphis was a magnet for anyone who had ever had the smell of bluegrass in their nostrils and the sound of a different kind of music in their ears. When the Presleys moved there from Tupelo in 1948, rock'n'roll had nothing to do with rhythm, but more to do with what was all too frequently happening on one of the river boats that plied the Mississippi river flowing through the middle of the city, a block or two from the Peabody Hotel, a place that the young Elvis had probably heard of and talked about to the pals he made as quickly as you could say mint julep, at least as quickly as he ever had in Tupelo. They immediately knew that, where Elvis went, his guitar went with him. On the other hand, ask any of those friends if they imagined he would become a professional entertainer, let alone a huge superstar, and they would sniff a word or two of regret at their own lack of prescience – unless they were among that gang of I-told-you-sos who inevitably knew all along that his talent would shine out. They would also, of course, have said they knew music styles were going to change.

Their teachers had no idea either, even though these days at one of his old schools, Humes High, there's a picture of Elvis on the backdrop of one of the stages that dominate academic establishment halls which are so well equipped they could double for professional theatres.

It was in one of those that two old-timers talked about the days when they sat at desks alongside that man with the greased curly hair and the long sideburns. One of them undid his coat and revealed he was carrying a gun – and that says a lot about this part of Memphis. It used to be a quiet, law-abiding district. 'Now,' Gene Bradbury told me, 'I wouldn't dream of coming here unarmed.' A couple of generations ago, the only kind of disturbance would have been caused by kids playing in the streets and upsetting the odd driver or pedestrian who got in their way. Their 'weapons' were their own guitars – or poor substitutes such as old tennis rackets – which they strummed as they pretended to be Elvis.

'He was amazing,' Bradbury recalled. 'I was in the band here. We would have variety shows and Elvis would perform at these shows ... a ballad like "Old Shep".' That was, I suppose, Elvis's proof that he had arrived, taken up residence in Memphis and was going to do what he wanted to do. Whether he wanted to appear in blackface in a minstrel show at Humes is perhaps another matter entirely. Or perhaps he thought about another performer who, in his time, was also known as 'the King', Al Jolson, who began his career doing just what Elvis was doing thirty or so years later. Perhaps there can be no better indication of how things have changed. At a minstrel show? In the Deep South?

'He came on a band trip and he started singing a cappella to a couple of girls. I thought he had a really great voice. Then he came back in my senior year. We had a male beauty show called "Musical Hats", guys in drag, competing in grades.'

There were no Xerox machines around at Humes High in those days, but there was a duplicated programme sheet which Bradbury still owns and is able to produce. It says, 'A Special Attraction, Elvis Presley and his guitar'. 'That was in February 1956.'

Just as the young folks in Tupelo had concluded, Elvis was the fellow to be with. 'But he was quiet, unassuming, easygoing, mild, friendly, a ladies' man.' All part of the Presley package. 'He wore long hair and fancy shirts, not the norm at that time. He also wore black slacks. We wore khakis or blue jeans.'

His days of dungarees and plaid shirts were plainly over. He didn't have any enemies, either. Or did he? 'A couple of football players made fun of his hair – and that was how Red West got involved.' West was another of the Presley crowd and, as Bradbury said, 'you didn't mess with Red. He was an All-Memphis football player, as tough as nails.' Tough enough to see off other players of his game who thought – ever so briefly – that Elvis was going to be 'easy meat'.

Red's cousin Sonny West would be the first to vouch for the abilities of his relative. 'Red protected him at school. Red stopped thugs from cutting off Elvis's hair. Red was a tough guy. He had a flat top. He told them they'd have to cut off his hair, too'

The consequences of that were not to be taken lightly by anyone at Humes. As for Elvis himself, did he have any real friends there? Sonny West is sure that he did not. He was different, but he had some cousins around. And he was a loner. 'I didn't know him at school. I was younger than he. The first time I saw him I said, "Here comes Elvis, carrying his guitar …".'

If any one name could be said to rival that of Elvis Presley in Humes, it was surely that of Red West. As his cousin told me: 'Another time, Red found [Elvis] leaning against the lockers avoiding guys who wanted to beat him up. So they walked out of there, Elvis and Red. Red threatened them, hence Red being taken on when the career got started.'

Another name that crops up constantly in this part of our story is that of Fred Frederick, a one-time policeman-turned-investment banker. He was the other man I met at Humes.

Gene Bradbury was a policeman, too – when, as he said, he

'handled several of the guys from our school'. Guys who, like some of the alumni of Tupelo, did well for themselves. 'Charles Controse, who's CEO of Cisco Foods, Paul Duncan, CEO of Reebok, Ed Butler, a judge in Houston. Several went into law.' And Elvis didn't have it all his own way either. 'Thomas Wayne Perkins had a million-seller before Elvis Presley.' Only he became known as Carl.

So what was there about that school to provide such a crop of talent of so many sorts? 'I don't know,' said Bradbury. 'We were just a bunch of guys.' And again there with the stock line: 'We were poor, but we didn't know it. We didn't go hungry. We grew up wearing clothes from the Goodwill [charity]. We didn't know anything else. Yes sir. If you've never tasted caviar, peanut butter is just fine.'

If Gene Bradbury carried his gun as a matter of course in the twenty-first century, I was intrigued to know in what way the neighbourhood had changed. There was a great story to prove how good things had been in that peanut butter age. '[One of the "gang"] parked his bike in 1947. Nobody moved it till 1956.'

There was another alumnus of Humes who went into show business. Jimmy Angel sang with Elvis on records, just as he had with Gene Vincent and Buddy Holly. Before long, he entertained in his own right, thanks to his disc 'Teenager in Love'. He would claim that he followed the Presley code – 'I had to be nice, like Elvis, don't cause problems, don't hit on audience girls. Kiss them on the hand, from the dolls to the dogs. Don't embarrass anybody,' he told my colleague Barbra Paskin.

If the other alumni of Humes think it is now a different environment from the one they knew when they sat at the desks and smiled nicely at their teachers, Angel puts them right. 'Humes was a tough school. Blacks weren't popular there. You could get your head handed to you.' Elvis made an impact, he says. 'You couldn't miss him. He looked like a pimp.' Angel was the first one to say things about Presley that wouldn't feature in a fan magazine put out by his own office. 'Elvis Presley was dressed up in a zoot suit. He was always singing "Your Cheatin' Heart". He loved Hank Williams.'

What becomes clear is that, when Elvis found friends who had something in common with him they stayed friends. There was, for instance, the loyal unofficial chairman of what would become known as the Memphis Mafia, George Klein, joint president of his class along with Elvis. 'The cat George Klein was president of our high school. He was a good cat. Elvis was very fortunate to have a friend in George Klein,' says Angel, 'Not a yes-man.'

Of course, no one would have known that at the time. 'We bonded,' George told me, a phrase he would use again and again in our conversations. 'We were going to do Christmas carols and Elvis asked if he could bring his guitar and sing. It wasn't cool to do that in 1948. I produced the senior class talent show and he won it. I wondered whether he'd go anywhere in music.'

Klein says it wasn't easy for the Presleys when they moved to Memphis.

They were very poor. Elvis himself had to adapt to a very big school. He wasn't used to all that regimented stuff we had at Humes. He was a quiet guy in high school. We called him the 'Velvet Hammer'. Now, people do piercings, coloured hair.

He was making a statement with his black pants with a white stripe or a black sport coat with the collar turned up. When he graduated in 1953, his hair was longer than the Beatles [would have theirs] – and people were not wearing their hair long then. But he wasn't a pushy guy.

Were the initial settling-in difficulties simply part of moving from a small town to a big city, from Tupelo to Memphis? 'No, I think he was happy to be in Memphis, away from Tupelo. He was living in a better place.'

The other two Humes old-timers to whom I spoke, Gene Bradbury and Fred Frederick, remembered when Elvis wanted to emulate them and become a policeman.

Frederick recalled for me: 'He just liked the police. He became a friend of [a local sheriff] Bill Morris.' Morris had been at school with Elvis. He eventually became part of the security team at a Memphis place far grander than any that the child Presley could possibly have imagined, one I'll come to before very long.

Perhaps another reason for Elvis's love of the police was the respect in which the force was held by his own parents. Perhaps particularly in the case of Vernon, once he had served his jail sentence.

On the other hand, the man who would famously take as his motto 'Taking Care of Business' proved from those very early days that he could also take care of himself. Even when faced with contemporaries who were probably showing signs of envy.

What was not known by his fans was that, as soon as he could, Elvis, like Gene Bradbury, always carried a gun. He loved the idea of the power it gave him – although he never actually used the weapon. He seems to have preferred gentler ways of persuasion.

'He was always a giving person, giving cars [when he became an international success]. He probably gave away as many as he kept.' But that's for later on in the story. For the moment, it was a chance for me to meet the people who at a certain time in his life knew and remembered him best. Among them were the ones who gathered in a room overlooking the yard at Lauderdale Courts, the apartment block – more like a collection of barracks until it had a recent refit – at 185 Winchester in Memphis, where the young Elvis grew up. Many of them, now sixty years or so older, have become highly successful; others are not on so very different a rung on the economic ladder now than they were when they were living there. But for them all, Elvis Presley was simply a neighbour and, to some of them at least, a pal. It was a very long time ago, but they keep coming back. Every week, they meet for a cup of coffee to chat about the old times that they and only they remember. For my benefit, they gathered on a Sunday morning in what used to be the Presley apartment at Lauderdale Courts. Then, the subject was entirely ... Elvis.

It was a family home, the first 'decent' living quarters they had – available to them as public housing provided only for people with incomes below $3,000.

By all accounts, Gladys seems to have liked living there more than anywhere else she hung her poor cotton dresses, including Graceland. Elvis, they believe, felt the same way – at least in those days long before his fame and his money began to make a difference to everything about his life and its style.

But there's more to the place than that. To many of the people whose lives seem to be built exclusively around worshipping the man in the jumpsuits, going to Lauderdale is one of those close-to-religious experiences.

You can now go and visit the rooms where the Presleys lived in the Courts – as the buildings are known by these veterans – just as they did that morning. And the fans, those who know about the old homestead and don't think life began for Elvis at Graceland, come and study the settee, the old radio and the bedrooms as though going there would somehow bring about a second coming. 'To the fans, this is a shrine, yes,' I was told. Not quite Lourdes but I'm sure to some of them the rooms have healing properties.

'The fans have been waiting for a long time for this to open,' I was told by my guide. 'Fans came in and were extremely emotional. There are extreme fan reactions. They see their Elvis here. A woman dug up dirt and sold it on eBay.'

It is said that a van-load of Elvis impersonators got stuck in the soil in front of the building trying to peer in through the window.

And if they are not extreme fans or faux-religious extremists, the historical angle is inescapable. As my guide said: 'There's something here for every Elvis Presley fan. People who believe Elvis was a family man, a philanthropist, religious man.' As she said: 'They see their Elvis here. Elvis used to drive people by here and say he used to live here. He wasn't ashamed of having been in public housing.'

Fred Frederick lived here at the same time as Elvis, and it was from the Courts that both walked to Humes High School. We were sitting in the living room of what had been the

Presley apartment, now revamped and looking rather more comfortable than it did when Elvis lived there. Now it is a kind of museum; nobody is actually living there anymore. If that is what it is, this is the village museum, because the Courts are and were in those days a kind of village. Neil Niker, who is three years younger than Elvis would be now, looked up to him, a kid who was one of those in 'the same boat, economically speaking'. He doesn't claim to have been a Presley friend. 'I just had one encounter with him. I was on a motorcycle with a friend called Arthur. Arthur looked over at Elvis and said he'd race him. Elvis said, "No. My butt won't get put together if I'm dead."'

The former residents were honest about things like that.

Niker told me he had first seen Elvis on a variety show in 1954. 'He was number fourteen on the bill – it was a fund-raiser for our school. He was good ... great.'

So that inspired the question: did he know Elvis was going to be famous, a superstar? 'Oh no. He was just a boy from the "hood".' Did he talk about his plans for the future? 'Not that I know.'

Ken Black excludes his and Elvis's contemporaries, but he says that there was a lot of jealousy among the older residents of Lauderdale. 'Most of those people weren't going to college; being in the police or fire department was a step up. People out East were doctors and so on and they resented the fact that an inner-city boy [from their own area] could make it big.'

On the other hand, his old pal Fred Frederick jumps to Elvis's aid and is determined that nothing detrimental could be perceived as casting a bad light on him. It wasn't at all like Frank Sinatra and his own home town of Hoboken, New Jersey, where the citizens were so jealous of him he almost never went back – in case the time when cabbages were thrown at him by his erstwhile contemporaries would be repeated. Not Elvis, says Fred. 'Elvis was so nice and so they weren't at all jealous. He was like the rest of us.' And he knew the rest pretty well.

'Things were different back then,' explained Jack Berelson looking out of the window at the courtyard of the block where we were. Once again, there was the familiar mantra: 'We were poor, but we didn't know we were poor. We had friends, good times together. We didn't fight and always helped each other. A time you don't see today. There are no long-term friendships today.'

But no fights? Well, yes, there were some. So who did Jack Berelson fight? 'No comment.'

Neil Niker went to Jack's assistance. 'Everyone's going to fight at some time. We didn't have cars. We walked. We had parties in the neighbourhood.'

They, however, all seem to know that Elvis had plans to go on some stage or other – wherever it was. Blanche Gordon Scott was certainly one of them. 'Elvis had a plan to be an entertainer,' she told me.

From the age of thirteen, he was working on that plan. There weren't gangs. Elvis wanted to impress an audience right from the first minute. He came up with wearing a special suit or something to grab people. Even then, if you were with Elvis Presley for a few minutes, you'd be a fan.

She wasn't actually an Elvis girlfriend, but, as she said, she 'walked with him' when he lived at Lauderdale and she was a cashier collecting rents for local landlords.

If Lauderdale was a village, and it was, one of the nice things about it was how the locals gave each other nicknames and how those names stuck – to the extent that even today no one thinks of calling them anything else. That is, if they ever knew any other name – like that of Buzzy Forbess. 'Every day we got up, we had fun,' he recalls. And then he and the others chuckled. 'We didn't crack the books too well.' Which said a great deal about priorities thereabouts. 'We did a lot of partying.' And then he added: 'The first party we had was in this apartment – right here.' Elvis, the host with the most.

'Paul Dougher, Guy, Elvis and me ... everyone in the Courts was friends. But us four were together all the time.' That was three fans and a star in the making. 'The first time I heard Elvis Presley singing was after about two months of knowing him [and it was] in this room. His voice was progressing all the time. This was in 1948.'

'It didn't take long to understand that Elvis Presley had a good voice,' said Buzzy Forbess. 'Elvis was thirteen.' But none of them saw Elvis's parents very often – or anyone's for that matter. 'Moms and Dads worked and the kids took care of everyone. You didn't see your parents.'

But maybe they didn't need to. As Neil Niker pointed out:

If you go shopping today, you drive fifteen miles to a mall. But from here, then, you could walk for a few minutes and find everything you wanted. Our whole world was a mile wide. We'd collect coat hangers, soda bottles, milk bottles and sell them. We didn't have cars. We knew each other. We fought together. We loved each other.

And they had plenty of exercise. 'In the parking lot, we played – football, baseball. There were not many cars then. And, yes, we got our exercise. We used to walk to the swimming pool.'

It would be nice to think of Elvis as a nascent football player, that somehow pictures of him in his pads and helmet had got lost in the darkness of antiquity. Truth is, there are no pictures because Elvis was better at watching his pals play than he was at playing himself. But there were times when he did. 'We had our own football team here in the Courts. He played for about six weeks,' recalled Nick. But in those six weeks he was a member of that team. 'It was knock-down drag here. He was part of it. You were all part of the community.'

If exercise was not everyone's fancy, well, that was when Fred Frederick came in. He used to work in the Rialto cinema – or, rather, movie theatre as they called it. So he always provided his employers with new customers. Except that they never had to pay. 'I let them all in and gave them popcorn,' he remembered. Even Elvis worked as an usher at one time. And that was one of the few times he had trouble. And one of the few times when Elvis plainly lost his temper.

'We were walking home from the Rialto and some black boys hollered remarks. We stopped. It was explosive. Elvis was the tallest one in the group, so the black guys didn't push it. It wouldn't have been a good scrap.' But the mind boggles as to what would have happened had that actually turned into a 'scrap' and the boys only realised a little while afterwards that it was Elvis Presley with whom they had had the spat. What a story to tell their grandchildren!

For a time, it seemed to Elvis that life revolved around Lauderdale Courts. Today, the Courts seem like a series of

quite nice buildings. 'Not then, it wasn't,' said the singer Jimmy
Angel, who wasn't a Lauderdale resident but lived nearby. He
actually started off as an Elvis-type performer. His mother
was a famous gossip writer, working for Hedda Hopper, the
doyenne of Hollywood gossip columnists. But we were interested in his relationship with Elvis in the Memphis of the early
1950s. 'He was struggling.' But it would have been difficult
to do otherwise in that area. 'It was a housing project, the
cheapest housing.' Elvis's mother liked her boy talking to other
residents. Perhaps because it was a way for him to become
recognised as more than just the kid in overalls. Angel remembers both Elvis's parents.

His mother was a good mommy. His father, too, Vernon. He
was very protective of his son and that was the reason that
'Colonel' Parker got him. I don't think his mother was into him
at all. He was a flim-flam kid. I think he was one of the greatest
managers in the world, maybe the greatest. Without him, Elvis
would have had the same fate as Charley Rich, Carl Perkins,
Jerry Lee … very successful and then … Col. Parker, he saw
the light.

That was, though, a peep into the future. There was plenty in
the past at the Courts to make life, shall we say, interesting,
even doing simple things like going to the Rialto.

Sometimes, the fellers wanted to take girls with them. But
that was difficult. They couldn't sneak them in the way they
could each other. So they had to find money to do so. They cut
lawns (a mower still stands outside the Presley apartment).
They did paper rounds. A friend named Farleigh worked at a

supermarket. But they scraped the coins together so that they'd go to the nearby Ellis Auditorium. And then, when the circus came to town, they did, too. And there were those fights. One of the other ones that people will talk about – and they don't like giving bad news – is the one Elvis had with Farleigh. But it was rare. As Buzzy Forbess recalled: 'Elvis usually handled things better.'

And the row at the gas station, we mentioned before, came into our conversation.

Ken Black called out:

I want to comment on the fight. They were two older men, the gas station staff, who were jealous of him and his car. We had picked up some girls – from a boarding house where girls came to get a job. We picked up a girl, smooched around. Those girls are grandmothers now and I'm sure neither remembers my name.

What becomes abundantly clear about those days at the Lauderdale 'village' was that the memories would have been there even without an Elvis Presley to talk about. Sure, some stories get embellished, but the core confirms the truth behind them. Lauderdale veterans talk about it the way that immigrant New Yorkers talked about the Lower East Side and their London cousins romanced about the tenements of the East End. As the writer Emanuel Litvinoff once told me: 'They think it was wonderful, but they forget the poverty, the lack of food, sanitation and the smell of cat's piss.' It was better than that at Lauderdale Courts, but it wasn't beautiful. The people were poor – or they wouldn't have been living there in the first place. Their conditions were not the most pleasant

– although 100 per cent better than in Tupelo. And, probably, so were the friendships, although those of the people I met in his birthplace town were strong enough.

But there was something about life in this kind of village. This was not unlike the Tenement Symphony immortalised by the singer Tony Martin.

The nationalities and the religions mixed in what the song called a 'confusion'. 'There wasn't any place you couldn't knock on the door and go and eat – especially in an Italian house,' said Fred Frederick.

> The first wine I ever tasted was in an Italian house. It was comfort-able here. You'd go to the movies to see a story – no other reason. You had religious areas – Catholic, Jewish. It was all a big mix up when they came back from the war. It used to be that schools were divided, that was due to religion. But this was different from other areas because we were all mixed up. We were everyday Joes.

The 'everyday Joes' are a sentimental bunch. They remembered a lot of the furniture in the Presley apartment, although much of it has been replaced so that it looked a lot like the way it used to before. The people in the living room the day I was there lingered over the things they recalled – that lawnmower which Vernon Presley used, Gladys's rocking chair – always an iconic feature of rags-to-riches stories. There was a radiogram, the one Vernon had bought, two electric fans, a plaque labelled 'Chalkware', which Elvis had won at a fairground and which he brought for his mother, a toy gun, even a television set. All bought with hard cash provided by hard work.

I looked around the room that is being celebrated as a Presley museum. 'This is nice,' I said often enough. But another alumnus of what could double as part of a forgotten university of life, who didn't want his name quoted, told me: 'It wasn't nice when I was there. Vernon had problems finding money. That's why they left Tupelo.'

He remembered Gladys's occasionally legendary cooking – good food from poor scraps. Her speciality when there were more than scraps available? 'Cheeseburgers.'

So how did Elvis's connection with Lauderdale Courts, or 185 Winchester, get started? It was a story they all could tell.

'There was virtually no housing for any of us. It was hard getting into the projects after the war. Our old slums had to be demolished because the furniture was supporting the ceilings – so people were pleased to get here.'

And they were pleased to be able to say that knowing everyone else was in its way a ticket to a good meal. The connection between Lauderdale and Humes High School was constantly referred to. It had been at Humes High that a development in the Presley youth was first mentioned.

Gene Bradbury told me: 'In the fall of 1956, Derry Bilions – he was the lieutenant colonel in the ROTC [the Reserve Officers' Training Corps] here – wanted a special drill team, so someone suggested Elvis. He went to see him and took care of it.' In other words, Elvis joined.

That struck many a chord during my visit to the Courts. The old neighbours were looking at the pictures dotted around the room. Sure enough, there was one of Elvis in his ROTC uniform.

Buzzy Forbess remembered for me.

It was a good chance for him to dress better. He had no fancy clothes at school. Just a couple of shirts at $3 each. You wore what you could get. But the uniforms – for him and for me – it was the best clothes we had. The Armed Forces paid for that. But we had to buy the polish for our shoes.

That was a lesson to be learnt – and full-time troops on both sides of the Atlantic would recognise that. He didn't have much choice about joining the Reserve Officers' Training Corps. Elvis had no ambition to be an officer – which was just as well since he didn't become one. The idea was to give people a chance to learn about military matters. No one can be sure whether it did him any good when he eventually put on his uniform and took that little trip to Germany.

But certainly the Lauderdale residents knew that there was something special about Elvis when he put on that uniform. At least, that was what Blanche Gordon Scott believed. And she has believed it for a long time.

I walked with Elvis to school, all the way through high school, and we continued our relationship after we went to work. And he talked to me of his hopes and dreams. We talked behind the library by the river. He'd spread out his shirt for me to sit on. He said God had given him his voice and he knew he was going to be an entertainer and he said he wanted to make a million dollars so his mom wouldn't have to work.

And together they listened to the Grand Ole Opry which in Tennessee is a kind of cathedral to the great God country and western. 'We all dreamed,' said Blanche, 'of being an Opry star to get out of the cotton fields and my family carried round a guitar and I thought it was natural – although the kids at school thought he was strange.'

Strange? Elvis? They had plenty of chances to think again. I asked Blanche if she really believed he was going to be successful. She had listened to others who liked to sing as they strummed a guitar, including people in her own family.

> He was better than them. They were good, but he was better. He had such a voice range. I was listening to the Grand Ole Opry, to people like Ernest Tubb [their big star at the time] and he valued my opinion. Elvis would use me as his sounding board – even up to 'Love Me Tender'. He was starting to get gigs then.

The abiding memory for Fred Frederick was going out with him to a bar or a run-down restaurant where they had a juke-box. 'He'd play a song and he'd turn his collar up. He'd laugh and enjoy it. I'd never seen anyone that talented,' especially one who was so loyal.

> He never forgot his friends. [Years later] he would phone from the mansion and say come out to the movies or the fairgrounds. We went to a travelling good-time show and he paid for every-thing. The only problem was if you got on the roller coaster with him, he'd never stop it all night long. It never stopped. He'd rent the whole fairground, dodgem cars.

There were two kinds of people they saw there when Elvis was paying – 'the good guys and the bad guys'. For two years, he would rent those grounds – taking it over for himself and his

pals, giving them all free rides all night and more than a song
or two in between. The long sideburns, the front quiff, the tight
pants and the swivelling hips competing with the roller coaster;
the pals from Lauderdale frequently more interested in the rolling ride than the rocking singer. Oh, how things would change
– and how people would chide them when the trips stopped.

By then, however, community life was about to change. The
Presley family had to move – and for the best of reasons. They
had too much money in the bank – an income that had passed
that magic and disappointingly low $3,000 figure. So the
Courts became part of their past. They changed homes, first to
Alabama Street, half a mile away, and then to places that were
somewhat plusher.

Sometimes business and social life got mixed up – Blanche
Gordon Scott's (Elvis's school companion from Lauderdale)
business: 'We were very close for six years, dreaming the
dream.' It would have been nice, she might have dreamed, to
stop having to collect rents. But she told Elvis about that, too
– and about a shop that she had to visit during her normal
working week. It was a place he already knew something
about, run by people who paid their rent to her on time.

This was a menswear store called Lansky's – or, to give it
its full name, Lansky Brothers, run at the time I was there by
Bernard Lansky (who has since died) and his son Hal, who
called his father 'Mr B'. The shop was bought for Bernard
and his brother (whom Bernard had then bought out) by their
father, a local grocer, in 1946. Originally, it specialised in World
War Two forces' surplus goods, but then it changed. Now it
was homing in on the sort of clothes that led the young Elvis to
think of dressing the way he sang – with originality and style.

These days, Lansky's is smart, slightly expensive, with an air of quality about it, not at all the kind of emporium usually associated with the rock'n'roll crowd. The carpets are deep, as is the conversation between proprietors and customers coming into the ultra-fashionable Peabody Hotel where the shop is now situated.

What distinguishes this shop from most others is that it still caters for that rock'n'roll crowd, but plainly the better heeled ones. Everywhere you look you see guitars: big guitars, small guitars, medium guitars. You might think they are the kind you could pick up at any friendly neighbourhood music store. Well, not quite. They don't sell guitars here. They're pure decoration. And pure public relations. The same might be said of the pairs of blue suede shoes – except that they *do* sell shoes here, as well as the hippest outfits this side of Nashville. Everything in the shop is there as part of the big deal that this place is important. Each of the guitars is autographed – with Elvis's heading a list that also includes names that are familiar even to people who care nothing about rock'n'roll, but which for those who do would make them salivate. Names like Roy Orbison, Carl Perkins, B. B. King, Van Morrison, James Taylor ... even the Sex Pistols. Because the instruments are for the decoration of their own place, the Lanskys bought them for themselves.

All the names are of customers, customers who signed instruments rather than autograph books. All of them wrote their signatures.

There are huge portraits of Elvis and, at the snap of a guitar string, they will show you a picture of him shaking hands with the senior proprietor or 'Mr B' fitting a blue jacket and adjusting its brown collar. If you ask nicely, they'll give you a copy of that snap to take home with you – although they might be happier if you also take an Elvis-type jumpsuit, too. If it's going to make you drool at the prospect of joining the other cats in the business, they'll be very happy. There is always a special label on whatever it is you buy, stressing the Presley connection. Why else would the label – and the one on a string that hangs from every jacket and pair of trousers in the shop – declare the fact that Lansky Brothers were 'Clothiers to the King'? They couldn't allow that connection to disappear – and neither could the customers.

By this time, you would have learnt that the Lanskys long ago took Elvis to their hearts. But probably no more than he took them to his. They themselves form a part of the Elvis story that is different from any other, but which, in its way, is one of the most important. Stretch the imagination and you could say that all those shows in which the sweat dropped from the forehead and cheeks of the King have a lot to do with the men, father and son, who run Lansky's. They aren't your usual idea of the rock'n'roll crowd either. They are soberly dressed and have the air of the businessmen they are, except that they dot their conversation with the 'right' phrases such as 'he's cool in the pool'.

And they do it with thick Southern accents, which is some-how unexpected, coming from the lips of the elder Lansky, whose family hailed – he was one of nine children – from Grodno in what is now Belarus and who is a pillar of the local Jewish community. If he could talk the talk, it wasn't just rock speak. He peppers his conversation with Yiddish and what at one time would have been called jive talk. There was no better way of saying that things continued, more of the same, than using Mr B's favourite expression, 'noch a mol'. It came naturally to him, although it didn't sound quite so traditional with that Deep South accent. Talking about their favourite customer, Elvis Presley, Mr Lansky Sr says they always gave him what they believed he needed. 'We walk his walk, talk his talk, eat his mash and talk his trash,' he told me. I just about understood. They didn't talk like that in Grodno, or in the Lower East Side of New York, where most of the Jewish immigrants to America settled on arrival.

Elvis shopped with the Lanskys in the days when their shop was situated just a stone's throw from the Peabody. That was at the corner of Beale Street, the street that sums up Memphis as much as the music played there. It now boasts a wall plaque recalling when it also meant Lansky's. In those days, young Elvis Presley could be seen hanging around outside and every now and again, just like other small boys of his age admiring the ice cream in the parlours they could not afford to patronise or the toy shops they would never dream of entering, standing with his nose pressed to the window. He was studying the clothes he only wished he had the money to buy so that he could really look the part when he had his next gig. What he really wanted the first time he dared walk the walk into the store was a tuxedo for his school prom. And a white tuxedo at that. He knew he'd never afford it. But a look in his direction and he succumbed to the entreaties of the proprietor.

Or, to be more precise, the Lanskys succumbed to him. It was the beginning of a beautiful friendship. And a very profitable one for both parties – although it might not have seemed it when Elvis made that first purchase. Said 'Mr B': 'He told me he'd buy me out when he got rich. I said we would not be for sale, but my clothes always were.' He said he admired the cheek – or as they don't say too often Down South, chutzpah – of the lad who was now working part-time as an usher at the nearby Loews Theater.

I asked if the firm ever told Elvis that a particular outfit didn't suit him. 'No,' Hal told me. 'Everything suited him.'

Later, he could honestly boast that Elvis was the best PR man in the world for his outfits. But that was not immediately obvious. Maybe Bernard Lansky (calling him 'Mr B', Hal says, sounds more professional than 'Dad') saw young Elvis as a kid with talent and ambitions to do so much better, in a way not unlike his own family's flight from European pogroms to work towards making a success in business. Or perhaps it was simply that he wanted to do a good turn for a youngster who needed a break, but, who, nevertheless, he believed, had enough talent in his guitar fingers to be a huge success. So he gave Elvis a discount and allowed him to pay on his own instalment plan.

Blanche has never forgotten the day the introduction took place. 'I was with him when he set up the account with Lansky's.'

She remembers what he looked like that day. For Elvis, it was like being on stage, a gig, a performance.

Blanche remembered what happened when old Mr Lansky – then, of course, young Mr Lansky – beckoned him to come in. Elvis had never seemed happier – at least, not since his visit to the Tupelo hardware store. For 'Mr B' it was a moment that helped put his business on the map – and keep it that way. As his son Hal told me, without them knowing it they were soon going to be facing difficult times. 'Memphis shut down after a certain gentleman was shot,' said Hal. That 'certain gentleman' was Martin Luther King, assassinated in Memphis in April 1968. 'It took thirty-four years for business to recover,' Hal told me. Business in general, that is. Lansky's had Elvis Presley. Said Hal: 'He had his dreams – to be a star.'

That being so, neither of them, father or son, can claim to have had any prophetic vision when the young man whom they regarded as a kid stared enviously at the white tuxedo in their Beale Street window. 'He had no money, but no money, no fun,' said the older proprietor.

> I had no idea he was going to be a star but I trusted him, yes, man. We did it for lots of people. He didn't have money to pay for the tuxedo but you have to be good to people. Word of mouth would bring people to come to the store. People know I can give you what you want, man. [With Elvis] from then on, it's just boom-boom. We had no idea Elvis was going to be a star.

But maybe Elvis did – if only because it would give him a chance to become a regular Lansky customer. 'He came back for other things,' said Hal. 'Yeh,' came in his dad, 'he would come in all the time.'

In fact, they maintain he came in every day. 'He worked at Loews, which was just a block away,' Hal explained. 'You'd see him looking in the window.' When he saw something he wanted – and there was always something he wanted – he shyly approached the owners and came to a deal.

'From then on,' said Mr B, talking in the vernacular once more, 'it was boom-boom.'

They knew he needed to pay on the instalment plan. 'I

once asked, "Have you got money?" He said, "I got money." I said, "Put it away",' Mr B recalled. He said he knew the young fellow would pay him back. 'I said, "You've got it [the item he coveted] just so long as you bring in Mr Green".' Mr Green came in various forms – but always resembled dollar bills. That was part of the service. As 'Mr Green's' friend 'Mr B' put it: 'He'd say, "What you got this time?"' He knew there would always be something Elvis wanted – and so did Elvis.

They'd sell him bolero jackets. Sometimes a pair of pants. Hal has looked up the receipts for those trousers. He paid $3.95 for them and $1.95 for a cap. 'He could buy a shirt for $2.95. It seemed like a lot of money in those days.'

As Elvis's success grew, so did the bill for his clothes. They have them on display in Lansky's at the Peabody Hotel. You have to realise there are two sides to Memphis – the rock'n'roll and blues Memphis where you are asked to leave your guns behind, and the luxurious Peabody.

There, proudly on view in a glass case is a vast (it would be classed as 'extra-large plus plus' in some places) pink leather overcoat with a mink collar. 'Coats like that became popular with the African American movies of the time when it seemed that only pimps wore them.' Hal Lansky says Presley was offered $30,000 for it, which they regarded as a fair price. However, Elvis originally bought it from them for $300. It came back to the store to be mended a short time before he died. 'The back of it was ripped. We repaired it but he never came back for the coat.' The firm might sell it if someone else came along with $30,000. For the moment, though, it stands on display, further proof that their place was 'By Appointment to the King'.

The Peabody is just the right place for such an establishment
as Lansky's. In another part of the hotel is a cabinet showing a
receipt attached to a letter – from 'Colonel' Parker to Elvis on
Peabody notepaper. For $4,500, a bonus from RCA Records.
The hotel adds that this forms a legal document 'as good as
money in the bank'.

In a way, the Lanskys are unexpectedly modest about some
aspects of their Presley associations. They made him the first
specially-for-the-stage outfits. But the first jumpsuits they sold
him were fairly conservative. Said Hal:

> In the late 1960s we sold him some jumpsuits, but not as wild
> as the ones he wore in his later years, but we might have had
> some influence on those outfits. But we don't take credit for
> later on. We like to take credit for the 1950s when he was
> young and innocent.

Bernard Lansky says he knew what the star wanted when he
was not so young and far less innocent. He made clothes to
measure for him. 'We made them specially. Man, I'm good.
I know what I want to do. You come in Monday, you want
it Friday, we've got it covered Papa. You get out of here. We
clean up. That's what Elvis knew.'

But a lot of the clothes he bought in those early years were
strictly off-the-peg. As Hal Lansky recalls:

> In those days he was just an ordinary guy, but he knew [to
> look in] our windows because our clothes were bright. They
> were above the ordinary. The bright colours brought Elvis into
> our store, the pinks and the blacks. We like to take credit for

the blacks and pinks that he wore. Everything was pink in that era – like the pink Cadillacs that he bought.

Hal's father likes to remember that he always thought of Elvis as someone very special even when he was buying clothes on what people on the other side in Britain used to call 'the never-never'.

There were fifteen tailors working for the Lanskys at the time – with Bernard Sr, 'Mr B', supervising and making sure that his best customers, including young Mr Presley, had exactly what they wanted – not just the ever-changing styles, but the never-changing quality of material and stitching he knew Elvis wanted. To them he was a perfectionist and they wanted to keep his custom – even though it sometimes took a few weeks before they got their money.

The strange thing was that until they saw him on television, the Lanskys really didn't know anything about him. 'I didn't know what the hell he did,' said 'Mr B'. That was a recommendation of Elvis's honesty on the one hand and of his own idea of business ethics on the other.

Back in the 1950s, once they did discover who he was, the Lanskys were notified of every development in the Presley career. They knew that for them all there was a part to play. Elvis told 'Mr B' that he had a contract to sing on *The Ed Sullivan Show*. 'I'm gonna need some clothes because I am going to have several gigs on television,' he told them. 'I showed him what we had – all the clothes I thought he'd want. He told me he had a problem with money,' said the senior Mr Lansky. 'I knew that Mr Green would soon help him out, so I gave him what he needed. Sure enough, Mr Green came.' And kept coming.

'He was fantastic,' he says, possibly with the benefit of folk memory, rubbed-off fame and success and appreciation for the effect the man had on his business. 'He was quiet – a real gentleman. I told him to call me "Bernard". He said – and that was because his mother brought him up properly – "Thank you, Mr Lansky." All the time, he was nice to us. He was cool in the pool. He talked the talk.'

And, indeed, they did business together affectionately. When Elvis clocked up million-dollar sales for his singles and albums, RCA Victor records not only gave him a gold disc, but also a 'small' gift in kind, too. One time it was that early 1960s sensation a Messerschmitt bubble car. Elvis passed it on to the Lanskys – 'in return for a two-hour shopping spree in our store'.

That would be before Hal was old enough to go into the business himself, let alone drive the tiny vehicle. 'In the early years,' Hal recalled,

every Sunday my dad used to take me out. I was nine, ten, eleven and my dad used to take me out horseback riding. But in later years, I graduated to being a delivery boy to the king of rock'n'roll. I would go to the mansion [Graceland]. The door opened magically and the next thing I knew, the King came down those steps. He had a bathrobe on. He had his hand in his pockets – and I knew there was a pistol in his pocket. That kinda put a spin on things. It made the trip a little more exciting. It was the early 1970s.

Said Hal:

> He was so anxious to try on his Lansky clothes. We had a thing
> called 'Super Fly'. Long coats [like the pink $30,000 one in
> the store] that people thought were only worn by pimps. So
> we tried one of those coats with fur collars on Elvis. We had
> a furrier working in the store to make those collars. Elvis put
> that coat on – with a top hat to match the coat. He walked into
> the dining room and swung open the doors to the kitchen and
> showed the coat and hat to his housekeeper and chef.

Even then, though, Elvis bought more conventional clothes,
too. 'He bought shirts with button-down collars, with a pick
stitch around the collars and cuffs. We sold lace-up-front shirts,
ruffled shirts, the short bolero coats had a high roll collar.'

Sometimes, they actually gave him clothes – which shows
just how much of a good customer he was. He was also a
customer who recommended the shop to his friends and,
sometimes, his rivals. The older Lansky told me: 'He'd say
[to his friends], "Man, this jacket looks good on you." The
other cats would say, "Where did you get that from?" He'd
tell them "From Beale Street".' Those other 'cats' included a
certain Frank Sinatra, although it's Elvis whom 'Mr B' and his
son enjoy talking about and who they thank for their position
in business. Vernon, Elvis's father, did well out of the relationship. The Lanskys made him suits, too – three at a time.

Elvis paid. Of course.

When Bernard was invited to Graceland, they gave him the
full treatment – including breakfast at five o'clock in the evening.
Lansky wasn't impressed: 'I told them I'm going home for dinner.'

If Elvis influenced other entertainers, he was not beyond being influenced by people himself – and not just those in show business. 'Mr B' liked to tell of the time he went really conservative. 'He showed me a tobacco can – with a picture of the British King Edward [VII] on it. He said "make me a suit like this". So I did a black cutaway cut with black trousers, just like royalty wore.'

As Hal put it: 'He was a clothes horse. He looked good in everything and he'd buy everything. Like a kid in a candy store.' And his father rejoined: 'Every time he came here, he wanted to buy something. He'd come back an hour later with the money.'

All that began soon after Blanche Gordon Scott introduced him to Lansky's and suggested he go there for the white dinner jacket he was going to wear at the prom. Up to then, all they had talked about was just to wonder at the way he reacted to the tunes he heard. 'He felt the black music he heard in Tupelo and on the Delta,' Blanche told me. 'We'd walk to WC Handy Park.' It was the place favoured by both musicians and courting couples, named in honour of the writer of 'St Louis Blues' and their own 'Beale Street Blues'. There, the talk about aspirations got all the hotter.

It helped shape the look of Elvis's appearances as well as his talents. When he made the trip to Lansky's, he was, in his mind, dressed as close to kill as it would have been possible without having the police ready to take him to jail. Blanche recalled for me:

[At the park] we'd see the black musicians feeling this music. The blacks were wearing their pink shirts and black pants. Elvis wore his hair long, like the blacks but only because his parents couldn't afford to pay for a haircut. His hair always ended up in a ducktail at the back. He was always looking for something different, so he would be distinctive.

But was that more because he actually liked the style or simply because he really couldn't afford to do anything else? She saw the two sides of his situation. 'Both,' Blanche said.

In Memphis, there is so much to show of how far the fellow who had stood with his nose virtually glued to the Lansky's window had come. It really all started for him with a certain recording studio whose logo was a rising sun. Elvis went to the building to cut a disc. The result of that visit by the lanky, unknown youngster was that the relatively tiny label never looked back and the sun on those old 78 rpm records shone ever brighter. But no one at the time thought it was going to turn out that way.

Sun Records was a fairly small operation, nothing like the big boys then like Columbia, RCA or even Verve. But they had good equipment in a rather shabby building, and in the somewhat limited country music market in the South and West they were beginning to be an important name. The studios on Union Avenue look today as if they could do with a coat of paint, and the floor needs a bit of polish. But, then, it always did. It looked that way the day Elvis called and said he had a tune he wanted to record. Not quite the puffed-up idea that such a statement would suggest. The company that filled jukeboxes throughout the South with discs waxed (the wax used for those old breakable records was to be in use until the late 1950s) by people like Johnny Cash and Carl Perkins also had a side line in recording numbers by people who just walked in, paid $4 and went home with a disc under their arms. These were mostly young people who never expected the records to be heard by anyone outside their own families – and then only until they were worn out by being overplayed. Very few people had tape recorders in their homes when Elvis called at the studio, went into a booth and nervously recorded a tune especially for his mother, 'My Happiness'. It was the very first recording with the name Elvis Presley on the label – handwritten.

Guy Thomas Harris remembered when that happened and the reaction to it back in the old home town in Tupelo.

In 1953, he came back here and Odell Clarke and I went to the fair with Elvis. I asked him what he'd been doing and he said he'd stopped at Sun and asked if he could cut a record. I said, what did they say? 'They asked me if I could sing', he told me. He asked me what I thought and he said he wanted to cut it for his mother's birthday. And he cut 'My Happiness'. We were all proud. We were all for him 100 per cent.

This was the start of everything. But it took some time. As my guide in the Sun recording studio, Matt Ross-Spang, told me: 'Sam Phillips [who ran the studio] had heard Elvis sing "My Happiness". But this wasn't country music. "This is not going on Sun Records",' he said. Yet Elvis was a recording star – although no one knew it. And certainly Sam Phillips didn't – at first. Of course, his mother did. But Phillips was just about persuaded and allowed him to come into the studio and play around with his resident bass player Bill Black and the guitarist Scotty Moore.

No recordings were planned, but in his mind Sam Phillips had decided that he might not lose too much money getting him in to make a 'proper' recording. The three of them – Elvis, Scotty and Bill – started jamming a song called 'That's All Right', giving it an upbeat sound never heard before. It had been written by a blues singer called Arthur Crudup and recorded by him as 'That's All Right, Mama'.

Phillips heard what they were doing and instantly told them to go through it again, this time with the recording machines switched on. Phillips's risk was to get Elvis to do the song (any song), but with the word 'Mama' omitted on the label – although that would come later. It was backed by 'Blue Moon of Kentucky' – exactly the same pairing chosen by Crudup. No one had any idea what would happen to it. It was only a matter of days before they found out.

The record was released on 19 July 1954. Virtually instantly, Elvis's version did a great deal better than Crudup's original.

The studio boss sent a copy to the DJ Dewey Phillips (no relation) who started playing it on his radio show *Red, Hot and Blue*. It was the very first airing of a commercial Presley song.

Dewey played "That's All Right" seventeen times. Sam Phillips heard the show, was amazed at the number of fan letters that came in and was convinced – to the tune of 20,000 copies' worth of mind-changing.

He immediately put the very young Elvis Presley on a two-year contract. Every one of his current friends and those who had been around him in the old days got to hear about it. 'And his popularity flipped,' as one devotee put it. One record after the other began the long, long trail of Presley hits.

Sitting in the control room at Sun, next to one of his old

recording machines, sound engineer Stan Kesler recalled for me what happened after the success of 'That's All Right'. He didn't actually twiddle the knobs on that machine when Elvis was there, but, in a way, he had a much closer relationship with the burgeoning star. He was to write five of his songs: 'I'm Left, You're Right, She's Gone', 'I Forgot to Remember to Forget', 'Thrill of Your Love', 'Playing for Keeps' and 'If I'm a Fool for Loving You'.

The royalties were to keep him happy for a long time. I asked Kesler what it was like hearing Elvis Presley singing his material. He gave the same answer that many another songwriter would have done: 'Unforgettable.' He says he remembered him as 'one of the guys, a musician. But he couldn't be himself, so many people around him.'

I asked if he had really thought that Elvis would one day be the superstar that he became. 'No. I knew he had loads of talent but didn't know he'd be so big.'

DJ 'Cowboy' Jack Clement, who was to be a radio star in his own right, was a producer at Sun in those early days of the Elvis triumphs, as well as a singer.

'I saw him a lot. He was big right from the start. I used to play the Eagle's Nest and he was the floorshow. One night I was singing there and he came up to sing. He was flirting with my beautiful girl while I was on stage.'

That wasn't very nice to see, I suggested. 'Oh, I got my own back,' he answered. 'I married her.'

An affectionate comment perhaps, helped by his own feelings for Elvis. 'I liked him – oh yes, right from day one or two. I was in the Marine Corps and one morning went back to Memphis. The DJ Sleepy-Eyed John played "Blue Moon of

Kentucky" and Dewey Phillips had played it the night before and everyone went nuts. Before the end of the day, everyone was talking about Elvis Presley.' It was, he recognised, a voice with style. 'Yeh. Right in your face. Everyone was talking about it.'

Clement himself gave up singing. 'I think I had decided that I didn't want to be an artist myself. Too many pitfalls. I didn't realise that anyone could just cut a record. I didn't know of any record companies till Sam Phillips was around.' And, he added, Elvis didn't know much about records and what they could do for his career. 'After all, he got famous on the radio. But everyone was buying his records – kids and older people, too: 45s and 78s.'

I asked what he thought Elvis was best at. 'Just getting up there and singing his butt off,' he answered without batting an eyelid or cupping an ear. 'He was good at most things.' But what drove him? Was it the showmanship or the music? 'All he wanted to do was cut a record for his mom. Sam was still doing that kind of music. Cutting a record for $4 a time. That kind of business was a bunch of trouble.'

'That's All Right' was played on the jukebox at the Blues Shop, where most of his gang hung out. 'He was excited. He was proud for his mother. He really enjoyed that.'

But if it didn't lead to Clement himself joining the pantheon of other great rock'n'roll discoveries, thanks to him, others did join it.

I cut out that sort of business. I phased that out. The most momentous artist I discovered was Jerry Lee Lewis. Chap came in and said he could play the piano like Chet Atkins. Well,

Atkins was a guitar player and sure enough Jerry Lee played the piano like Atkins's guitar style.

So Jerry Lee was good but, he said, 'Oh! Elvis was unique.' Not, however, that Elvis ever made a fuss over what he was doing. 'He'd tell people you could get on the radio and fart.' But that didn't mean that Elvis was necessarily the best of the bunch who went into a Sun recording studio and performed. I asked him whether, if he put Elvis in a group with Johnny Cash and Jerry Lee Lewis, Elvis would be on top. I thought I could anticipate the answer. 'I wouldn't want to rank him. He loved Bill Monro and he sang a lot of bluegrass.'

Actually, it was a woman called Marion Keisker who is perhaps responsible for Elvis's success at Sun. She was Sam Phillips's assistant and should be credited with more than that, finding Elvis and making his career – much as legendary Hollywood film producer Louis B. Mayer's assistant, Ida Koveman, used to act as his talent scout and came up with names she had discovered such as Clark Gable and Judy Garland.

Ms Keisker knew, even if Sam didn't at first, that Elvis could have been the answer to Phillips's prayers.

All Elvis's old friends claim to know the story. For instance, Jimmy Angel. Of course, Sam Phillips had a lot to answer for, too – without him, there possibly would never have been an Elvis Presley outside of the poor quarter of Memphis. As Angel said:

Times were hard. Sam Phillips liked the black cats. Phillips was looking for something that sounded black but would [also] get the white folks – because he couldn't get the white stations.

Fats Domino sold 200,000 in two years for 'I'm Walkin''. Rick Nelson sold two million in a week. Sam himself was a music cat, a brave guy.

Brave enough to take an unknown whom he is convinced led to a certain British sensation known ... yes ... as the Beatles. That may or may not be true. But certainly Elvis was just waiting, ready to be just as big a hit. Was Phillips really brave in booking Presley? Probably not. It didn't exactly cost a fortune to press a record or two, but he was certainly brave in another way. Angel told Barbra Paskin for my radio series, *The Elvis Trail*: 'The Ku Klux Klan tried to shut him down time after time.' That was the penalty down South for a white man marketing blacks. It was another reason, perhaps for Jimmy Angel's – even belated – enthusiasm for Elvis Presley.

It all started at the same time as 'That's All Right'. 'At first when Elvis walked into Sun and said he wanted to make a record for his mom, he sang "My Happiness". She gave it to Sam. Elvis wanted to do ballads but Sam provoked him and that's when they cut "Blue Moon of Kentucky".'

It turned out to be a huge hit. As John Rumbole, senior historian at the Country Music Hall of Fame, told me:

Elvis synthesised country, gospel and pop. He came up through country, and performed on the *Louisiana Hayride* [radio show]. He toured the country with acts such as Hank Snow. When we come to 1954 when Elvis's hits were coming out, country music was shaken by this new music of rock'n'roll. Radio stations were adopting rock formats.

In the world of rock'n'roll, nobody knew that Presley was about to become king. But, for the moment, as Rumbole said, 'he helped to nationalise country music. He had a great impact on country music. Prior to him, there were very new nationally famous country stars – just perhaps Red Foley, Gene Autrey, Eddie Arnold and Roy Acuff, maybe.' But, as he did not say, none of them had an impact to compare with that of Elvis.

It was into that world that a whole new tranche of music professionals and hangers-on came.

The engineers at the recording studios on Union Avenue took it all in their stride. But the response of people who heard it was enough for it to be played on night-time radio shows all over the South. Some copies strayed over the Mason–Dixon Line into the North, which was the real beginning of the Elvis Presley revolution. The disc was marketed, not originally optimistically, by Sun and in days everything changed. Memphis youngsters lined up to buy newly minted copies and Elvis made live performances at the country and western jamboree at nearby Overton Park. Word spread – and so did Elvis's fame. Now, for the first time, Elvis Presley was a star outside his home town (both of them). Now he could afford to pay the Lanskys and buy a new outfit.

And the local teenagers – particularly the girls – just wanted to be around him. As one of the pals recalled:

> We went in Elvis's car [things were really getting better; now he had his own transport] and we went to the Community Center. Everyone rushed to Elvis Presley. We were ghosts. Nobody noticed us. He always said he wanted a Cadillac – a pink Cadillac; when he had some money. He got one.

When he did get that very expensive car, it was to be another trademark, to go side by side with his clothes. It was also a mark that he had arrived, a prestige point.

There was an even more significant result of the steamroller called 'That's All Right' – the establishment of a new and bigger coterie around him. Some of its members were out for all they could get. Others were cementing existing friendships or establishing new ones that would outlive Elvis in life. Because of his fame and because of the fact that he loved to keep people together, the Presley set came into their own. Together, they became known by a title that could have seemed dangerously insulting – the Memphis Mafia. Instead, it turned into a badge of honour, one they wore beside the brooch Elvis gave them and would himself wear, a monogram of three letters, 'TCB', the famous 'Taking Care of Business' legend. To those in the know, it was a trademark as prestigious as Coca-Cola or Cadillac.

The business of the Mafia was to take care of the head of that business, Elvis himself. Put simply, it was to be his friend and do what friends are supposed to do. It was, in effect, the Presley version of Frank Sinatra's Rat Pack.

If Elvis was the godfather (or even the monarch) of the Memphis Mafia, the chairman of the board was his old schoolmate, the class president, George Klein.

As we have seen, it was at Humes High School that they first met. 'He was at my music class and we bonded,' Klein told me.

The friendship developed further as Elvis's career zoomed. George Klein was at the beginning of that, too. He saw it from the inside because, as he put it, 'I was a flunky for various radio stations.' Most significantly, he worked with Dewey Phillips on his radio programme.

'Elvis was driving a truck then – for Crown Electric. He said he wanted to get with a band, have an audition.' He didn't know yet about 'That's All Right'.

There's an argument to be made – a fairly thin one, admittedly – that Klein, doing his 'flunky' job, was the first person outside the Presley family to have heard that record.

When I got out of Humes, I wanted to get into radio. I didn't have the money to go to radio college. But I was approached to be a sit-in, help-out guy for Dewey Phillips. [In Memphis], he was like Alan Freed or Hunter Hancock in Los Angeles. So, 'yes', I said. I'd do that. I was Dewey's gofer. And I began to do presentation. I couldn't be a gofer all the time so I cut some demo tapes and sent them out and I got hired by a station in Arkansas. I went over there and I came home on the weekend and I went by WHBO and saw Dewey and he played me Elvis Presley singing and I said, 'Who is that?' Dewey said, 'You went to school with him?' I said, 'Great! My man Elvis has a record out!'

The fact that he heard that record at that time might also – just might – have been responsible for the Presley career taking off with the boom and lurch that it now did. And certainly for Klein himself getting a new life.

I got a job at KWEM, a part-time job. The morning jock was playing rhythm and blues and he left, so I took over that spot. I took off straight away, getting a hundred letters a day and I got a call from Bill Grumbles at Dewey's station. I went to see him and he asked me about my morning ratings. Apparently I was number two in the morning.

It was a good enough position for him to get yet another new job and for Elvis to take another giant leap forward.

Klein fronted a popular show called *The Rock'n'Roll Ballroom* – 'live on stage, kids dancing. Elvis used to come and see me.' But Klein lost his radio job. 'They said rock'n'roll wouldn't last and they sacked me.' Elvis then stepped into the breach. 'He said, "You're going to work for me." I said, "Oh, man!"' His job? As Elvis's travelling companion, a job usually reserved for young ladies going on trips with lonely old women. In this case, it was part of a command performance.

'We were to go to Hawaii and to Canada. There were three of us with Elvis at that time – Gene Smith and Arthur Hooton. I was the third guy.'

And they all had a job to do – which, in less polite language that was used outside of Memphis, was known as pimping. 'I wouldn't call it that,' said George, 'I'd go out and ask ten to twenty girls to come back.' They were girls who knew what they were wanted for, even if they didn't know on whose behalf the 'travelling companions' were providing this particular individual service. They soon would, however.

Sonny West, who through the years would be involved in the Presley career, for good or bad, and who was also on hand, said that he and his fellow Mafia members would go

what we called 'trolling' and we'd go down in our car and see a couple of girls and say, 'Hi, howya doin?'

A few minutes later we were heading back in two or three cars to the house. The only time I remembered going out and getting them without Elvis himself choosing which girl he wanted was in

Lake Tahoe. There was a very pretty girl sitting there beside the stage, at a table, and I was watching her and I looked at Elvis and I could see that Elvis was looking at her, flirting with her from the stage. So when the stage curtains closed, I went right next to him and he said, 'Sonny, there's a girl …' I knew what he wanted. 'OK, boss,' I said. 'I know which one.' I went up to the girl and asked her, 'Would you like to meet Elvis? He saw you were enjoying yourself. Would you like to come back and see him in his dressing room?' and she said, 'Oh yes.' So I took her back to his dressing room. They dated for a while. He saw her more than just one time.

It was a frequently occurring tale.

Once in Vegas, he said to me, 'Sonny, we need some girls.' We were playing at the Hilton. So I would go out and invite some girls we found down there who were attractive. And we'd ask them, 'Are you with anyone – a boyfriend or a husband or anything?' They said, 'No. We are just here from LA.' I'd say, 'Would you like to meet Elvis?' and they would. We had a little party and they would enjoy it. There were eight or ten people up there. Just sitting around talking. He might pick one up who was special and make a connection if he found someone who was inviting to him. It's hard to believe, but there were times when he did not make a connection.

He said he never saw Elvis line girls up and choose which one he wanted to spend the night with. But, as we shall see, there were others who did witness it and that is more or less what he was confirming. But then there were always the 'special' ones.

There's a great little story about Shelley Fabares. She was an actress he made three pictures with her. He thought she was adorable. First picture, I saw him flirt with her and goes up to her and she says, 'Sorry, I cannot. I have a boyfriend.' He said, 'OK.' He honoured that. A couple of years later, he made another picture with her. I heard him say, 'Are you still going with that boyfriend?' She said, 'Yes, I am. But I'm engaged to him.' He said, 'Oh boy.' And the last time, on the last picture he made with her, *Clambake*. He said to her: 'You still engaged to that guy?' And she said, 'No. I'm married to him.' And he said: 'You were weakening, weren't you?' They had great chemistry. He had been around long enough to know if a girl wanted to be with him. The girl was always given the choice.

Sometimes, Elvis himself was offering services of the kind to those in his entourage. Years later, when Klein got married, Elvis let it be known that he would have been offended had he not been allowed to be best man. George had been a grooms-man at the star's own wedding and so to Presley it seemed the most natural thing in the world to stand with him side by side. 'He offered to pay for the whole wedding in Las Vegas. My woman was beside herself. Elvis put us up at the Hilton, it was amazing.'

'Amazing' was a word that applied equally to Elvis's former and only wife, the very young Priscilla. It was to be another of those vital moments in the Presley career – the time the boy from Tupelo, now a multi-millionaire, announced he had found the love of his life, the woman who would soon become the mother of his only child and then have no mean show-biz career herself. 'Elvis was gorgeous, a movie star. Priscilla was drop-dead gorgeous ... when she was fifteen, sixteen. Unbelievable.'

That was all to come – when the former class president-cum-travelling companion had become more of a mentor and sounding board than just a hanger-on. When Elvis was set to divorce Priscilla, Klein knew before most other people. He was surprised. 'I was shocked when it went wrong. Priscilla grew up. They grew apart. It was the most beautiful divorce I have ever seen. Elvis told her they would be friends for ever. He gave her $1 million in cash and child support.'

But that is really jumping ahead. It was not the kind of episode of which George Klein expected to be a part when he first signed on as a charter member of the Memphis Mafia, who bore little resemblance to the men with twisted noses who wore long overcoats and hailed from Sicily – when they weren't running the 'saloons' where a certain Mr Sinatra performed, that is. This made-to-measure group was not interested in extortion, had no desire to rub anyone out. Nor were they ready to treat people as publicity fodder the way Sinatra's Rat Pack did. 'Yes, we were a bit like them, but closer. We were all regular guys. Elvis was the only star.' That made a profound difference.

They did things for each other – and not just introducing women, says Klein. 'Sure [we helped each other] and, apart from Elvis, I was the only guy in show business.'

Anyone used to the Elvis Presley stories might be forgiven for thinking that he rode roughshod over his 'helpers' and was happy only when he got his own way. On the contrary, it seems that he was much more a kind of father confessor. Said Klein: 'We wouldn't help each other. No, we'd go to Elvis. He'd solve it. He'd talk to you. He'd bail you out. A health problem, he'd pay for it. He was the best friend I ever had.'

According to him, Elvis remained that way all through their association, which lasted until Elvis's death. Certainly it covered his Hollywood years.

He wasn't into the Hollywood scene. He went to see Robert Mitchum because he liked him. After making a picture he always went back to Memphis. He bought houses in Bel Air and Palm Springs. His movies took two months to shoot and then he'd go back to Memphis. He'd quit touring at that time.

For all the kindness and the joys that being with Elvis brought, there was always another side. The young Mrs (Priscilla) Presley saw that. As Elvis's friend George said: 'She didn't want to be in the goldfish bowl. Once Elvis Presley touched you, your life changed. It was like being in another family.'

But for Klein and most of the other people in his set, there was never a question of Klein himself wanting to get out.

'Also being in radio [he had another job at the same time as being an Elvis buddy] I had access to one of the greatest stars. It was a wonderful situation.'

Part of that 'wonderful situation' was watching the way Elvis dealt with his own problems – particularly his health. It was obvious that, as his fame grew, so did his waistline. 'He didn't take care of himself,' he recalled. 'He didn't eat fancy. Typical Southern stuff – meatloaf, pork chops. Fried chicken mash and greens. And he liked those peanut butter sandwiches – with bananas. He wasn't a sweet-eater, though sometimes he got into ice cream.'

Nobody knows if Priscilla tried to get him on to some kind of diet. 'We all casually mentioned it. But you had to be diplomatic, you know, drop hints.' You had to know how to drop those hints, however. He never told Klein, unlike some of the other mafiosi, to mind his own business. 'I was smart enough to be private about it, tactful.'

Not that Elvis didn't show his temper from time to time. 'But it was short-lived. If he was really upset, he'd stay in his room. He didn't become mean-spirited.'

Klein was to write his own book, called, appropriately enough, *Elvis Was My Best Man.*

I said in that it was a great ride for me. He gave me material things. What he gave me [best of all] was his friendship. He was the most versatile, most handsome and most charismatic. There are two men ... who were known only by their first names – Jesus and Elvis.

It was an interesting juxtaposition of names. Klein is Jewish and Elvis was at times accused of being anti-Semitic. His friend denies it totally. So does his fellow mafioso Sonny West.

He always had Jewish people around him. I asked my pastor about Alan Fortis and his uncle Abe, who was in the Supreme Court [after being Lyndon Johnson's principal adviser] and George Klein, because they were Jewish. I worried about them not being in the afterlife. I talked to my priest. He said it would be as if they had never existed.

Which must have worried Elvis's Jewish friends and fans.

A book would later claim that Presley was concerned about so-called Jewish power. 'I never said that,' West told me. 'That didn't come from me.'

As for George Klein, there's no doubt he wouldn't have been so close to him had he been so racist. And, after all, Elvis wore, as a lucky charm, the Hebrew letter 'chai', which means 'life', around his neck – alongside a cross. Klein thinks it quite possible that he had some Jewish roots, despite what the genealogist believed. What Elvis really was an internationalist, his friend maintains.

> There are Elvis statues in Japan, in Jerusalem. There's one of the head guys in China who sings like Elvis. He was a kind, kind person. Generous. He could sing in five styles – country, rock'n'roll, ballad, rhythm and blues, and gospel. That sums him up – the greatest entertainer the world has ever seen.

There were, of course, others who lay claim to that title. Al Jolson, who, to the surprise of many Presley fans, was the first to sing 'Are You Lonesome Tonight?' (in the same arrangement as Elvis would use years later, long after Jolson's death in 1950) called himself 'the World's Greatest Entertainer' and nobody dared correct him. It has always been a toss-up as to who could take over that role in the second half of the twentieth century – Frank Sinatra or Elvis. Since they each had very different styles, it is probably quite reasonable for them to share the accolade.

Not surprisingly, with success came wealth. But, as we shall see, money was slipping through Elvis's fingers like sand poured from a child's seaside bucket. His records, his stage appearances had from the late 1950s been bringing in the dollars to an extent rarely known before. Like some 21st-century computerised implement, every time he opened his mouth it was as if it automatically pressed a key on a cash register.

Every record he cut, every time he swivelled those hips, each scream from a young girl in the audience represented a kind of success not seen in the Deep South before. There had been brilliantly popular country stars like Hank Williams, and the Grand Ole Opry was, in those parts, the most listened-to event on steam radio and present at the burgeoning of the TV phenomenon, but this was essentially entertainment for folks (as they would say down there) living below that invisible Mason–Dixon Line.

The kind of success Elvis had now had previously been reserved strictly for Southern audiences. He was now proving he could cross not just that line, but the Atlantic and Pacific oceans, too. Sinatra didn't yet look as if he was going to be shaken from the throne that he had inherited from Jolson – who sang about the South but was in his forties before he saw what was familiarly known as the Swanee River. Now this still young kid with the greasy long hair, sideburns and what was so frequently – if unkindly – called the snarl of his lips was selling as many records in New York as in Memphis.

This situation was changed in a way that few could have anticipated. Ed Sullivan, the biggest talent maker in the country, invited Elvis on to his show and achieved a record of a kind not restricted to the 12-inch vinyl discs, which had taken over from the 78s. Tests showed that fifty-five million people watched the programme – an astonishing 83 per cent of the available audience (it was, of course, long before cable TV).

He was a hugely important investment for Phillips and his

Sun label. They were good for each other, as record producer 'Cowboy' Jack Clement remembered. And as was 'Colonel' Parker, who was shortly to come on the scene.

Elvis was so big that the record business was beginning to wonder how long Sun could keep him. Did they have the facilities, let alone the money needed to exploit Elvis, to sustain him as one of their artists?

Anyone with any 20:20 hindsight and a spattering of knowledge of the music scene at the time would say they realised that Elvis Presley was a million-dollar personality, worth every cent of that huge figure. But Sam thought he was being clever and did a deal to sell his biggest star to what was then the biggest name in the record business – RCA. The price? A whacking $40,000, which Phillips soon realised was enough peanuts to start people wondering if he had lost his sanity.

I asked Clement, who knew more than a thing about that business and who was a witness to that evening of history, if he thought Sam Phillips had regretted that sale.

'Sure he did,' he told me. 'But he made a lot of money and $40,000 was a lot of money at that time.'

It was also recognised in the business at the time as a fortune. 'That was the most money anyone paid for an artist back then.'

Clement himself appreciated the value of a name like Presley's on the (Sun) label. 'I think he should have kept him. Sam said, "Well, at least if you're going to make a mistake, you might as well have made a $12 million, perhaps $12 BILLION one." But Elvis didn't want to leave.' Phillips admitted that himself.

'I asked Sam once, "Did Elvis want to leave?" "No," he said. "Elvis would have been happy to stay there."' But $40,000 ensured that was not to be.

And, for the time being, Sam Phillips was certainly riding high. 'It was exciting for me there,' Clement added. 'Sam Phillips was as famous as Elvis was.'

Clement says that Elvis would have enjoyed staying. But he went.

Clement thought they could do anything with the kind of talent they had. Even when accidents happened, as they did, they were lucky ones. None luckier – though it wasn't realised at the time – than when Clement was producing a record featuring Carl Perkins and a young, unknown, somewhat eccentric piano player called Jerry Lee Lewis. It was a night in 1956 that would result in what has become one of the historic moments in the Elvis story, to say nothing of that of rock'n'roll itself – but it took almost forty years before anyone realised what happened on 4 December that year.

Perkins was there to record not just with Jerry Lee, but also with his brothers Clayton and Jay and the drummer named W. S. Holland. He didn't have any set schedule. He thought he'd play around and see what happened. He had no idea what would actually result. The session finished and then something approaching a college alumni reunion developed.

Johnny Cash was in the Sun building, too. While there, he heard the Perkins recording, liked what he was listening to and decided to pay a courtesy call, as they might have called it then. Before long, he was joining in. And then, Elvis, now very much the number one star of RCA – his sales far outstripped those of Sinatra at Capitol – decided to pop in as well. He was accompanied by his then current girlfriend Marilyn Evans. He also liked what he heard. And also liked the idea of joining in.

That session and the artists 'jamming', to use an expression

coined in the world of jazz, became known as the night of the
Million Dollar Quartet. It was, if anything, an understatement.
You couldn't put a value on these four.

On reflection, it seems it would have been the easiest thing in
the world to arrange to make the record and a million dollars
in the process. As Clement recalled the scene for me:

> I was doing a Carl Perkins session with Jerry Lee and Cash and
> Elvis came in. I turned on the pots [the controls] and they were
> messing around and I said to them that it would be remiss if
> I didn't record it. We recorded it in an hour and a half. Here I
> was listening to all these people performing together, like
> never before.

Plainly the basis for the hit of all time? One would think so.
But it was not quite as easy to make that bit of history come
to life, even though the event got the publicity it needed right
from the start.

A photographer from the *Memphis Press-Scimitar* came
along and took some pictures that have since become iconic.
The next day, an article appeared in that newspaper under the
heading 'Million Dollar Quartet'. For some strange reason, no
one at the time thought of taking up the idea of releasing it all
as a record.

As Clement told me: 'The tapes just sat around. Eventually,
it was bootlegged and now you can buy it on RCA.' If it hadn't
been for those bootlegged versions, one of the really huge
events in the story of rock'n'roll would have been, to all intents
and purposes, forgotten. 'RCA just weren't that interested in
putting it out.'

It couldn't be released on the Sun label, because Elvis was already committed to his new RCA bosses. But things eventually got moving – slowly, slowly. In 1969, Sam Phillips did his deal to sell Sun, an event which caused almost as much excitement as the time he sold Elvis's contract. The new owner, a man named Shelby Singleton, decided he needed to go through every bit of recording that Sun had ever produced – distributed or otherwise. He literally stumbled on the Quartet tapes – at least, most of them.

There were enough numbers on the tapes to turn into an LP, but probably for reasons of copyright – nothing of Elvis's could go out on anything but an RCA label in America – it was only issued in Europe on Singleton's Charly/Sun label. But it took thirteen years for that to happen. In 1987, more tapes were discovered and issued on a new Charly/Sun disc. That was the 'bootlegged' disc to which Clement was referring.

The question is, why did RCA themselves take so long? Plainly, they had the rights to all Elvis recordings in the United States, no matter how long or short and with whom he was performing. They issued their *Million Dollar Quartet* album in 1990. Sixteen years later, another twelve tracks never before heard were added as a fiftieth anniversary album special.

These are fascinating details in the story of what otherwise would not be considered a brilliant piece of music. 'Cowboy' Jack was quite right when he said it had to be taped, and the final result proves his judgement. The fascinating parts are a series of duets between Elvis and Jerry Lee Lewis – and the arrival and departure of Presley are featured, too. It was indeed an historic moment as Clement recalled: 'Elvis would drop in to the Sun studios regularly and we would talk about music and stuff, you know. And when Jerry Lee was in he wanted to meet him, so he dropped in. Actually, I only saw Elvis one more time after he came out of the army.'

Clement likes to give the impression of being a rough diamond. People who hear him on the radio love his humour – exemplified by the numerous references to the art of breaking wind on display in his home.

No one can doubt that this was the principal era of Elvis's triumphs. And triumphs they were, ones that led inevitably to the expansion of the Memphis Mafia, which was, by its very nature, a symptom of the growth of the Elvis empire.

Sonny West was one of the Mafia's stalwarts who paid due deference to Godfather Elvis. As a result, he was to claim that he was the first mafioso to be awarded the Order of Elvis, otherwise known as that TCB badge. 'It was the identification for being close to him. He also gave it to other celebrities, like Tom Jones.' More than that. 'It was everything. Like a boy getting a Christmas present.'

To this day, it is one of Sonny's proudest possessions. 'He had twelve of them made at first. They were beautiful on black velvet. He put mine round my neck.'

The TCB legend was a 'code', he says. 'It meant that Elvis Presley was doing something naughty. Something to tell one girl when he was with another one.' That took a bit of deciphering, but it seemed to mean that mention of the three letters was enough to put some anxious female on to other things – often with other members of the Mafia. Officially, West was one of Elvis's bodyguards.

He remembers how he, too, participated in the provision of girls for the boss. 'There were always a lot of girls around him.

Oh yes ... see, he didn't have them when he was younger. So he wanted to try a lot of different candy.'

The girl-hunt ballet reached its zenith when Elvis was away from Memphis and had bought houses in Los Angeles and Palm Springs. 'We didn't keep girls away. We did "trolling" in Palm Springs, driving around, picking up girls. He chose them himself.'

When people gather to talk about Elvis, they are for the most part proud of their associations with him. They like to talk about the private moments – and, indeed, that is what this book is about. But most of those associations came about as a result of Tupelo and Memphis creating a superstar. 'Superstar' is a much abused term, but that's what he was. By now, he only had to walk on to a stage to satisfy the customers out front. If he chose to stand and do no more than move his lips without saying anything they would have been satisfied. Had he gone on to recite – without singing it – 'Little Bo Peep', they would have been in ecstasy. As it was, he did sing and he twirled his hips and snarled his lips and the girls (and not just the girls) swooned as though they were enjoying a religious experience. Maybe they were. There was a lot of what he did that brought back memories of Jolson and the other greats of his era.

Of course, a lot of the plaudits and a lot of the blame for the good and the bad things in Elvis's career is attributed to the man known as 'Colonel' Parker, who, as we have seen, was neither a real army colonel nor legally called Parker. 'The title had been given him by a governor,' said Sam West. 'I myself was made a colonel in Kentucky, Louisiana and Tennessee.' In other words, a colonel like a certain Mr Sanders. 'A lot of people called Parker "Tom".'

Actually, the rank, in the Louisiana State Militia, was awarded him by the Louisiana Governor Jimmie Davis for working in his election campaign (Davis was a former country and gospel singer, who claimed to have written the 1940s hit 'You Are My Sunshine'). He would never have got the title from the Defense Department – his own time in the 'real' army was badly marred when he deserted, an offence for which he was jailed.

The man born Andreas Cornelis van Kuijk was the Svengali-like figure who tried to make Elvis Presley into a kind of Trilby – at a price: he always took more than the usual 10 per cent commission from the time he became Elvis's agent in 1955.

That was the least of the charges levelled against Parker. He was born in the Dutch town of Breda in 1909 – a place from which he ran away after a murder charge was levelled against him. He entered the United States illegally (after jumping ship) and refused to apply for American citizenship because he was afraid of too much information leading to his being extradited to Holland.

There were those who hated the 'Colonel'. But not everyone did – including members of the Memphis Mafia – and few people among the many to whom I talked deny his influence on, or usefulness to, Elvis and his career. Some even admired him.

Sonny West really liked the 'Colonel'. 'He was a carnival man. Working in carnivals was the first job he had after coming to America.' But if he was not only not a member of the Mafia, he was distinctly outside the Presley pack. Yet he did have his own group of acolytes. Says West: 'He was the Godfather on his side and Elvis was the Godfather on his and they really did get on well. And when he said, "Be there", you went and if you didn't, he'd get all over you.'

Sam Thompson, another Elvis bodyguard in his later years, describes the 'Colonel' as

a complex man. I thought I knew him. I was young – only twenty-nine – when Elvis died. The 'Colonel' was a wily man. He and Elvis had their ups and downs. He made Elvis in the early days. The latter days there was tension … I liked 'the Colonel'. Parker wrote me a letter attesting to my good character.

Thompson himself says he never thought of Parker as being a phoney. 'No. We knew he wasn't a colonel. He produced, he delivered. He'd done things. He'd managed Hank Snow, Eddie Arnold, and he'd made a ton of money. The colonel was no phoney. He was a manager.'

His own Mafia was an intimidating set, much less relaxed than Elvis's, but even he had a softer side. Said West:

He had a guy called Al Labore and he'd ask Al who was out there and Al would tell him that the Elvis Presley promotion [people and the] stuff they were selling was bad, bootleg stuff. So he gave them $200 and told them to go home. These were carnie guys whom the colonel knew. If it were good stuff, he'd let them go on selling.

George Klein says that, all in all, he liked Parker, too. 'But we fell out later. After Elvis died, we made up and I saw a softer side to him.'

Sonny West saw what was known as 'the game' – or, as he and his pals got to call it, 'war'. The idea was to introduce a kind of blood sport to the Elvis entourage – fighting to the finish and shaking hands afterwards. For Elvis, it was like watching a dog- or a cockfight. Sometimes, it was a bit more like bouts at an English public school.

> War was what it was called. That's where I met Elvis. I was introduced as 'new meat'. What I saw made me think I'd die when I got out there. There was one girl, Melinda, who Elvis Presley allowed to play. She was tough. She kept on hitting me. Eventually, I stayed on the floor because Melinda kept on knocking me over and Elvis told her to lay off me.

He had the wounds to prove that he hadn't come out the better from their fight. 'At the end of the night, I thanked him for inviting me and he asked if I had had fun. He said, "See you tomorrow."'

They went skating. 'I told Melinda I don't skate good. Years later, at Graceland, I saw Elvis working out with [another man] on karate. I said I'd recovered from my injuries. He said, "Korea?" I said, "No, the Rainbow Skating Rink."'

All in all, it worked out well for this particular member of the Memphis Mafia. 'That's why I was good bodyguard material, because I didn't get mad when Melinda knocked me over. I asked Elvis whether he'd put Melinda up to knock me down to test me and he said, "No". But I don't know. He did test guys.'

Hand in hand with Elvis's success came that of other people around him – the success in meeting the Presley standards and the rewards that came with that seal of approval. Such success came in the form of presents, gifts so precious that they, too, form part of the Elvis Presley story; not, as some may think, the Presley legend, because there was nothing legendary about the cars he gave people or the jewellery he distributed like sweets to children at a tea party.

We had a talk about all that at the session at Humes High School. Fred Frederick referred to what he described as 'the story everyone knows' – everyone who knew Elvis, that is. It is a tale that forms the bedrock of the genuine memories that his old pals have of the person they say, without prompting, was 'the most generous guy [I] ever knew'. As Fred Frederick recalled: 'He was passing a Cadillac showroom when he saw a lady looking through the window at one of the models. "Would you like one of those?" he asked her. She said, "Yes, of course." So he bought one for her.'

That black woman was a complete stranger and, contrary to what people might normally think, Elvis had no ulterior motive in mind when he made her the offer. He simply took the woman by the hand, went up to a salesman, got out his chequebook and handed the astonished woman a set of keys. As far as anyone knows, once she had settled herself in one of those deep leather seats and satisfied herself that the steering wheel was sufficiently comfortable for her height and bulk, their paths never crossed again. Nor is it known if she kept the car or was persuaded by her family to sell it. Such vehicles were not common in the part of Memphis in which she lived.

Gene Bradbury says that one talking point among his friends

was Elvis's relationship with their classmate George Klein, recipient himself, as he told me, of his generosity, to say nothing of his cars. 'Elvis gave George loads of cars. George and I used to ride together to Memphis State University. George was given a Cadillac convertible and George's mom was so strict on him, she didn't want him to have it.' But Elvis wouldn't have had that. 'He knew who was genuine.' As for Elvis himself, 'a damned good guy to know'.

People knew of Elvis's generosity and some tried to take advantage of it. Said Gene: 'I'm sure he was taken advantage of. He was so sharing and giving. I am sure he gave away more than he kept.'

There were a lot of other people – outside the Mafia – who claimed to be right when it came to organising Elvis's life. The real estate agents who sold him and his parents their first really good house in Memphis, for instance. This was in Audubon Drive – a green, ranch-style bungalow very much in the wealthy Hollywood mould, but far from the madding crowd. Mike Freeman – the man who bought the house and knew what he was buying, the house that Elvis made his home – is glad that, unlike so many other Presley places, this has not become a shrine. 'It's too far off the tourist track,' he says.

In a way it *should* be a shrine – if only for what it represented. This was the reward for one of the great Presley successes, the product of the fortune that came to Elvis as a result of his big hit 'Heartbreak Hotel'. He bought it in March 1956 for the now ridiculous sounding sum of $29,000 (although the average price for a Memphis house at the time was only $6,000). As Freeman remembers: 'In March 1957, he was the most famous 22-year-old in the world.'

'Middle-class kids used to come here and go to Elvis's first bedroom.' It was a time when he built a brick and iron fence – with musical notes engraved on it. 'It's all gone now. There were always people looking in at windows. Gladys would hang out the wash and they would disappear.'

It was, however, too good for a success story like Elvis's. 'This is when fame had robbed him of his privacy.' When Elvis first became more than just one of the boys, this was not something he had contemplated. Life had become so sweet that nothing could change things for him. But this lack of privacy made him and his parents think again, to think other thoughts about the Presley fame.

It was a strange dichotomy, one familiar to other great stars, those who craved the attention that brought them their success but then realised there was sometimes too high a price to pay, and not one that was counted in dollars.

His neighbours weren't happy with him either. In fact, there was even talk that they were clubbing together to buy the house, so as not to have to put up with the noise. But it was put on the market because Elvis and his mother had come to a decision – to buy another house, one that, when Elvis and Gladys met the real estate agent, they insisted on having a stone wall built around for privacy and security.

It was the house called Graceland.

GRACELAND

If there weren't the crowds outside, this might have been a mansion straight out of *Gone With the Wind*, a plantation house where the owner would expect his slaves to doff their caps as he took off his own big hat and aimlessly stroked his big boots with a whip, the one which they were always afraid he might use to hit them.

The connection is not merely peripheral. Today, there is a different kind of slave walking around. The kind who, even if he didn't see Elvis as a god, knew him as an idol. The pillars and the bricks represent the Presley most of them knew best.

As far as Elvis was concerned, Graceland came with success. Which is like saying that Buckingham Palace came with being Queen. That word 'success' should be outlawed when talking about Elvis Presley. It is the understatement of showbiz history. By the time he moved himself, his belongings, his entourage and his family, he was already the epitome of the superstar – with the exception that he was perhaps not wholly comfortable with the role. He started giving away those expensive gifts, possibly in the belief that with these he could buy himself a friendship that he could never be sure he deserved.

Graceland was living confirmation for Elvis that he had embarked on a fantastic voyage and that Graceland was his home port.

The Mafia and the rest of the Elvis crowd loved Graceland. There was much to love about it. It was big, it was elegant, it allowed him to realise all his fantasies. His mother wasn't so happy. Not that she would have really wanted to go back to Tupelo and the birthplace. That was never on the cards. But as was constantly said at both Tupelo and Lauderdale Courts: 'Gladys wasn't happy at Graceland. He [Elvis] was away all the time and she didn't have friends like she did before.'

That must have been a problem for her son. As Fred Frederick told me: 'Elvis was such a family man and loved his mother so much.' But in the matter of buying and then enjoying Graceland, there was no competition between mother love and career love. He needed a big house – and one that would not necessarily be appreciated by other people. The stone wall that Elvis created around the rolling acres was cleverly built. There was plenty of room for the wall to be almost invisible – as it was from the mansion itself. And it was unobtrusive even if you got close to it.

Those who knew the place simply called it 'the Mansion'. To the Memphis tourist board, and to millions of fans on every continent in the world, it is indeed 'Graceland'. To those who are part of the Presley industry – historians, music professionals, writers – it's a place that sums up Elvis himself. It is where he lived – and where he died. But, as the stories are told, it was the living Elvis who encapsulated the place, where his extravagances, his peccadillos, his kindnesses and his awkward moments were all on display.

Even today, more than three and a half decades since he died, this could be a real grace land – a mansion that outwardly bespeaks elegance, a place for a duke perhaps, at least for a moneyed plantation owner who takes care of his staff. A land of grace, indeed. Except that, to echo Elvis's own *cri de coeur*, it was where he took care of business. But with its pillars and its steps, it could also have the air of a cathedral, this building in its beautiful grounds on what is now Elvis Presley Boulevard, the road, the hostelry that is, inevitably, called the Heartbreak Hotel. Certainly, not all who come here, the ones who have just as inevitably changed for ever the appearance of Graceland, are just gawpers. So many of them are the worshippers we have already met in this story, people for whom this is a kind of rich man's Bethlehem. They come to the house and they stand in line to weep at the grave of their god and his parents, the Mary and Joseph of Memphis. Some will also stand and marvel at the lush fields where Elvis, his wife and child would enjoy their horses and try to ignore the traffic and the crowds outside who in those days only dreamed of actually being able to peep over the fence and perhaps, just perhaps, find an excuse to go inside. But that was fanciful. This was also home to the Memphis Mafia and the bodyguards there to prevent such a thing ever happening.

It was the place to which the old Tupelo crowd would come – although their visits and the length of their stay would gradually decline. Guy Thomas Harris was one of that crowd. 'It ended in 1958 when I got married. He was as hospitable as he was in Tupelo. Gladys told us, "Just tell the cook what you want to eat and you'll have it."'

All the visitors were fascinated by the dress adopted by their host. 'Sometimes,' said Harris, 'he wore the fancier clothes, but just for football he wore jeans.'

Certainly, he made them feel at home. 'One Sunday he took us to the piano room and asked me to sit down next to him. It was good because I had started taking piano lessons at school, but they used to tease me and so I stopped, because I liked the tough-guy image.'

This is the house – there are plans for a theme park, which a lot of the real fans might not like so much; they could see it as one step of commercialisation too far for the house that Elvis bought when he was twenty-two in 1957 – for the hugely expensive price of $100,000.

The combination of Elvis and his Mafia began to resemble a royal court. The king was in residence and his pals were there – just to be around and, if they weren't bodyguards, some had nothing to do but be around – and answer to their lord's needs. To some, Graceland was not just the mansion but the palace. And Elvis? Well, they did call him the King.

My guide to the house, Kevin Kern of Elvis Presley Enterprises, was a little more prosaic: 'We consider it a museum, a unique historic home, a rags-to-riches story of a man born in Tupelo in two rooms and within a few years was living in this grand Southern-style mansion in thirteen acres.'

There are 17,000 square feet of Graceland, the house itself, the one to which the Presley family moved after taking over from a family called Moore. The Presley family? Elvis, his parents, his grandmother, his daughter, his aunt Delta and always a string of relatives who turned up from time to time and were given the freedom of the place.

It was a very different scene when Elvis bought the house.

It wasn't situated alongside the massive highway that is today named after him. Neither was it a street of big, elegant houses like Graceland itself. Buying the house was a demonstration that Elvis had arrived and was very much in the good books of the big banks – as well as of showbiz.

In his attempt at finding a home where people wouldn't 'gawp' at him, as my guide, Kern, put it, he had created a tourist attraction – and one that none of his advisers or Presley himself had envisaged.

'When he bought Graceland,' said my guide,

when the Moores sold it to him, it was on a farm of 600 acres. They sold him thirteen acres. The surrounding land was sold off to developers and he soon had neighbours. Highway 52 was just a two-lane road, now it's the huge Elvis Presley Boulevard – and Elvis had neighbours once more peeking at him.

It was not only something he didn't plan on happening, it was to be the cause of regret and attempts to change things round – attempts that didn't work. 'He regretted not buying more land. He eventually did buy more and now, even though we're in a large metropolitan area, it's still peaceful.' Indeed it is – although no one would want the area around the mansion itself to be that way. The very lifeblood of Graceland is the throngs of people who come every day. You get the impression they'd only be quiet looking down the barrel of a gun. Of course, if by some miracle not yet devised, Elvis himself were at the other end of that gun, one could only imagine ...

We went to the racquet court – or, as they like to call it, the racquetball building. 'He loved playing here,' said Kern. 'He played racquetball the night before he died.'

Elvis and his mother, grandmother and the various women in his life were only the second family ever to live there – and took over the name of the mansion from the previous people.

He lived there, thinking that life could never get better – or worse. But for a time his stay there was interrupted, care of the President of the United States, Dwight D. Eisenhower, who sent him a letter beginning with the word 'Greetings'.

It was 1958 and those 'greetings' ushered in the biggest change in Elvis's life since he had recorded 'That's All Right'. It sent not just him but a few million fans into moments of near despair. Mr Presley was about to become Private Presley.

But Elvis had to get used to the idea. He didn't complain – openly, that is. But he wasn't exactly enthusiastic. As his DJ friend 'Cowboy' Jack Clement told me:

> I was the first person he told that he was going in the army. I told him about the Marine Corps and I said it was the best thing I'd ever done. After I told him, he seemed happier with the idea. He was a bit bewildered. I told him that it could be a positive thing.

He was drafted and before long was being photographed having his head shaved, the sideburns removed and the jump-suits replaced by a green uniform – admittedly a very nicely tailored and pressed green uniform that would have pleased the Lanskys very much indeed.

The stories are that he was a normal soldier, earning a soldier's income (enhanced, of course, by his record royalties), doing a soldier's job. The Defense Department certainly said that and Elvis told his fellow soldiers that was what was happening. But it has to be faced that calling him up was a very smart move. Not only did it attempt to show that there was no favouritism in the draft process, which was basically a lottery for which he got a 'winning' ticket, but it was totally democratic. Nevertheless, once in uniform Elvis was a wonderful PR man. Every time he was photographed in those clothes – either that smart green uniform or in fatigues and also in freezing weather conditions complete with the appropriately padded clothing, they figured hundreds if not thousands of other young men would volunteer without being conscripted.

It was notable, too, for one important factor as far as Elvis was concerned: it was the first time he had left American shores – to serve in Germany. The 'Colonel' had refused to allow him to make any overseas jaunts. The reason was obvious – if not the one he gave: he was frightened himself of being arrested by Interpol on behalf of the Dutch police and made to face that murder charge. He had always been lucky in the United States. For reasons that are difficult to explain – apart, perhaps, from the sort of negligence which was more likely in a pre-computer age, or possibly because he was considered an important influence in the country – nobody in America asked questions. Parker had no desire to chance his luck by risking a trip across the Atlantic.

Nevertheless, as far as Elvis's career was concerned, the very fact that it was his first overseas trip was also useful publicity.

Personal factors in his life were hardly ignored. As Fred Frederick told me:

> There was always a soft side to Elvis's personality. He was in the army when he heard that Gladys, his mother, had died. He got permission from the army to come home. I had a friend in the hospital where she was taken and I was there with him when he was told that she didn't make it. He wept, of course. He was very normal – and anyone who loves his mother is all right by me. Yes, he behaved normally – cried a lot.

That added to the legend of Elvis Presley and his service to president and country. Even Sonny West, the member of the Mafia least likely to say nice things about Elvis, acknowledges how Presley behaved while in the army. The answer from all sources seems to be – impeccably.

'After he had done his service,' West says, 'he was more respected. He'd been made a buck sergeant in two years. He was a regular guy. He asked for no special favours. He could have asked for special treatment, but he never did.'

In the America of the late 1950s being a regular guy was the most a man could hope for.

It made a lasting impression on the Defense Department which, throughout the two years that Elvis served, kept up a constant barrage of Presley stories and pictures, which he himself accepted with more equanimity than enthusiasm. As a loyal American he agreed that he could be helping the country. What was more, Parker insisted that every bit of publicity that his client got while a soldier was important for selling the records that were in the stores – including a whole batch

that were saved up for release, bit by bit, during his service
time, so that he could keep sales – and along with them, his
name – buzzing.

In that, Parker was right. The fans would never forget him
and counted the days perhaps even more enthusiastically than
he did himself.

Army service enabled Elvis to make friends. Inevitably, there
were some buddies who were anything but buddy-like. But on
the surface, he was one of the boys, that regular guy. But there
were jealousies. He expected them and took it all the way that
he took the grub served in the mess halls – not quite like his
own cook's cuisine at Graceland, but OK. He wouldn't accept
the idea of eating by himself, although he could have done
so if he'd complained that he was being plagued by envious
soldiers sitting by his side. The one compromise was that he
had his own house to go to at night. Sleeping in a barrack room
would not only be uncomfortable, but also a security risk. As
for friendships, a few stayed. One in particular was very strong.

Joe Esposito would become a kind of road manager for
Elvis and, by virtue of that fact, one of the Memphis Mafia.
But there was little in his background that fitted the usual
pattern. He was a townee, not a country boy. He came from
the Midwest, not the Deep South. But they hit it off once they
were both posted to Germany.

'We were drafted at the same time and I was posted to
Freiberg a few weeks before he was,' Esposito, the former
office worker, told me.

I'm from Chicago and I was drafted at the age of twenty. The
army photographer, Wes Daniels, was asked to follow Elvis

around and take pictures of him. Wes and I became friends and I asked him to introduce me to Elvis to play football. I was very nervous but he came straight up and introduced himself and said, 'Hi, I'm Elvis Presley' – as if I didn't know who he was, but that was the kind of gentleman he was. And he asked me to play on his team. We chatted later and he invited me to see him again. He asked me questions about my life. There was something about the look in his eyes, the smile. The minute I shook his hand, I knew we would be friends.

Esposito seemed the perfect person to ask about that 'regular guy' business. Was he really like an ordinary soldier?

He really was. That was very true. Elvis was a very patriotic man. He loved the United States. After his basic training, the army actually came to him and offered him to do special service, to go overseas and entertain the troops. But he said he wanted to be with the other guys, do his two years and serve America. That's what he did. An ordinary soldier. He was out in the field, in the cold, in the snow, in the rain, and I was working in the office!

Elvis was trained as a tank driver, which was not quite the sort of driving he had been doing in one of his pink Cadillacs. 'He then became a reconnaissance driver, driving a jeep to go in front of the tanks.'

He maintains that he was not the only friend Presley made while in the service. 'He met Charlie Hodge, who was an entertainer. They became close friends. And then there was Rex Mansfield. They were very close, too.'

As for the guys who either fawned on Elvis or mocked him,

Esposito is sure that he had the right approach. 'Well, Elvis would pick and choose who he wanted to be with.'

Then, there were the officers – among them the first colonels he'd met who were not called Parker and who were really entitled to the rank. 'Some good officers got on well with him. People worried about Elvis being an egomaniac, but he wasn't.' A few officers, on the one hand, tried to throw their weight around, while others were always trying to get into his good books. 'A few did both, but most liked him. When you met Elvis, you couldn't help liking him.'

The change in Elvis's persona was evident across the generations. 'That was because he was out there in the field. Before the army, parents [of young girls] were not happy about Elvis being too sexual. But once, he was in the army, the adults liked him, became fans.'

What Esposito realised was that becoming a serious Presley friend required giving up a portion of his life to the star. He took that joyfully. 'Before we left the service, Elvis asked me what I was going to do. And he asked me to work for him. I became his right-hand guy. My family exited.' That was, indeed, quite a commitment.

Becoming road manager was more than just organising transport to and from gigs.

Before that, I was known as 'the foreman'. I organised the guys. Before he went in the army the guys around him were just friends. But when he left, he knew he had to have people around him to organise him. I'm a very well organised individual and I had to tell the guys where they had to be and what they had to do, that was my job – to make sure he knew where to go.

Back home, there were parties. But not wild ones. His secretary, Becky Yancey, doesn't like it to be thought that people
gathered at Graceland and tore the place up. 'No,' she told me.
'It's a misconception that they had wild parties at Graceland. I
went to parties there, but it was never wild. His grandmother
lived there. His aunt lived there.'

Wild or not, the Mafia and their friends had a great time
when they partied, not least Joe Esposito, whom some called
the godfather of the Mafia men.

No, Elvis Presley was the godfather. Do you know how he got
that name? In those days in Vegas, everybody got dressed up.
The women wore long dresses, the guys wore black mohair
suits with black shirts and white ties. We'd get a limousine to
the hotel and Elvis would get out of the limousine, the don of the
Mafia. Well, the press gave us all that name, 'Elvis is in town
this week with the Memphis Mafia'. So we called ourselves that.

Plainly, he also made them offers they could not refuse.

Yes. But you didn't want to refuse. Once you'd met him you
never wanted to leave. He helped you with problems. But
he never opened up about his own problems. That was not
good, because you have to be able to open up. I can't believe it
is all those years since he's been gone – and that the kids still
love him today.

I wondered how difficult it was for Esposito, born seemingly a million miles from Memphis, to fit in with the rest of
the Mafia.

At first, I thought they might not like me. After all, I wasn't a Southerner. I was a Chicago Italian. I had a feeling they were not going to be too happy with me, because I was in charge of things. I was the only Yankee. But once they got to know me and I got to know them we became good friends.

In some ways, he and the others were living in something similar to a British stately home, with Mr Presley the peer of the realm who graciously allowed the proletariat to walk through his residence, wondering at the portraits of his ancestors. But Graceland wasn't quite like that. In many ways, it was very different indeed.

There was never that problem with Elvis. He met people and talked to them. And, said Kern, 'he rode his horse to the gates to sign autographs'.

Long before he died, and long before the house was opened to what is usually referred to as 'the public', tongues were wagging that Graceland might better be called the real 'Heartbreak Hotel'. Judging by the number of love affairs conducted there – and the number of women who were sent away with a diamond necklace but no promise of permanent adoration – it might have been suitable.

When Elvis lived there, he could never have known there would be a part of the site that would be called the Meditation Garden – the site of his own grave and those of his parents and grandmother. As Kevin Kern told me: 'Elvis constructed this himself, but he never intended to be buried here.' Nor was it ever going to be a bespoke private cemetery.

'He was originally entombed in a mausoleum at Forest Hill Cemetery. There were attempts to rob the grave and so they buried him here and then they exhumed Gladys and put her here and then Vernon and then his grandmother who had outlived everybody.'

No, Graceland was and is intended as a place of fun. He had the garden built as a place of quiet meditation. But now it is somewhere that allows fans to pay their respect. Indeed, a visit to Graceland can often be combined with watching people bringing and laying wreaths. 'We receive flowers daily from all over the world.'

As he says: 'Coming to Graceland is always a unique experience.' And he added: 'It was always evolving. [Like with] the peacock stained glass he had brought in. Always in a state of evolution – like his music. He was such an icon to the fans.'

Elvis was not just a singer. When you go through the house you are studying the results of Presley the interior designer. As Kern told me: 'Apart from the basement, he designed everything. The department stores would have had decorators on staff to help him match the furniture. But Elvis was always involved. He chose the chandeliers here. It was his home. It made him feel comfortable.'

Comfortable in the form of a fifteen-foot couch he designed along with his blue curtains, his white cloth wallpaper, lots of mirrors, a white television, a white piano. But the custodians of Graceland are wary that regular visitors – and there are people who go there time after time – could get a little tired of what they see. So Mr Kern and his colleagues have an answer. As he told me: 'We rotate the furniture. The television is an RCA set. He didn't pay for it. All the speakers and so on are RCA.' So even Elvis Presley wasn't shy of accepting what are commonly known as jollies.

Today, only the ground floor is open to the public, but that is enough to alter the place. A shrine is not a home and, even when the fans see the glass chandeliers and the long dining table, this is at best that stately home Elvis himself would probably not have wanted it to be. It is no longer the kind of establishment that they could honestly call a house.

There's only one bedroom on view – Gladys's room. A purple bed.

> Yes, purple was Gladys's favourite colour. The dining room was another centre of activity – with its mirrored walls that make it look bigger. As you see, there are French doors leading to the garden. But they are barred and leaded. It was [a demonstration of] concern for security when [his daughter] Lisa Marie was here.

Everyone with any connection with either Elvis or Graceland was frightened of a possible kidnapping. If Frank Sinatra Jr could be kidnapped at just this time, the idea was distinctly possible. When people mentioned the Lindbergh kidnapping and killing thirty years before, the thought sent shivers down everyone's spine.

What was remarkable about Graceland was how it was, despite all that, so often open house. 'Yes,' said Kern, 'that's true but the welcome mat stopped before the upper floors. It's the same today.'

That is partly out of respect for the memory of the man who was the idol of many of the people who go to the house, but not completely. 'Yes, but to have 600,000 visitors upstairs would have been difficult.'

Not so difficult to visit the kitchen. Of course, people want to see where the meatloaf was cooked and the peanut butter sandwiches cut. 'It was open 24/7,' he said using a term certainly not in common parlance when Elvis Presley lived at Graceland. 'There were two cooks always on duty, someone on duty twenty-four hours a day – along with the Memphis Mafia, the garden staff, friends and family, security staff. No one had a separate dining area.'

I wondered if, for instance, he ever cooked his hamburgers himself. 'No. When you are a superstar, you don't do it yourself.'

It was from Memphis that he set off for his first Las Vegas show (more of which later). Fred Frederick was one of those of whom Elvis asked a special favour. 'He was scared to death,' he told me, 'and flew two planeloads of his friends out there – to make sure he had an audience.'

It was easier to understand, just by knowing who those friends were, when Elvis had reached what most people would have regarded as the pinnacle of fame. As Gene Bradbury told me: 'Elvis had to live a secluded life and he had to live a little differently. He'd get mobbed just walking down the street.' Memphis in the 1960s witnessed that to an inordinate degree. As Bradbury put it, 'one of his main faults was simply not being able to handle fame – he might not have become so secluded [as he often was]. That slipped down a step at a time. It was hard for him and it slipped slowly, bit by bit.'

Just how secluded was the sense that some rooms were inner sanctums – such as Elvis's Jungle Room, full of exhibits that an explorer might have brought home, but which Presley would never have had time to collect. They were bought the way he bought everything else – including, so often, love. It is just a funky museum piece.

The comparison with the English stately home seemed obvious. Previous generations of peers of the realm would go on grand tours, or, in the days of the Raj, take trips 'up country' in India, which always included violently ending the life of some poor animal otherwise minding its own business. Elvis never went hunting – at least, not for lion heads or tiger skins. This stuff had a Hawaiian feel about it. The furniture, of course, was picked out and designed by Elvis himself to serve as a reminder of his days in the jungle? No. Not exactly. It came from a Memphis store – all massed-produced. And, of course, he made all those Hawaiian movies. It was known originally as the Den and only later became known as the Jungle Room. It also doubled up as a recording studio. He made three LPs in here. The shag-pile carpet on the walls and ceiling all helped. He got fed up with going to the studios. As Kern said: 'He was tired and had been doing it for twenty years. He was touring a lot and Elvis felt safe here. It was his home – and his refuge. So RCA brought the studio to him – and blanked out the windows. His last LP, *Moody Blue*, was recorded here.'

That was probably a very good idea, since working with Elvis Presley in the studio was not always the simplest thing. An RCA executive told me: 'He was always late. He liked to tell stories, visiting. Finally, we got around to recording. But he wanted to feel comfortable in his recording.'

Did that mean that, like others, Sinatra in particular, he was a one-take man? 'No,' he said, and then added: 'Sometimes.' There is a lot to be read into that word 'sometimes'.

Strangely, perhaps, there were no production problems in
the Jungle Room or the Den.

> There was not much rehearsing. Elvis said he wanted to just
> do his own thing. He knew when it was right. There was no
> producer calling the shots. He'd stand at the mike and joke
> around. Sometimes, he'd stop and start over. He was in control.
> Sessions often started late at night.

He would indeed feel more comfortable and in charge at
Graceland – the place where he was also Elvis the daddy.
There's a large teddy bear sitting in a chair. A very large
panda. Kern explained: 'It was Lisa Marie's teddy. It was Lisa's
favourite napping spot. They had to take out a window to get
the teddy in.'

The room that the historians and music aficionados love is
more than just a room. It is like an atrium with records instead
of trees, although in fact, his hits, his million or more sellers,
seem to have grown like trees for so long. Here is every gold,
every platinum, every single and every album that deserved
a precious-metal pressing with its sleeve on display, covering
seemingly every inch of a wall two storeys high. It is perhaps
as though an art gallery has been transferred to this corner
of Tennessee.

There are surprises here. As my guide said:

> I don't think you can play any of them. They were not made for
> that. We've got his first million-seller, 'Heartbreak Hotel'. The
> power of Elvis is still amazing. Here you can see a gold record
> for 'Good Rockin' Tonight'. That was a sophomore record for

Elvis on Sun in 1954 and only a few years ago did it go gold. He still sells. Usually around his birthday. He still gets awards. A lot of the awards we have here were awarded posthumously.

There were so many of them and all are on show here. 'A Little Less Conversation' had been remixed – it was the last worldwide hit. The last number one was 'Burning Love'. All the big ones are with RCA. 'Elvis was popular when Phillips sold them his contract. But he only became such a massive star after RCA took him up.'

Also on show are his jumpsuits. It is plain that as the years went by and his fame increased, the outfits got more and more elaborate. 'That,' said Kevin Kern, 'depended on the designers. The designers would sketch out what they had in mind and then show them to Elvis.' They were elaborate. And heavy. 'Yes, they weighed forty-five to fifty pounds [so much heavier than his earlier outfits], depending on the number of jewels.' It seemed equally clear that the weight of these garments contributed to all that sweat pouring from him during his performances, to say nothing of his subsequent ill health.

Kern didn't agree. 'No, he gave a great heck of a show all the time and he was bound to sweat.'

Much of what is on show is more tasteful than some people might expect. But there are other things that might not warrant that description. But it all needs to fit into the picture the people who look after Elvis's image have in mind when it comes to selling merchandise. 'We are charged,' said Kern,

with the name, image and likeness of Elvis Presley worldwide. We keep a tab on merchandise, to make sure it's respectful.

T-shirts etc., the tour experience. When a song is used in a movie or an advertisement, we don't own the rights but we have a say. We have greetings cards, watches, wrapping papers, calendars. We have 65,000 images of Elvis Presley.

All that helps make up Graceland – and the way Elvis is portrayed.

But did the star want his home to be opened to the public? Kern is not totally sure about that.

But he would have appreciated the fans being here. You can see [the descendants of] some of Elvis's horses, which the fans loved to watch. He loved the equestrian activities. He got into horses with Priscilla. He was a busy man with films, touring etc., and horses were a peaceful activity. Elvis would escape here [the fields where the horses roamed] from all the activity. But he was aware of the world around him. They let people come to the front door and take pictures if Elvis wasn't there.

This place is a piece of pop culture – and music history. You get a piece of America and Americana here. The fans can see it all. At an average entrance price of $28 for the tour.

They can hear his singing on the headphones they pick up, describing the artefacts in eight languages. They can also see Vernon's office – which to those students of history is important in itself. It was the room where he handled the fan mail. 'Yes, Parker was the manager but Vernon and two secretaries answered the mail,' Kern told me.

It was a quiet, peaceful life for the family. But it shouldn't be forgotten that there was always a bodyguard on hand. But why did he need a bodyguard? It was a question to which I constantly returned. I asked it of Sam Thompson, who entered Elvis's life not just as head of security – not a title he likes: 'I was his bodyguard' – but as the brother of his boss's long-standing girlfriend, Linda Thompson.

Sam came to Elvis's mansion in June 1973 after working at the county jail as a guard and sheriff's deputy. 'But I'd had an accident,' he says.

Elvis loved motorcycles and he would call in the middle of the night and ask me to come over. I would always beg off because I lived the other side of the county, about an hour or so away. One day he and my sister Linda came over to my apartment and I had a plaster cast on my leg. They were in their black 'Stuts'.

They went out in a car, he and Linda in front, Sam and his wife in the back, with Thompson's plaster cast-covered leg between Elvis and Linda.

'Elvis was smoking his cigar and every now and again he'd lean back and drop ash on the cast. Under the pretence of looking for a property, we drew up at a place and ...' I waited for the surprise that was coming.

He knocked on the door and the lady [who opened it] screamed. He said to my wife, 'Do you like this house?' She said she loved it. 'Oh good,' Elvis said. He pulled out the key from his pocket and said, 'Good, it's yours. No more excuses – so when I want to go ride motorcycles, you come.' I was no longer too far away.

He bought me a motorcycle, so I had one to ride. He called quite often. He would come by and there's a recording of him and Linda singing in my house.

Once Priscilla had gone – to star in *Dallas* among other things – Linda was to be the one really important woman in his life, Said Thompson:

He and Linda were together and, as it morphed into something more, I was like a brother-in-law to him. And then when he and Linda broke up, we had a whole different relationship. All in all, I stayed with him till he died. I liked Elvis through it all. Relationships are very difficult at the best of times and are more difficult when you have family involved. But Elvis always made sure he took care of the people around him. But he was his own man and I appreciated that. He understood that, as we say in the South, blood is thicker than water, and he always respected that.

'The fans loved Elvis to death', reason enough for his position as bodyguard-in-chief.

They mobbed him, pulling his hair and his clothes. One night, they actually pulled some of his hair out. The woman turned to her friends and said, 'Look.' It was like a trophy. He adored his fans, but he'd have been hurt. He had Band Aids on his fingers. After every concert, his hands would be scratched from all the women trying to get the scarves he handed out. My job was not as a knuckle-cruncher, not to beat people up, but to get Elvis in and out of venues and protect the fans, too. I'd dress up the wardrobe man in a jumpsuit as a decoy and run into a second limousine. We saw back staircases, kitchens everywhere – all to try to avoid confrontations.

He ultimately decided that, rather than call himself a body-guard, he was indeed more that 'security specialist'. As he said: 'I approached it from a law enforcement professional perspective, because I was with the dignitary protection department.' And part of the self-dignity he protected (to alter the word slightly) was not to be involved in the principal sport of the Memphis Mafia, bringing girls for Elvis's approval.

Through it all, he insisted there was no nepotism involved. 'It was coincidental that I was Linda's brother.'

And it was obviously true that, no matter how close he was to Elvis, neither he nor anyone else could really compete with Linda. The beautiful Ms Thompson shared so much of the Presley life and lifestyle after the departure of Priscilla that the word 'relationship' barely covers what they meant to each other.

As she told my colleague and friend Neil Rosser for our project, 1972 was the big year for both of them. She *was* actually one of the girls presented to Presley by a member of the Mafia. Those were, on the whole, women who were there for one-night stands. Linda had other ideas – and so, it turned out, did Elvis.

She says that she hadn't always been a Presley fan and, as a girl from Memphis, 'we knew each other before we knew each other, if you see what I mean'. I think I did. 'We had a kindred spirit.'

Linda, in fact, knows the precise date they met – 6 July 1972.

I was Miss Tennessee Universe and T. G. Sheppard [another
Mafia stalwart] invited me to the Memphian Theater after
midnight. I wasn't going to go at that time. I was a good Baptist
girl and thought, 'Gee, after midnight. That doesn't sound on
the up and up.' I had a lot of trepidation about it. But my girlfriend, who was Miss Rhode Island, said we had to go. She
wanted to meet Elvis. So if we hadn't have gone, I probably
would never have met Elvis. I probably would have said, 'NO
thank you. I don't go anywhere after midnight, unescorted' –
because I was a bit of a prude.

It was the beginning of what seemed to be a typical Presley
performance. 'Elvis swept through the door in this black
suede cape, red lining made of red silk satin, high collar with
sunglasses on. My first impression was "Why is he dressed like
that? It's hot outside." It was July.' Only a showman could
meet a girl dressed like that – and only a girl from Memphis
who was used to shows like Elvis's could react as she did. 'I
made a joke about the Dracula look.' He wasn't fazed. 'He
sat down and was very sweet. It was as if we had known each
other our whole lives – and, in a sense, we had.'
But the doubts resurfaced that night.

I got home at about four o'clock in the morning and the phone
rang. It was Elvis. His speech was slurred. I didn't understand
that. I had never been around anyone who was incapacitated
like that. Not that he was incapacitated, but he was definitely
affected. I said, 'Are you drunk? Why is your voice slurred?' He
said, 'Oh, honey, I'm just tired.' Of course, later on, I found out

he took sleeping medication – and I am sure he had taken a sleeping pill before talking to me.

In her way, she had had enough successes of her own not to be intimidated by the man already being imitated all over the world – let alone going round and round on record players in a hundred or more different countries. 'I had won several contests and had met celebrities. I wasn't nervous because he was so down home and down to earth – kind and gracious [with] humility.' Which, it has to be said, was the reaction of a lot of people. 'There really WAS a sense of humility about him, a wonder that people think so much of him.'

A lot of that was to rub off on Linda herself.

I never felt more loved and more listened to and more known than when I was with him. He had a beautiful humility about him. One of the most beautiful qualities a person can have is humility and Elvis personified that. I always felt that he took the time to listen, to engage in conversation, to look you in the eye, to get tears in his eyes when the subject got to something sentimental …

For Elvis it was the conventional love at first sight – if anything connected with Presley could ever fit such a cliché. 'He invited me to meet his father. Right away, he was saying, "Where have you been all my life?"' Another cliché, but it was a perfect performance in the Elvis wooing game. She protests today that she was slow at first to accept the situation at face value, but then, nobody did – or could.

'I was distant because I thought he was married and he told me, "You know, I'm not married any more." I said, "No. I did not know that." "Well," he said, "we haven't told the press yet."' It was part of her personality to want to hear things straight. 'I told him that he should have married a Southern girl and he took that to heart. He really should have married someone who grew up as he did and have a real assurance of understanding of who he was.'

Very few had talked to Elvis, face to face, like that before. 'Yes, I was full of myself, confident and I like to laugh. I met Vernon [Presley Sr] and then I left town for two weeks. I told him I was going on vacation, but I don't think it registered.' If that was playing hard to get – and she wasn't saying it was – the message got home.

> He tried to call me for two weeks. The moment I walked through the door of my aunt's house, the phone was ringing and he said, 'Where have you been? I want you on the plane tonight.' It was an invitation to join him in Nevada. He said, 'Well, tomorrow morning then.'

And? 'I was up all night, packing my little college things and flew to Los Angeles. Then we went straight to Las Vegas, where he was rehearsing for his shows at the Hilton.' She was on the Presley bandwagon as it rolled. 'It was an amazing relationship because I was a bit younger than he. There were times when he was very paternal with me and very nurturing and very caring. And there were times when I was very maternal to him because he was such a big baby.'

The affection bred pet names for each other, none of which

seems to have much explanation attached to them. 'I called him "Gullion" and "Bunton" and he called me "Adriadne" and "Mommy".' As she said, 'He was paternal and I was maternal. We were brother and sister sometimes, lovers sometimes, friends always. A consummate relationship.'

All the Mafia knew how close they were. They also knew she was not the only companion he took to his bed. And so did she. She didn't accept that he wasn't always the most faithful of lovers.

> Not really. But I tried to understand it. I was very young and it was oppressive. After that, it was a welcome relief to have time for myself even though I knew he would have someone else there, he was very needy. There were times when it was [really] oppressive. Elvis wanted me to be with him all the time. In the first year, he did not even go to a dentist without my accompanying him. I was with him twenty-four hours a day in that first year. Apparently, he broke his record for fidelity. I knew he was faithful because he never left my side and I never left his.

But it was a two-way street. 'I adored him and so was happy to be there most of the time.'

Which indicates a rather unusual woman in a not so very unusual situation. 'I don't think I ever fully accepted it, but I tried to understand [the infidelity],' she repeated. 'He was a prisoner, sequestered with the same thirteen people [the Mafia members] all the time. He was a prisoner. So more than ever, I felt he felt oppressed by his own fame.' Not least by the fact that there were often other women in his life, while he was swearing unwavering devotion to her. But it wasn't sex all the time when he was not with her, she maintains. As she said:

> He [didn't] always sleep with these women. He often just wanted to talk or to read a spiritual book to them, though he did date women. He always said he only loved me; he wasn't unfaithful. I certainly felt very loved by him. He would say that in his own way, 'I am completely faithful to you and I don't love anyone else.' And I never felt that he did. I always felt very loved and very treasured and respected by him.

She saw the two sides of the man called Elvis Presley. Intimately. She saw him watching other entertainers – mostly on TV – as we shall see, once with potentially drastic consequences. But on the whole he enjoyed sitting back and watching the (then very) small screen. 'We watched *Monty Python*. He memorised the lines. He had an insane sense of humour. He loved British comedy [like the work of] Peter Sellers.' Actually, he would have loved to have gone to Britain – something he never did, apart from the time he landed in Scotland briefly on his way to military service in Germany.

If humour was a passion – and at times it was – there were others. Linda also knew about them – like karate, which he took to and practised more and more. 'He was so involved with karate he wanted to star in a karate movie. The self-discipline in karate attracted him.' Whether it would have attracted the 'Colonel' is a different matter. Banning Elvis appearing in a musical called *A Star Is Born*, as he did, was one thing (and we shall return to that); taking part in a martial arts film would have been going too far. The risk to Parker's 'property' wouldn't have been worth thinking about.

One feature of Elvis's life that has hitherto not come under the microscope much is his attitude to babies. He and Thompson never married, but that was not the main reason they had no children. His view on the matter was very different from hers.

He loved his own daughter Lisa Marie, and Linda insists the two got on well together.

I loved her. Contrary to popular belief we never saw Priscilla. When Lisa Marie was with us, I took care of her. I realised I didn't want this kind of family life. It was exhausting. I couldn't live with him and take care of a child. We lived like vampires [asleep in the day, with him at night], Elvis and I. Not a great way to live. We were very pale.

It wasn't as though she acted as a kind of surrogate stepmother. 'I was a kid, too, and we'd have fun together. Priscilla called and told me off for giving Lisa Marie lipstick.' Not that she always kept to a strictly girlie routine. 'I grew up with a big brother and most of the [Mafia] guys were a lot of fun. They gave Elvis security. We didn't always agree. But we got on. I like men.' And she said,

When I look back, the thing I most remember about Elvis is his tenderness, his kindness. When he told me he loved me, he had tears in his eyes. He had great passion. He was so sensitive. And very funny. He had a bracelet that said 'Elvis' in diamonds and he flipped it over and it said 'Crazy'. He did crazy things, like set off fireworks at Graceland and people got their ears burned. He was lucky that he didn't damage people.

Linda always took Elvis seriously. And so did the Mafia. 'The men were on the payroll,' Linda recalled. 'They tried to do their best, given their level of understanding of his position. But when you're looking after your own interests, you don't want to take a chance of getting fired. They don't always do the right thing, but they all loved him. All of those around him.'

She had no doubt about her status with him. Above all, she remembered, she said, 'his tenderness, his kindness. [He was] sensitive, passionate. Also very funny.'

Well, that's something nobody else had said before.

There was another side to him, she always recognised, which to many people would seem in direct contradiction to his womanising and unruly behaviour. 'He had a very distinct spiritual side,' she emphasised. He really felt the need for a God – and, of course, there were always the songs he sang. 'He grew up in a spiritual environment in Tupelo,' she recalled. 'It was very fervent among the people in the South. The Baptist, Pentecostal, musicality, gospel, black music, rock'n'roll, the blues.' She saw a spiritual connection with all that.

He got filled with the Holy Spirit at the age of nine and he ran out and gave away his comic books. It was his way of sharing with the world. He felt very connected to God. He respected all religions, which is why he wore the Star of David and a crucifix. Sometimes to search for things you get off the beaten track. Elvis would disperse clouds.

That also explained, said Linda, the love he felt for his mother – which seemed to her to be a totally mutual love. 'She shaped who he was. She baby-talked him. Very nurturing, very spiritual.'

He also talked about the twin who was never to share his life. But he thought that he did. 'He felt there were two natures in one. He felt he was [still] a twin.'

Spiritual or not, they had more fun moments than serious ones, it appears. 'I used to write him silly poems. We laughed a lot,' she repeated.

He was interested in everyone around – even in the labour ward of the hospital. He never tried to be anyone but himself there. 'He walked around as Elvis. He put his hand on the belly of a woman in labour. She said, "Oh my goodness, I'm hallucinating. I imagined Elvis Presley was here." And he said, "OK, honey. I am Elvis Presley." She got him to sign her much enlarged stomach.'

The question of their becoming parents together themselves did crop up, she says. But, as she has also said, while she loved Lisa Marie she didn't want to think of her as more than some-one to play with.

Playing was what both Elvis and Linda liked most. Even when there were more violent moments.

It is not difficult to imagine what kind of 'enjoyment' Linda experienced the day she witnessed a bullet fired through the wall by her angry boyfriend seeking some kind of vicarious revenge. The revenge was not against her, it has to be said immediately. It was directed at another singer, Robert Goulet. He shot him – or at least the televised image of Goulet – on his RCA-donated TV.

Linda's brother Sam remembered: 'He said: "He's got a lovely voice, but there's no feeling there. It's like, vocally, you sing an opera and you have to have feeling in your voice, like when you're talking."' Goulet didn't have enough feeling for him. And he didn't like the way he sang the national anthem, 'The Star-Spangled Banner'. Sonny West was with him that day. 'Goulet messed up the words. Elvis looked at the TV screen and said, "You learn the words of our national anthem, you SOB!" and then whoosh!'

Goulet, an easy-listening singer for whom rock'n'roll was close to anathema, was not Elvis's kind of performer at all. So Presley did what he considered a man ought to do. For him, there was no choice. He took out his favourite reliable Derringer .45 and shot the television. He saw this entertainer, who was in no way a competitor, compromising something that he believed represented the country he loved.

'It was a goofy thing to do,' George Klein commented. But why, even if it were 'goofy', did Elvis do it? Sonny West thinks he knows the answer. 'He shot the TV when Goulet forgot the words. Lisa Marie once asked him why he did that – because he didn't want to get up and turn it off.'

The results could have been a lot more sinister, according to West. 'We panicked. Freaked out. Radio activity. There's stuff in there. But he had another television set there in an hour.'

Years later, Sam Thompson met Goulet at a fundraising function and was asked in the kind, gentlemanly way for which that singer was famous, why he had been a target for Elvis's bullet. 'A very gracious man, he looked at me rather plaintively and asked, "Why didn't Elvis like my singing?"' The former bodyguard was too polite to tell him. 'I honestly don't think it was that Elvis didn't like his singing. It was a momentary thing about something else. The .45 comes out, four rounds go into the television.'

It was not the only time this happened. On the other occasion, the bullet failed to penetrate the TV but did some rather expensive damage to the hotel where they were staying, to say nothing of the pride of his girlfriend Linda as it smashed into the bathroom where she was in the course of doing something no one else could do for her. It missed her by an inch. She was not happy. 'She told him off,' said her brother, somewhat nonchalantly, I thought. But, then, people in his position are frequently known to underplay events. But he later on did expand on this.

'We were at the Las Vegas Hilton,' said Thompson. 'He missed [the TV] and it went right through the wall as Linda was sitting on the toilet. Of course, she got up, went in there and gave him holy hell.' Needless to say, she remembers the occasion pretty well, too. As she recalled: 'I stepped in front of the wall where a bullet went through when he was doing target practice. The glass door was shattered. Had I been sitting on the loo, it could have gone through my legs because it shattered the metal toilet paper holder.' It was all part of the famed momentary Presley temper. 'Lisa Marie said, "Oh, Daddy just didn't want to turn the television off."'

Linda accepted this explanation, supposedly with equanimity. That is probably putting her views slightly less than truthfully.

All in all, when he wasn't shooting, the affair with Linda seems to have been a pretty perfect arrangement. Here was, to many people, one of the most exciting men in America and a girl who to this day is still exceedingly beautiful. Everything to make the perfect relationship. But one day she packed up her things and drove out of Graceland. The Mafia were stunned. How could this apparently permanent fixture in Elvis's life suddenly give it all up? Linda says it wasn't so sudden.

It is at this point that she introduces to the story what began as a secret but before long was public knowledge, something neither pleasant nor a cause for indulgent smiles – his drug dependency. It would be some time before the people to whom I spoke reached this period in Elvis's life. But for Linda this was when the drugs and the excessive eating provided the reason for her saying goodbye and his losing such a constituent part of his whole existence.

It was at the time when other people were starting to talk about Elvis's health, too. His doctor, Dr George Nichopoulos, whom everyone at Graceland knew as 'Dr Nick', told me that there was no way he himself could take responsibility for the prescription drugs everyone knew Elvis was taking. As we shall see, he stands by his conviction that all the other doctors Presley consulted when he himself wasn't around were responsible.

Linda left when an addiction seemed to have become a vital part of her lover's life. She felt she had no alternative. 'Yes,' she says,

I feel like I made the choice to leave, knowing that he probably wouldn't live much longer. He was in a lot of trouble with prescription drugs. But there was no Betty Ford [the clinic founded by the former American First Lady to which people like Elizabeth Taylor and Liza Minnelli went when their addictions were making them dangerously ill]. You couldn't get help

with drugs. It was kind of embarrassing and he was ashamed
he was addicted to prescription drugs. I didn't want to be the
one to wake up one day and find him dead. I loved him too
much to watch him destruct like that and I had to make a
choice to leave, knowing he probably wouldn't last a lot longer.

There was another, not altogether unrelated, reason for her
leaving. 'I knew that I took amazing care of him. I followed
him all around. I knew that if he fell asleep I would get him
back to bed and attend to all his needs. Honestly, it was wearing me out.'

She told Neil Rosser that she had one advantage over the
Mafia men.

I wasn't on the payroll so he couldn't fire me and I could tell
him he needed to get help. I could tell him straight out that
this is a problem and a couple of times in the hospital, he was
with two doctors, a Dr Nott and Dr Fink who helped him get
off this prescription drugs. It's not an uncommon thing even
today, but there was a stigma attached to it then. And he was
all-American, apple pie, loved his mom, good clean and didn't
even drink. So it was difficult for him to admit that he had a pill
problem. The two psychiatrists helped him but pretty soon he
got back into the same predicament.

She saw people actually giving him drugs, without realising the
consequences. 'I had no understanding of addictive behaviour.
It was difficult to watch someone you loved self-destruct.'

No matter how much she loved her Elvis, in 1976 it was all
over. 'Linda and he had problems,' her brother Sam recalled

for me. 'But she stayed with him for as long as she could. They broke up in November 1976 and she never saw him again.'

I asked Thompson, who himself remained with Elvis until the star died, what was really responsible for the break-up. 'He was a womaniser,' Linda's brother explained. 'He was never a one-woman man. He had a number of ladies.'

Linda was particularly close to her brother, one of those who, to use her own term, gave her erstwhile lover security. As for Sam himself, he was caught up in the big Presley tours. 'My partner,' said Sam,

was Dick Grove who [had been] a Palm Springs policeman. We had the same type of training. We'd go on the road, check the hotels, arenas, run the routes, liaise with local police. We had the whole tour set up. We'd leapfrog. Staying with Elvis was exhausting. I'd take a few cities, Dick would take the next few. Staying with the 'Colonel' was also exhausting – so no one would go with the 'Colonel'. Everyone wanted to go with Elvis.

All in all, he liked this Mafia's 'godfather'. 'Yes, I did. Relationships were difficult but Elvis made sure he took care of people around him.' And in turn he tried to take care of Elvis – in particular, his diet.

One of the big rows was over George Klein's plea for Elvis to have Memphis added to his tour programme.

Parker didn't want him to play in his home town, because they might not sell out. I said, 'Of course, we'd sell out.' A week later, Parker announced they would play Memphis and they sold out five shows in eight hours. I asked if I could ride in the

limousine. I looked at Parker and smiled and he walked away
– because he knew I was right.

Cynical people could say that Elvis's financial success was
engineered by the 'Colonel' and Elvis himself in a somewhat
deceitful way. Not all the ticket sales figures were precisely
accurate. A lot of them were bought by the Presley/Parker
partnership themselves. If they wanted tickets for their friends,
they actually paid for them.

Naturally, Elvis liked to see all the seats in the audience
taken – and that could have been one way of assuring that
that happened. But, as far as Elvis himself was concerned, it
was more than just a mere business transaction. It was all part
of a love affair. Like his predecessors Jolson and Sinatra, he
didn't just sing to the people out front. He made love to them.
If a girlfriend complained of there being another woman in his
life, there always was – his audience.

Said Sam Thompson,

At the end of a show at the back of the stage, he'd stand, looking
out. He had glaucoma and couldn't see well. He was sweating
from those canvas suits that didn't breathe. He'd have sweat
around his eyes, his eyes would be red. He would be blinded by
the lights. But we had a routine so that he knew where everybody was standing and if there were stairs involved, where they
were. It would be me or one of the other people who would
take him by the arm and put him back in the limo.

Larry Geller, later Elvis's close friend and mentor, recalled Elvis
having to lie down after a show with cold compresses on his eyes.

That was when another part of the bodyguards' job came
into play. Said Sam Thompson, 'We'd put him in the limo.
There was ice and water in the limo. He would put ice on
his eyes and ice on his face. Then after a few minutes, he'd
say, "How was the show tonight? Did the fans like it?"' It
might have been a sign of insecurity. In his case, it was a genuine inquiry. It was a love affair that needed consummating.
'There was no other way of asking the audience, "How was it
for you?"'

It has to be said that drugs and death were not on other
people's minds until it was too late. And if it was on their
minds, while they were kidding Elvis they were possibly
kidding themselves. It is perfectly true that other people didn't
watch and didn't know he was self-destructing. Yet. Many of
even his closest old friends had no idea. They still marvelled at
his success and at the way he was, during all his professional
years, demonstrating kindnesses that were far beyond the call
of normal friendship. If there was not so much evidence of that
kindness, it might easily be dismissed as a folk memory, a truth
that disintegrates into a kind of urban myth.

All this was mixed up with Elvis's other private life.

It shouldn't be forgotten that Graceland was where Priscilla
lived and the place their daughter Lisa Marie called home. It
was also where other women came to settle – and eventually
to leave. It was where, at the end of his life, there was another
woman in the life of Elvis called Ginger Alden. She was not
one of the fly-by-night girls or even the sleep-by-night girls

whom he kissed in the morning with the gift of a diamond (sometimes just a small diamond; sometimes bigger) bracelet to take away with them, the lady in question never to be seen again. The romance with Ginger was watched with excitement by the Mafia who knew she was giving him a hard time. As Sam Thompson told me, 'She was much younger and he had to pursue her. She was not that willing. And he had a quick temper. He would get mad and flash and then it was over. There was no apology, no acknowledgement.'

Sam Thompson describes Elvis's behaviour – 'we took quite a bit of that in the later years' – at the time as 'volatile'. It came to a head during his relationship with Ginger. 'She was not completely winning most of the time. So she would go home and we would see the frustration and the anger.'

As we have seen, a lot of big arguments Elvis got involved in seemed to happen at gas stations. On one occasion, Elvis got caught up in what became a notorious fight at a station in the city when two men who chose to fight him were arrested and spent time inside.

The men had been teasing Elvis about his car, a Lincoln Continental, somewhat different from the vehicles normally seen in the part of Memphis where Elvis and his once friends lived. There were girls with them – who had marked the car with lipstick.

Then there was the time he and Thompson were in Madison, Wisconsin. 'We were leaving the arena and stopped at midnight,' said Sam.

We were all pretty tired and as we pulled up, in the dim lights of that sodium vapour lighting, there were two fellows who had a man over a car and were beating him in the face. We all saw it at the same time. In the front seat was the limo driver and the chief of police and in the back there was Dick Grove and me and Elvis. Elvis said to the driver, 'Pull over.'

Before anyone could say anything, Elvis has dropped into a karate stance. And these fellows are just stunned. Elvis always carried his Derringer, even when he was on stage – it fell out a couple of times and caused a bit of consternation just then. He pulled out his pistol and the last thing I wanted was Elvis to shoot somebody with that Derringer. I stepped in front of him. I had a little .38 Smith and Wesson Special in my shoulder holster. Well, the fight was over by then and Elvis became the peacemaker and he made them shake hands and apologise to one another; gave them a little lecture on God's graces in this world and got back in the car and we drove off. It was surreal and as we drove off it hit me that this was very strange. And, by the way, they got Elvis's autograph and they're standing there with these pieces of paper with Elvis's autograph and they're watching this limo drive off into the night. I don't know what happened to these guys. But many years later, a judge contacted me – he had been a police officer – and said he was writing a story about this – because it was a story told for years. He had run down these guys and got them to tell their story. Whatever the dispute was, twenty-five years later these guys had formed a friendship.

Usually, Elvis was happy to confine his shooting expeditions to less risky occasions.

We'd have a target range behind Graceland. When I was with the sheriff's department, I'd take him down to the police range with Thompson sub-machine guns [the 'tommy gun' of World War Two fame, to say nothing of Al Capone, the Valentine's Day Massacre and all that]. He would come down there and have a ball – like a kid in the candy store. He loved it. The SWAT team would show up and he got to shoot everything.

That provided an opportunity for Elvis to show his generosity to someone outside the Mafia circle, a police lieutenant who had been particularly kind to him and was Sam Thompson's contact. As Thompson describes it:

> Elvis had this beautiful brand new Chevrolet Dooley pickup, you know the one with the big wheels at the back, very expensive, and we drew up in this and were shooting at everything and this lieutenant made the mistake or the propitious comment of admiring the pickup. Elvis turned to him and Billy Smith, his cousin, was with him and he said, 'Billy give me the keys.' Billy knew what was coming. He said, 'Give them to him.' The lieutenant was given the car and we had to call Graceland for a car to come and pick us up.

The Mafia did pretty well themselves. Not least the faithful bodyguard, Elvis's Sam. The recipient of Elvis's appreciation – and his generosity. I asked him what form that took. 'Two Cadillacs and a Lincoln and a motorcycle and a lifetime full of memories.' And a house in the grounds of Graceland. It was August 1973, a time of change. As Sam told me: 'He dismissed Red and Sonny, who were his long-time trouble-shooters and David Hebler [another bodyguard] so it was me and Dick Grove [also on the bodyguard payroll].'

In later years, Elvis would record an album for RCA at that

house of Thompson's. Sam liked that. After all, as he said, 'He was dating Linda and he was like a brother-in-law.'

Thompson got the job because Elvis fell out with the Wests (ending an association which began at Lauderdale Courts) and with Hebler. Sonny West thinks the bodyguards had in particular the blessing of the 'Colonel', for whom Elvis was more than just a client. 'The "Colonel" turned down prospective clients and only took on Ann-Margret as one other, because Elvis asked him to.' But it didn't last. 'They [Elvis and Parker] were more than client and manager. He told Elvis that [working with Ann-Margret] meant he'd have to divide his time between him and the beautiful red-headed star, so Elvis had to tell her that the "Colonel" couldn't do it.'

West is one of those who got on well with the 'Colonel' and, if you study the evidence, there do not appear to be many of those who did. 'I knew the "Colonel" well because I worked with him. He had a great sense of humour. Other guys had things against him because he jumped on them at times. The "Colonel" was the leader of the pack when it came to production, news conferences etc.'

West first came into professional contact with Elvis at the Rainbow Skating Rink in Memphis in 1958 – just before Elvis began his army service – and was later introduced to him by his cousin, Red. Elvis was in the middle of a karate session with his opponent Rex Mansfield. Elvis was struck by a man in the Texas town of Lubbock.

'Elvis chased after the guy.' Having a bodyguard helped him on occasions like this, says Sonny West. 'He needed a bodyguard. He had more trouble from women than men. But there were plenty of jealous guys who wanted to punch him.'

West partied with Elvis as well as fought for him, although sometimes one resembled the other.

'He adored his fans,' Sam repeated – even those women who scrambled to pick up the scarves he threw at them.

As we have seen, that was becoming a new tradition, something that was as important to his act as the songs he sang or the pelvis he wiggled. He would throw colourful silk-like scarves into the audience and the girls and women who caught them thought he had focused his attention on each of them alone. It was as if they felt that in some strange way they were marrying him – catching the scarves was akin to holding out for a bride's bouquet, even if it played havoc with their idol's fingers.

The bodyguards rarely had to strong-arm people. 'But we had to keep them away. They would scratch him, poke him accidentally. One girl got on stage [a reprise of what had happened at Tupelo] and she tried to kiss him. Their mouths hit and he got cut.'

This was one of the opportunities that Thompson had to take to show his own bodyguard methods.

I asked if the way fans behaved frightened Presley. Strangely, the man who depended on crowds to keep him alive was secretly scared of them. And, according to Thompson, always had been. 'In 1956, the largest crowd ever was in the Jacksonville, [Florida] Stadium. [There were] thirty cops around a stage. They couldn't stop people.'

The Elvis industry depended on those policemen – it was long before policewomen were drafted into this sort of work.

We worked with the police. Everywhere we appeared, I would go with 'Col.' Parker and meet the police in every city before

the gig. We'd check out security on the hotel floor. At Madison
Square Garden [New York] I worked the first two shows and
at the second show, Elvis was on a different level. So we had to
kick it up a different notch. [John] Lennon was there and [so
was] Elton John.

So we have established that Elvis needed bodyguards and
security people. But there were others, many who seemingly
wouldn't have had the strength to throw a peanut butter
sandwich (more about which later), whom he needed to have
around him. He simply wanted friends – as if the most popular
man in the country didn't have the self-confidence to believe
that people actually loved him for himself.

The interpretation of that manifestly did not apply to Sonny
West but it fits the picture perfectly.

When I was first taken on, I said to him that I didn't sing or
anything – and he said he needed someone to drive, keep a
jealous boyfriend away, all sorts of things ... I said I could do
all that and we both laughed. I grew up in the Marr Terrace
Housing Project, the baddest place in Memphis ... the baddest
gang in town. You didn't walk around there. Elvis asked me
about it, whether I was in the gang and I said, 'Yeh.' I told him
I would be honoured to be his friend.

And, to quote the old adage, a friend in need ... 'We were a
kind of safety blanket for him. We had trouble in 1969 – death
threats, bomb threats. He needed that blanket. He was proud
of us that we would take the knife, the bullet.'

One of those who was around to see all that was the man

who always signed himself simply as T. G. Sheppard, a music
executive who himself had been a successful singer, who first got
to know Elvis when he was sixteen and who says he was just
'sort of' a member of the Memphis Mafia. Then he corrected
himself: 'I was one of the "New Mafia". I got my TCB pin. I
spent a lot of years with Elvis. It was an incredible life.'

A joint life, as he saw it.

'I had run away to chase music, to escape a religious household. I had climbed out of the window. I was at a skating rink
and I met Elvis and he said, "I need you."' He wasn't offering
the kid a job but to join him in a game called 'Kill' – 'It was
like football on skates. We went back to Graceland and from
that night on, we were friends. I went from being a rock'n'roll
star, a record executive, a country star and then as a friend.'

He had a premonition, he said, that he and Elvis would be
getting on well. 'I told my mom we would become friends.'

As far as he was concerned it was a special relationship.
Special? Most people would understand that. But what WAS
so special?

I felt I was in the presence of greatness. Elvis was an energy
force, a kind of karma. People were drawn to him, a musical greatness. I drove past Graceland a few weeks after he had
gone. When Elvis was alive and he was home, the grass was
greener, the sky bluer. With Elvis everything was bright. The
colours vivid. And after he'd gone, everything was duller.
The energy had left.

It prompted a question. Why was it that people constantly use
faux-religious imagery when talking about Presley? Sheppard

thinks he knows the answer: 'Because Elvis was not bashful to be speaking about God. At the time, it may not have been kosher [to coin a phrase] to talk about religion. He was very open. Even on a Vegas stage, he did religious songs.'

It was almost as if he were talking about something from the Bible. 'Not really. I think Elvis, on more than one occasion, [thought] his music was a ministry. He healed people, made them think, dream. He thought of being a preacher, we discussed it.'

There were the stories of his laying on of hands. 'Oh, yes. I was there. He did it for several people. He went through a time of doing that – with many people. The person would feel changed.'

Wishful thinking? I suggested. 'Well, maybe. But in the presence of Elvis Presley you felt different. The karma, the energy, as if I could move my hands through the air and see it.'

Of course, a Revd Elvis might have become leader of a cult. 'Maybe. But he wouldn't have allowed that. It would have been dangerous.'

As we have seen, there were those who thought the 'cult' followers he already had were dangerous enough. 'He was unique with his friends. I've met loads. It was like Sinatra, but Elvis Presley was more accessible, certainly to his friends. He was different from other rock stars. He laid the ground plan for being a rock star.'

Sheppard saw Elvis's success working for RCA, the label to which he went after leaving Sun Records. He himself was, by then, an executive with the company. It was the 'Colonel' who ran the business side of things then. But, for the moment, that is another story.

The 'Colonel' himself, however, was never just another story. When Sheppard worked at RCA, Parker was always there with Elvis, organising his next product like a teacher planning her pupil's school curriculum. Was he a difficult customer? I asked. 'Oh, yes. He knew how to market Elvis. I lived in fear of the "Colonel". He could have your job in a heartbeat. Everyone wanted to please the "Colonel" and I did, thank God.' He said he was 'aware of how ruthless the man who called himself Parker could be'.

There was always the fear among his friends and closest associates that Elvis was being manipulated just that little bit too far. That wasn't Sheppard's view. 'Elvis was always his own man. Elvis was in control of his own destiny and he told the "Colonel" what he wanted. Elvis never wanted the business part. The "Colonel" made all the decisions. It left Elvis free to do what he wanted, the fun things.'

And to be generous. The legendary generosity touched Sheppard as much as anyone close to Presley.

> He gave me my first tour bus. He called me at midnight and he tells [sic] me to come over. I get to Graceland at 1 a.m. And we go to Dallas. He'd just bought his small Jetstar and we got to the plane. Marty Lacker [another member of the Memphis Mafia] and George Klein were there. He told me he had sent [the gospel singer] J. D. Sumner to buy a bus.

And not just that. 'You'd get diamond rings. He was a generous man.'

I asked how it was possible to repay that sort of generosity. The answer came instantly: 'Loyalty,' he said. But spending money on him? 'Sure, but what do you buy Elvis Presley? But what Elvis wanted was the moment of surprise when he gave you something. The gift you gave him back was the reaction. He loved to see your face.'

'I bought him a pistol one Christmas. We all got him something.'

That could have been expensive, but didn't compare with a tour bus or a diamond ring.

So, the obvious psychologist's answer to all that was that Mr Presley, king of showbiz, seemingly at the time everybody's favourite entertainer, was actually buying love. 'No, no, no,' says this mafioso. 'It came from being born poor himself. He learnt from his mom ... giving is more blessed than receiving. It made him feel good.'

Even with his huge income, giving so much could make big dents in a person's bank account. Was Elvis never worried about his funds drying up? 'No, because Elvis Presley could always make money.'

And he made it by doing what he liked to do best – although that was always an understatement. 'Entertaining? That was the biggest turn-on he had. He loved entertaining.'

They worked together on Elvis's 1969 comeback tour. 'I talked to the "Colonel" and he said, "I just want it done right, i.e. My Way."' But his way didn't include actually singing with Elvis. 'I did it – but only round the piano at the Vegas International.'

Despite all the big business involvement, Sheppard is sure that Parker cared about Elvis as a person, not just as a commodity. 'Elvis grew up with the "Colonel". There were good and bad times for the pair, ups and downs.' That, too, is another story.

What is also not another story – in fact, it's very much part of the whole thing – is the way whatever he did and wherever he did it, the fans went with him – right to the end, watching as every drop of sweat descended down his cheeks, as much as anything from the intolerable discomfort and heat brought on by his canvas jumpsuits. Dr Nick told me: 'Those clothes WERE too heavy. He couldn't breathe through those suits which weighed ten pounds.'

Frank Sinatra, of course, had experienced much the same thing with audience adulation (without the jumpsuits), although Sam Thompson, who in later years went everywhere with Elvis – always addressing him as 'Mr Elvis' – noted the difference between the two crowds. 'Sinatra had a more sophisticated, older audience.' Would Elvis not have been better if he left behind those remarkable, original and probably unhygienic outfits?

'Yes,' Sam Thompson told me, 'but the fans would have been disappointed if he hadn't worn them.' It was part of, the bodyguard emphasised, his 'animal magnetism'. 'Elvis was a bit like President Obama. He attracted a disenfranchised audience.' And sometimes, it seemed, a disenfranchised orchestra.

As Thompson noted: 'He'd do new songs. He planned the song list, the repertory and Elvis ran the stage. He probably had perfect pitch. If he heard a wrong note, he'd stop the show.' Now, how do you do that? Did he shout? Unlikely. With a wink or a stern look? I suggested. 'Yes, he did that. The band had a problem one night with the running order, so he began to accelerate the rate of the songs. It looked like a snowstorm of music back there. He didn't do it to be mean, just to get them as good as he was.'

Sometimes, it wasn't just the orchestra of whom he made demands – and lost his temper in the process. He did it when the West cousins and Dave Hebler wrote a book after being dismissed from the Presley service.

Sam Thompson remembered for me: 'He became very angry about it. He exploded.'

There were all sorts of reason why, eventually, they didn't get on. Some of them were obvious – Elvis, once he had established himself as the Laird of Graceland, needed to exert his authority. Others, quite surprising. 'He was very naïve. He couldn't do simple things, like find a telephone number.' That was not something he did very often in Tupelo.

Sonny West says his former boss was 'extremely street smart', but at the same time very naïve.

Once [when he was in Los Angeles] he wanted a cab. He couldn't get any answer from the phone. He told me that when, finally, he got through, he was asked what address and what street did he want to be picked up from – and he didn't know where he was. 'What's your address?' the dispatcher asked. 'I don't know,' he said. 'Well, what street are you on?' 'I don't know,' he said. 'Is this some sort of a joke?' she asked. 'No, Mam,' he said. She said she was going to hang up. 'Don't do that,' he said, 'I'm Elvis Presley and I'm at Jack L. Warner's home [which was the nearest he could come to it].' She told him that she would send a car to the film mogul's old house and that he had better be there when it arrived.

A cab arrived but then when he got home, Elvis didn't know how to open the electric gate. So he was trying to get the driver to stay on and wait for him. I then arrived and saw the cab. He was angry when I arrived because I [hadn't been] there. I'd gone to get food for his breakfast. He was aggravated then but the real bad tempers were much worse.

But the Mafia, said West, seemed to know that Elvis was changing.

We knew it was a matter of time before he was going to get sick and he warned us we would have to look for other jobs if we didn't stop saying things. But he meant more to us than the jobs, so we didn't stop being on at him about the drugs. After a tour we came back to Memphis and Graceland and he said, 'Happy Birthday, Sonny.' I said, 'X has made us a cake. You want some?' He said he did ...

... and plainly enjoyed the experience. As West told me: 'She had made four cakes and Elvis had eaten a whole cake, double-layer.'

There were others in Elvis's life who to this day see only good in an employer who looked after their interests, as much as they looked after his. None more so than Nancy Rooks, his maid, the black woman who was there to answer his calls – the needs he had for food and for another kind of subsistence.

Neil Rosser and I met Nancy in her small Memphis house,

sitting on a couch with her husband, a church minister who almost in every way seemed the stereotype of his calling. As for Nancy herself, her kindness and her adoration of the man who used to be her boss seemed to be oozing from her very pores.

'I cleaned, made his bed, put his socks out for him. I'd take his jumpsuits up to his room, put his toothbrush out ... I cleaned his hair comb, fixed his sun-tan lotion and towels.'

She was obviously going to give a different kind of interpretation of Elvis's life than the members of the Mafia. So what was he like as an employer? 'He was very nice to work for, easy to please. He'd say, though, if there was something he didn't like.' Which prompted thoughts of her acceding to his whims, doing all the bad things that were later to be seen as the causes of his early death.

'No. Like the peanut butter and banana sandwiches? People thought he ate them all the time. He didn't. He brought in the recipe from California, but he only ate them for about a week.'

Sam Thompson dismissed the idea of a peanut butter addiction, too. 'I never saw that,' he told me. 'Elvis had a good appetite. He had that personality of eating the same thing over and over again. Like meatloaf again and again.'

Nancy Rooks could confirm that. She made it for him – again and again.

She really did run the gamut of clichés about him. And about his complaints. 'On stage one night, he busted his pants. He asked me to sew them up, but I told him I wasn't a good sewer, but he said, "Try it" but when he put them on, the pants busted again. That was the end of that.' But not the end of her preparing his food or – as we shall soon see – other things. But what he was going to eat – and more significantly, what he wanted to eat – most of the time that was her primary consideration.

She was worried about his food consumption. 'He was put on a diet and I tried to cut down on his food. I tried to cut down his breakfast – three or four eggs, cheese, onions, twenty slices of bacon ...'

Twenty slices of bacon?

Yes, twenty slices of bacon. One day, I tried to take some food off his plate before I took it upstairs. He told me he'd seen me taking some of his food off his plate and he told me to go back down and put the food back. He said he'd do that himself when he was ready. He put some stuff in my freezer. He said he wanted soul food. Not Californian food.

Despite all that, she says she never felt he was really excessive in his food intake. 'There was one other man who sat with him and ate twice as much as he did.'

That man was not his medical adviser, Dr Nick. 'His eating was not that much of a problem,' he said of Elvis's consumption. 'He had a lot of people around him to wait on him. He didn't eat all the food he was brought. Occasionally, he'd get a sweet tooth. After a concert in Macon, he wanted a banana split. Someone opened up a place and got him five banana splits.'

Yes, it might have affected his work, said his doctor. And the 'Colonel' wanted Elvis to work more.

So what to do? The doctor wanted a big slowdown. The slowdown became a showdown. Perhaps, he suggested to the 'Colonel', still the all-powerful manager, that Elvis should consider stopping work for a time. 'The Colonel and I had a

real showdown. Elvis was doing two or three shows a day,
[which was] pushing him too hard. We reduced it all down.
One show a day for only a few weeks in Vegas, not months.
That helped with his nervousness.'

Elvis nervous? As we have seen, Mafia members denied he
was ever nervous. But George Klein saw it. 'He wanted to be
perfect on stage and he worried that he wouldn't be able to do
that. He thought he was above it, that he could handle it all.
But he realised he wasn't able to.'

The verbal battle between Dr Nick and Parker was serious.
'The "Colonel" and I didn't see eye to eye,' he told me. 'He
thought I was one of the ones who wanted to make money
from Elvis. I helped the "Colonel" once, though, when he had
bursitis and he was better the next day.'

Elvis and Dr Nick had first got together in 1967.

I was on call for a doctor's group on a Sunday afternoon.
And I got a phone call from one of the ladies who worked in
my office. She was a close friend of Elvis's. She said Elvis was
sick and they couldn't find his doctor. I said that I'd rather not
[go to him], that I was on call.

But go he did.

Elvis was not the conventional idea of hypochondriac. But
he liked, in fact needed, medical attention on tap. On this
occasion it was nothing serious, but Elvis wanted, as it were,
to get to the bottom of things.

He played too much. He'd bought a new ranch. He'd been
riding horses all week. He loved to ride. He'd ridden so much

he had trouble sitting down. He had saddle sores, bad blisters – and he was supposed to be leaving for LA to start a movie. He wanted a doctor's excuse to get out of travelling for a few days. I wrote a letter for him – for Parker and the producers in California.

Dr Nick describes it as 'the beginning of the end'. Not that he didn't appreciate the connection when it came to some of the perks of the job. As we have seen, he wasn't quite in the Mafia, but was close enough so that it made little difference. Yet he didn't jump at the chance of exercising the right – should such a thing exist in America, which, of course, it didn't – of putting up a plate outside his office declaring he was 'By Appointment – Doctor to the King'.

As far as the Mafia was concerned, while he was virtually an honorary member he was always on the side lines. But, very often, where Elvis went Dr Nick went, too. He drove with him in his car, sat with him in his aeroplane, watched him from the wings during a tour. But that wasn't always what he wanted to do. 'I tried very hard not to be part [of the Elvis entourage],' he told me. 'I didn't much care for him as a performer ... I was a Dean Martin, Frank Sinatra person.' The doctor's tastes would change. 'I got to love what he did. Oh yes, he was so involved with his audiences.'

And become part of the scene he did. 'Yes, it took a while. But he seemed to connect with me more than I did with him. He'd call me when I was too busy. But we developed an immediate trust. He'd ask me about all his ailments.'

So didn't that mean that his patient really was a hypochondriac? 'No. He was lonely. He loved being around people,

people he could talk to. His immediate crew began to tire him. He was educating himself – and his entourage was not educated.' Did that, I wondered, mean that he himself gave Elvis an intellectual stimulus? 'Yes,' he agreed, 'it did.'

And there were opportunities for travel – which for some people is a joy, for others a penance. Dr Nick was part of the travel scene, the peripatetic court. 'Initially, he'd call and say, "Can you get away from Memphis for a few days?" And I'd go to California and all he wanted to do was talk.'

For all that, Dr Nick never really had the official job of court physician. 'No, I kept my practice.' It was not easy, though, to deny the call from the top. And he got used to it. Used, that is, to spending more and more time with his patient. It started slowly. 'He was doing movies at first, so not so much time. But when he quit movies, to do Las Vegas, we spent more time together.'

The 'Colonel' treated Elvis as a commodity, he told me. 'He was very hard-nosed. A good businessman? Well, he had a good product and without that he would not have been a good businessman.'

It was due to the manager that only American audiences had a chance to see their idol performing live. 'He wanted to tour outside the States. We could never understand why he wouldn't tour Elvis [abroad]. The "Colonel" was scared to leave the country.' We now know why.

Elvis's eating habits had to be managed by someone like Ms Rooks, someone who swore him blind obedience coupled with equally blind devotion. And it all had to be managed according to Elvis's own ideas of time, which tended to resemble that of a Las Vegas hotel – when he was playing Vegas, certainly, but in Graceland, definitely. Breakfast, for instance, was at 5 p.m., cocktail hour in polite American circles, almost tea time for his fans across the Atlantic. She knew what she had to prepare – and in quantities that would have made many another man go in search of a sick bag – along with fresh orange juice, biscuits, half a grapefruit.'

Then she would prepare his next meal, which might not be until midnight.

'I wouldn't be in on that, but he'd have meatloaf [as Sam Thompson had said, again and again and again], baked potatoes, beef, all cut up in bites.' But why, I asked, would it all be cut up in bites? The answer, given deadpan and entirely reasonably, was simple: 'So he wouldn't have to cut it up himself.'

Of course, there weren't just two meals a day. 'Yes,' she said, 'he might snack in the night – 'you know, pies, like a lemon icebox pie, some chocolate.'

I asked if she thought he was nice to her. 'Yes, he was. And he taught me a lot. He showed me to say "thank you" a lot. He'd thank you for everything.'

She remembers Elvis like a lovable aunt recalling the sad loss of an adored nephew, but one who should have had a little more common sense. 'He was a nice intelligent person. A mama's boy who didn't really grow up like a real man. He was childish. He played with things, like trains, bubblegum machines. He didn't get them when he was a child. So when he had them, he played with them.' But that was only part of the story. 'When it came down to business, he meant what he said.'

Her memories cover almost every possible aspect of her

employer's life. Again and again, inevitably we talked about the women in his life (excluding, of course, Nancy herself).

In particular, she heard the rows, especially a spectacular one with Ginger. There were always rows with Ginger. Her very presence caused a row right from the start. 'Well, he wasn't supposed to be with Ginger. He really was supposed to be with her sister, a Miss USA. He had them all lined up and was asked which one he wanted and he picked Ginger. She was the youngest.'

That worried Elvis's family, Nancy told me. '[His] grandma told him, "She's too young", and he said, "Well, I'll teach her." He was in love with Ginger and he bought her a ring, a coat, a white fur hat.'

When things weren't going well with them, Nancy heard it. 'He told me had spent $50, on this ... it was a bad name [that he used] ... and she was messing up on him.' He complained to Nancy that she was never around when he needed Ginger by his side or in his bed. 'And he had me to call to try to catch her. She'd leave every morning and come back every evening.'

The big row, Nancy told me, was that 'she wanted to stay at Graceland, but go to California the next day'. Plainly, that was not Elvis's idea at all. Memphis was his home. If she wanted to be in Graceland, there could be no nonsense of going on to California.

And then, when she was around, she wasn't fitting into what the Presley maid considered being part of the household. She was able to define what that meant in a fairly simple way. 'I never washed her clothes,' she told me. But worse were the love tangle secrets that Nancy was told.

He told me she was cutting out on him and he was not going to marry her. And he told me to call her mother at her house to see if she was there. And I had to keep calling her mother until she was there. He had her followed and found out she was meeting someone else.

He always called her by her name. Nancy said she liked that. She always called him, 'Mr Elvis'. He didn't always like that, she told me. 'I didn't have to, he said. He was like my big brother. One time, he asked me to talk in his bedroom and we were up there a long time. I said there were dishes to do and he said, "Whose name is on your pay cheque? You stay here."'

On those occasions, he invoked their mutual feelings for religion, the search of the unknown.

We talked about life after death. Elvis said he was going to come back. He said God was going to allow him to come back in the flesh. So when he passed – I guess I dreamed this – I saw him and he said, 'Didn't I tell you I was coming back?' Was I dreaming? Somebody shook my foot and I shouted at him, 'Don't shake my foot.'

These were notable moments in his life. 'He'd wear his pyjamas, his house coat. And I said to him, "I'm going to treat you", and he said, "Yes. I want to be treated that way." And I said, "You got to be my big brother."'

She learnt, she said, that he liked her to be a little cheeky.

Despite all this good humour, she also saw the famous Presley temper at work. 'I mean, he could get upset – but not with us' – 'us' being the kitchen staff and two other maids, Mary and Lottie. 'Oh yes, he did at one time. He dialled a bodyguard and not us and so when we brought in the food, it was late.' Which was close to a capital offence in the Elvis code of conduct. But it wasn't Nancy's fault and the notion that it was still rankles.

She also remembered the time he got so angry that he tore the phone from the wall. 'His dog ran out and I ran up the steps.'

Very little, however, would stop him singing around the house, which was something that made Graceland not just a home but his own private concert hall, the place where he entertained for nothing – if you don't count the salaries and the perks enjoyed by his employees – all hours of the day or night when he wasn't on the road or in a local venue for what were then astronomical fees.

Sometimes, Nancy says, she and Elvis sang duets. 'He'd play the organ and together we'd sing, "Precious Lord, Take My Hand and Lead Me On".'

Often his aunt Delta was there when she was preparing Elvis's meals. 'I called her "Aunt Delta". She drank heavy. She treated me nice.'

Unlike some of the other retainers and mafiosi, Nancy herself didn't actually live in Graceland. She had a home not far away. And that presented a few problems. Her husband drove her to work each day – and night. The biggest difficulty of all was that she couldn't drive. A difficulty for which her boss had a solution.

If he had always been generous with his time, it was a generosity that spread. 'He gave me a car and a TCB pin,' she recalled.

But if she had a car, she had to learn how to drive it. He arranged for her to have driving lessons.

That was proof that she was accepted. Not quite a member of the Memphis Mafia, but close enough to be in the set. 'He'd buy cars for all of us every September.' The one she liked best was a yellow Pontiac.

Was she surprised when the keys of the first new car were handed to her? 'Yes, I was. One of the bodyguards told me to come to the front door. And I did and Elvis said, "Do you like that car?" And I said, "Yeh", and he said, "That car is yours."' The answer might have been worth a kiss, but Nancy Rooks, a proper, Bible-reading lady, knew her place. 'I patted him on the jaw. I always did when I brought him a drink.'

There were others who were responsible for a part of the Presley routine she saw regularly – supervising the girl line-up. Others like Sonny West. Elvis's favourite was always Ginger, Nancy said. But there was also one called Rose. 'He was choosing one. He would have girls lined up and pick one. It may not have been the one we wanted.'

It would all happen outside 'Grandma's room'. 'He had different girls coming in and out all the time. I had to make sure they went out the back gate. Not the front.'

On one occasion, she wouldn't have dared do that. She was on duty for Elvis's wedding party after his marriage to Priscilla. In her blue, white and yellow uniform, she served the drinks. Unlike, however, other big stars, those drinks – either then or on other occasions – were never taken in excess. 'He drank wine, but never a lot. Someone once sent him some wine in a funny bottle. We drank it together. I never saw him drink whisky or beer. And I never saw him drunk.'

Nor did any of the Mafia. Or a lady called Marian Cocke, Elvis's own personal nurse who was seemingly as much of a fixture at Graceland as Nancy and the other women who worked for him and were never lined up for purposes they would have considered anything but decent.

'When I met him,' she told me, sitting in the office of the enormous church and Christian centre where she worked, 'he didn't impress me. He had a broken finger that I attended when he was in hospital – I don't know why he was there. Then I met him when he was forty, many years later. He was a great guy. I told him I hadn't been a fan and he asked me whether I was now. And I said I was.'

She met him for a second time in January 1975 at the hospital. There would be another visit there. 'It was in August of that year. He said he was sick and tired. He was there for three weeks and when he left, Dr Nick said he needed a nurse and he asked me to be the nurse.'

A good idea, she thought. A flattering idea. But an impossible one.

I said I've got a job and he lived the other side of town. And I asked, 'For how long?' He said, 'A few weeks' and I said I'd go in the evenings. So I did and stayed there and went to work from Graceland. It turned into two and a half years.

When the man she called 'Babe' was living at the mansion, she was there every day, sleeping in his daughter Lisa Marie's bedroom, but still working in the hospital where she had been employed where they first met. That was for the first six months. 'And then he travelled a bit and I'd see him when he got back. Then in April 1977, it started again – up until our daughter got married [when she stayed at her own home] but he knew all he had to do was call and I would go.'

It was an unusual relationship. Marian was attractive, but he made no approaches to her – as we have seen, he wouldn't try even to flirt with a married woman and she was very happily married. 'People ask me if I have any pictures of us together and I say "No". I wasn't there for that.' Nor, she says, was she really there for the reasons she had been hired. 'He didn't need a nurse,' she said. 'He needed someone to talk to.'

She was never paid for that daily drive to Graceland. There were offers of presents.

> I refused [being paid]. He'd given me a car and a chain. I said I wouldn't take them if he wanted me paid. He also gave a ring and a fur coat. He said he wanted to give me another car. I said 'No' and he said, 'Well, have a diamond TLC chain' and I said, 'No'.

All in all, she says she sees him as that 'great guy' – and added for me: 'He was a wonderful young man. He has been abused and misused. People have told things about him that were stretched beyond belief.' I mentioned that few people said bad things about him. No, she agreed, 'There wasn't *anything* bad about him.' Even his famous temper had a reason behind it. She says she saw it twice, but won't give details. 'It was personal. I let him rant and then carried on.'

Was the real Elvis Presley like the little boy who loved his toys, as Nancy had claimed? Was he perhaps a little immature?

'I don't think so. He bought cars and gave them away. You'd be surprised at all the wonderful things this man did.' Not a little childish? 'Well, we all have a bit of the kid in us. I'm immature and I don't give a rat's ass.'

Then she said:

The nicest thing he ever did for me was when he reached over, touched me and said, 'Miss Cocke, you're one of the few people I know who only wants friendship from me.' I wanted to do something for him. I didn't need the money. If you're salaried, you have to do what the boss says. I wanted to do what I wanted to do.

Besides which, her role really wasn't to put Band Aids on his finger any more. (Sam Thompson said he put Band Aids on his fingers when he played the guitar.) 'It was the time when ladies had those long acrylic fingernails. He would have scratches all over his hands from women trying to grab the scarves that he handed out. Some people have said he put them [Band Aids] on to stop his rings from falling off.' Nor was she at his side for the thrill of the experience.

As she said:

There was something about him because as soon as you met him, your life changed. He certainly changed my life. Elvis Presley was a great guy because he was a wonderful human being. He had one fault – he cared more about others than he did about himself. People abused him because of his wealth. One girl came out of Graceland and asked: 'What car are you going to give me?'

The women who worked with Elvis continue to this day to remember a kind, affectionate man. Like his long-time secretary Becky Yancey, who plainly doesn't like dwelling too much on the past, but makes an exception for her years with Presley. She remains taciturn, but you get the picture: 'I liked him, yes. I liked his singing, his personality. He was a special person. What was not to like about him?'

Like so many others, she says it was always more than a mere working relationship. 'It was like a happy family,' she told me. If she could feel like that in a life devoted to dealing with Elvis's correspondence – including replying to fan mail, of which there was always an inordinate amount – paying all the bills for his various homes, dealing with insurance – then it says something about the working environment. 'If he wanted me to write letters, it would take all day.'

What she really liked about him, she says, was his intelligence. She knew that, she explains, by his conversation, his talk about books. Not many, she maintains, realise how many books her employer read on both religious and medical subjects – possibly because he worried about his own medical situation and thought of what was to come. She didn't have an opinion on that, but it fits in with the worries that others knew he had.

The intelligence is not at the top of the list of most of his fans' feelings for him, but this is no doubt the sort of thing that Elvis fans would like to hear about their idol – a man as clever as he was talented. It would be nice if she could confirm what Elvis addicts would have liked to have heard and which they believed summed him up as a man who sang for his soul. No, she said, he didn't sing all day long as he walked through the rooms of his mansion. 'He sang at the piano sometimes. But he didn't just walk around singing. When he had friends round, he usually sang the Presley trademark numbers and mostly gospel tunes.'

Hollywood parties are renowned for the gathering of stars performing as if the get-togethers were adjuncts of the shows and films in which they were currently appearing. That didn't happen at Graceland, says Becky. 'He was at home in Graceland.' Didn't he like the company of stars? 'Not really.'

Naturally, knowing the experiences of so many of the other people to whom I spoke, I wanted to hear about presents. So what did Becky get? Sorry: 'No comment.' And what did he call her: 'Becky.' And what did she call him? The answer in four words spoke what used to be called 'a book'. 'I called him Elvis.'

That was the sort of thing you wanted to hear about the man George Klein called 'the best friend I ever had'. Undoubtedly, the past remained vital to his personality. Relations between him and the Memphis Mafia were not so much about finding new friendships as maintaining old ones. Even those outside the Mafia were drawn into what could be called the grace of Graceland. Like Fred Frederick, no longer the poor boy from Lauderdale Courts, but now an investment banker.

It would be a continuing story. Joe Esposito would come into Elvis's life the way a lot of people did, working for him and finding they laughed at the same jokes, had the same tastes in many things. He, too, would go on the girl hunts. 'We'd be partying all the time. There'd be twenty or thirty girls and there were ten of us.'

So how were they chosen? 'Looks were important and [they also had to be] outgoing, a lot of fun.' His way of deciding which ones deserved Mr Presley's personal attention was 'he'd go around talking'. And then he confirmed what I had heard before. 'But he'd never touch a married woman. He loved women. He was close to his mother. He related better to women than to guys. But he enjoyed our company, too.'

As he stressed, he never had to fend off members of the opposite sex. 'No. We brought them in. Well, if I saw someone who I thought he'd like, then I'd introduce them.' Klein did that, too. 'Elvis Presley attracted all the women. We all got married. Our wives were married and we were all single! We were real bad boys.'

Fred Frederick, the fellow who remembered Elvis's performances in his teenage years, went to the mansion and was thrilled with something that would later be featured in magazines but which at the time was virtually unknown. He saw at first hand the singer's love of something other than gospel music – his motorcycles. Not just any old motorcycle, but the prince of the motorbike, the Rolls-Royce of two-wheelers with engines, the Harley-Davidson.

Frederick said that having the motorcycles was no surprise, but where he kept them was. However, their storage fell into place with what Presley intimates knew perfectly well. 'Elvis never threw anything away. The first shirt. The first stick of furniture.' After Elvis died, he was to go round the eight (yes, eight) warehouses where he stored these things.

It was full of them. We moved all the shirts and there was a Harley-Davidson underneath. There were enough shirts to cover a Harley but that wasn't all of them. There was a ninety-foot-long hangar full of them. All the stuff in the pile was unwashed shirts. He didn't have them washed, but he didn't throw them away.

(As other mega-rich people might do – Queen Victoria made a point of never wearing her bloomers more than once.)

Everyone around and about knew about the motorcycles – five of them. Frederick saw him ride them every time he went to Graceland, which was often. And Elvis riding fast machines wasn't limited to those five Harleys. 'He always had a Harley until he died. He had snowmobiles converted to wheels so he could ride around. He had six Harley golf carts. Later I repaired them. It took five of them to make three.'

He also had an ESL Mercedes, which for a time was his favourite car. Kevin Kern confirmed what Frederick said: Presley never threw anything away. 'We have the receipts, everything. All left in storage – like a clock from George Klein. It's a time capsule.'

Klein, like other members of the Memphis Mafia, shared the main living room as the centre of all their activities.

Frederick likes to put all this into perspective. 'More important, he was a damned good guy to know. People didn't know who he really was. It was difficult for him to demonstrate how good he was. It was almost as if he wanted to curry their friendship and support.'

Plainly, others felt the same way, especially the ones whose memories were vividly of a longer-ago past. Bill Halton sat in a luxurious wood-panelled board room in Memphis, not at all the sort of place frequented by those who remembered the boy in overalls in Tupelo or the kid who stood with his nose pressed against Lansky's Beale Street window. Halton is a highly successful – which, it goes without saying, means highly paid – lawyer, specialising in medical negligence. His own family's experience involved Halton's father and his young friend Elvis Presley – and there was not a shred of negligence involved in their relationship.

Halton Sr was the youth minister at the First Assembly of God church in Memphis and got to know Elvis when he was living in Lauderdale Courts. He would take the boy to church with him, for what the lawyer says were 'Pentecostal services, very alive, charismatic'. Analysing it, this was almost the experience of Elvis the performer; the man who, secluded, as we have seen, in his private life, had all the charisma of a preacher calling for congregants to come to him. Elvis had the biggest church of them all, with a pulpit lit by floodlights, a surplice white and glittering and an evangelical congregation counted in millions. He could never have dreamed of that as he saw Halton's 'audience' on those Sunday mornings in early youth. The magic rubbed off and he desperately wanted to be in the church's youth choir. It didn't happen. In a decision of momentous ill judgement, the minister said no. 'My dad said he didn't have a voice for it.' Stunning as it was, that was the verdict at a time when the name Elvis Presley was unknown outside his school and Lauderdale Courts – and, of course, parts of Tupelo.

There was perhaps in that an element of racism, indirectly, but the fact has to be faced. Bill Halton explained: 'First Assembly was all-white. Elvis brought together black and white music. The minister was taken aback by it. He couldn't handle the black mix in the music. It was almost [a kind of] apartheid. His music brought together hillbillies, black Memphians, poor white folks.'

No, not at all the kind of thing the nicer, richer white folks wanted for their church, the place where they prayed to God for the good of humanity – but a little bit more for their own distinct kind of humanity unsullied by too much knowledge or affection for people who weren't quite the same colour as they were. As Bill said, not the usual sort of thing to be heard in a church that was segregated. 'Segregated? It was very segregated. Almost apartheid,' he repeated.

Later, they got to know that Elvis was, in Halton's words, 'bringing together all those strands', the blacks, the hillbillies, the poor white folks. 'Those of us with roots in the Assembly of God were not surprised – he came from that background.'

I suggested to him that Elvis contributed towards making Memphis in particular more tolerant; that possibly his voice defeated racism. No such luck. 'No, because we still have problems like that. But he transcended race in this city and in the whole world.' And, according to Bill Halton, he is still regarded even by those snooty white folks as their own favourite son.

In fact, I always took him for granted. Like a local celebrity – and in so many ways he was a local boy and it wasn't until I was a grown man that [I realised] that everywhere in the world where I've said I come from Memphis everyone says, 'Oh, that's Elvisland.'

A situation that continues to this day, all those years after the King's death, he maintains. Memphis would be a very different place without an Elvis to whom people could pay homage. 'Oh, people come here from all over the world. We're very proud of Graceland. I thought for a while that it wouldn't continue, but it is. All my kids understand Elvis.'

Sadly for his family, the story has no happy ending. 'My late mother was very concerned about him. We tried to visit him at Graceland and we went out to see him. But the security man wouldn't let us in.'

To Elvis himself, his friends were always let in. Men like Ray Walker of the vocal team that backed so many of Elvis's records, the Jordanaires, the quartet who named themselves after a creek in Missouri. His first work with the group was with Elvis. They met in January 1956. Their sides, 'I'm Counting on You' and 'I Was the One', recorded earlier that year, were their first together – and the first Elvis ever did with a vocal backing. They also worked with him in his live shows.

Walker joined the Jordanaires two years later after giving up a tour with the USO, the organisation specialising in troop entertainment. It was a good relationship, but right from the beginning he was conscious of people taking advantage of the star. 'He had an insight [regarding] people, but he was gullible. He always backed off. He didn't fight. He was a good listener. He would respect all people. "The only thing a person has is himself," said Elvis.'

But apparently he respected the Jordanaires. 'He'd been listening to them for years. They'd been going since 1948. He listened to them on the [Grand Ole] Opry. He loved the spiritual side of the Jordanaires. He loved country, he thought he *was* country.'

There were no arguments to be had about that. But there was something controversial about something else, Ray Walker said: 'But he wouldn't qualify for country now. Because ...' That 'because ...' takes some believing. 'Because,' he went on, 'he didn't have a good voice.' Elvis Presley not having a good voice? Astounding! Incredible. Insulting – since it came from a singer who worked with him. 'Like Johnny Cash he could tell a story, but not sing, he was so versatile. He loved Mario Lanza. You could always tell his voice. He loved opera, Italian artists.' We hadn't heard that one before.

He is sure that Elvis was conscious of not having a good *enough* voice.

He asked me, 'You teach singing, don't you?' I said, 'What do you need?' He said he wanted to go high on the word 'tonight' [in the song 'Surrender']. We were in the studio ... now Elvis rarely took a break, but he did this time. He said he wouldn't be able to make the word 'tonight'. I asked him whether he could vomit – and he got tickled. We ran through the vowels as if he was going to retch. I told him to put an 'h' in front of 'tonight' and it worked.

Apparently, Elvis knew what that meant even if no one else did.

But there were other songs that had no problems – and Ray Walker saw some of them at work. Such as 'Can't Help Falling In Love'. 'He told me he had just met Priscilla and he dedicated that to her.' Then there was his version of 'O Sole Mio', 'It's Now or Never'. And the iconic 'Return to Sender'. 'That one changed the atmosphere of his work. It was the first time he used a saxophone.'

But there were other influences. Always. 'Elvis loved Mario Lanza,' he repeated.

And he asked Hill and Range for a song that sounded like ['O Sole Mio']. In the end, Lieber and Stoller wrote that song. Elvis recorded it. They said he needed to change the notes, otherwise there would have been copyright problems. But he just sang it like Lanza and told Lieber and Stoller not to bother him any more. 'That's your problem.'

He may not have had the best voice, according to the gospel of Ray Walker, but there was much in this vocal group leader's view that was good about Elvis Presley's presentations.

He sang as he talked. He was the best communicator I know. That's why the kids today are as wild about him as ever. An English woman came up to me in Australia and said her granddaughter was an Elvis nut. I asked her whether she had heard him, his records. Yes, but she hadn't seen him perform. And I said, 'What's the difference between you and your granddaughter?' In other words, the notion of Presley through the generations was there for him to see.

And as for the Jordanaires themselves ... 'He was in awe of our harmony,' he said somewhat immodestly. 'When he looked at you, you knew you were the focus of him.' That seems to have had its effect on a man who, despite the reservations, has no doubt about the effect that he had on those in his 'focus'. 'All problems,' he told me, 'disappeared when you were with him.'

They had fairly intimate (but not sexual) discussions. 'I asked him about his clothes. He said he dressed according to what people expected. He liked dressing up of course, though.'

Walker was one of the people who thought Elvis worked too hard. 'Yes, but he didn't know it. He got despondent.' The reason was the same one I had just heard from George Bradbury. 'He couldn't go anywhere. He was worried about other people hurting themselves.' He had heard a story about Rick Nelson, how kids had bent metal posts in order to get to him. 'And Elvis didn't want anyone hurt.'

Being with Elvis was, in many ways, the culmination of a long-held dream. Ray Walker had first met his idol soon after he had recorded, 'That's All Right'.

> I'd heard it on the *Red, Hot and Blue* Dewey Phillips show and he came up and offered to sing that and other songs for us, [like 'Blue Moon of Kentucky', 'I Don't Care If the Sun Don't Shine']. Next time I saw him was in 1956 at Tucson Rodeo Grounds. I kidded him in 1958 and I said he took my girl's heart.

That would have been what Elvis Presley himself would have wanted to hear and which could be repeated a millionfold. But not all those millions boasted a TCB badge like the one he wore proudly on his lapel.

But that did not explain why Elvis and the Jordanaires were such a good combination – so good that it is sometimes surprising that he didn't want to record with them more often. Walker doesn't believe in focusing too much on the combination of Presley and the Jordanaires. How different, I asked him, was the Elvis who performed with them and the one who sang solo. Walker could have emphasised how important he and his fellow singers were. He didn't.

'He was always a solo,' Walker insisted. 'He drew from us and we drew from him.' You could tell that, he said, just by watching him at work. 'If you watch the videos [you can see that] if he heard a good horn line he would get a twinkle. If someone made a mistake, he would also indicate that he heard it. He was very aware of the physical surroundings when he was performing.'

Walker saw Elvis at work even when he wasn't singing with him. So that brought me to the obvious question: how much of it was the art of a man with a good voice (despite what he himself thought of that voice's quality, singing sometimes great songs – and sometimes terrible ones) – and how much was it simply showmanship? There were those clothes, for instance – the jumpsuits, the ones that we had heard made him drip with sweat and eventual exhaustion? (Some he had worn several times, some rarely. Some were obvious favourites, not just for the fans, but for Elvis himself. 'The Aloha from Hawaii one was the least frequently worn,' said Kevin Kern. It was very well jewelled and worn in the 1973 concert.)

'It was all-important to Elvis. It was an individual style. If you have a certain task, dress for that task. He sang differently according to how he was dressed. He sounded differently when he sang in Las Vegas.' We shall discover that later on.

What we have already discovered is that Elvis could be quick to anger. 'I saw his temper flash,' said Walker. 'But never a negative side. I've seen times when he should have put his foot down and didn't. But if Elvis asked for something, it was like a cannon going off, even if he asked quietly.'

I myself had another take on Elvis and his outfits. I had mentioned the link with a previous generation, of the man who sang what was eventually to be known as an Elvis song. Al Jolson was a bundle of nerves before he went on stage and somehow felt a different person when he put on the black-face make-up that would later sully memories of him in some quarters (even though there was a strong case that he did more for the black man than any other on stage – he always had to have the upper hand, frequently at the expense of white actors playing white villains). For Jolson it was a kind of disguise. Wasn't Elvis's extravagant dress a similar disguise for a man who, as we have already heard, was essentially a shy man?

'No, he never hid [behind anything]. When a shy person dresses up, that's an exultant moment. He did it as a service. It gave him conversation points.' So, then, the jumpsuits gave him confidence? 'No, no, no. He had as much confidence, naked!'

But it is possible that the man who, like everyone else, Walker calls the 'Colonel' could have drained that confidence. According to him, Elvis constantly asked his advice – which sometimes, although the singer didn't say so, was more than merely that. And sometimes the shiny boots were on Elvis's feet.

I knew the 'Colonel'. He knew exactly what he could pull off and what he couldn't. He never went past that point. But he always kept control. Once, at Warners, he was asked to do [work on a film on] a Saturday. He asked the 'Colonel'. The 'Colonel' said, 'Get out of here.' And he told the man, 'You ask ME if you want to know what Elvis Presley does.'

Did Elvis lose by that sort of attitude from his manager? 'No.
Certainly not.'

Walker says, not unreasonably, that he doesn't know what
went wrong with Elvis's only marriage. 'It was not good for
Lisa Marie. Elvis was caught up in a tsunami. He always
honoured a contract whether he wanted to or not. All the guys
around, the hubbub wasn't good for Lisa Marie. So Priscilla
took her away to raise her in a neighbourhood situation.'

The relationship between Elvis and his groups, like the
Jordanaires, is perhaps not stressed enough. It was so strong, it
was like that between him and his childhood buddies. A feeling
of mutual respect and, surprisingly perhaps, not that of master
and servants. Sure, they knew what he wanted, but he appreciated what they did for him. The Jordanaires were enshrined as
partners through their work. The Blackwood Brothers, a quartet that had its roots in a group under that name established
in 1934, were merely admirers. Actually, more correctly, they
joined Elvis in a mutual admiration society.

It was in Memphis, on Elvis Presley Boulevard, in the shadow
of Graceland (as if there could be shadows in Graceland other
than those thrown by Elvis himself – as his spirit, if not his
ghost, roams the place, and the weather growing dull would,
seemingly, be against state laws) that I met Jimmy Blackwood,
grandson of the founder, Doyle Blackwood, and the leader of
the quartet since 1969.

Elvis plays a big part in his story, even though there are no
recordings of their singing together. In doing so, he was adding

cachet to a group that was always as much a family as a quartet. 'I myself have been singing for forty-six years – originally with the Junior Blackwood Brothers – and my dad had been singing for seventy-five of his eighty-two years. This is what my family does. My family were sharecroppers in Mississippi.' So almost with something in common with the Presleys.

> Unfortunately, we never sang with him, but we had regular gigs at the Memphis Auditorium and he used to see us. Occasionally, he'd step out on the stage and wave. But his contract wouldn't allow him to do that in later years. It was classed as an appearance. In the early days, he would come out on stage and sing. But when he was famous, he wasn't allowed to and it would have caused too much of a stir because of his fame.

The Blackwoods still do what they always did – performing gospel songs like 'How Great Thou Art', which Elvis would often say was his favourite of all songs, and not just from his gospel repertoire. Johnny Cash performed with the group. To this day, Jimmy regrets that Presley didn't follow his example. However, it was the music that made Jimmy, his father and the various members of the group such great friends with Elvis. 'Gladys [Elvis's mother] used to listen to the radio every day and the Blackwood Brothers were her favourite group.' As for Elvis himself, they influenced Presley and he was influenced by them. 'It was the original approach of his music,' Jimmy Blackwood insisted.

> He had no training but he sang as he felt it. If that's allowed to be expressed, it's going to influence a lot of people. It all went

back a long way. The quartet used to attend the First Assembly of God, as did Elvis. They used to bus kids to the church. Elvis and a cousin of mine were in a local group in the church and Elvis used to hang around with them. He was influenced by the radio, by his traditional Pentecostal family, and that was the music he would have heard.

He casts an expert eye over a list of Elvis's songs. He is convinced that the best Presley songs really were gospel. 'The only Grammy Awards were for his gospel songs. That shows where his heart was.'

It really did go back a long way. 'Some of the quartet members used to go down to Graceland to sing round the piano but I was too young for that.' But they did perform more publicly under Elvis's gaze. 'He sent one of his planes when Gladys died – to pick up the Blackwoods to sing at her funeral.'

That was, of course, part of the pilgrimage made by people who were used to that sort of religious terminology.

For others, it is a trip back to the days when Presley himself wasn't just a man on a stage, behind the label of a 33 rpm long playing record.

'We have a lot of people who say they knew Elvis well,' said Kevin Kern at Graceland. 'You get all sorts.'

Those 'all sorts' love to talk about knowing Elvis – including a lot who didn't know him at all. Few actual friends deny that friendship. When the Blackwoods and Elvis got together, it was indeed a meeting of friends. Others, like Fred Frederick and some of the gang from Tupelo, like Guy Thomas Harris, used to be among them, too, most of them in the early days at Graceland.

His cousin Edie Hood went there and is proud to this day of the distinction afforded her by the relationship.

'His grandmother was Minnie Mae Hood Presley and my grandmother Alice Hood Presley was her niece.'

She was sixteen when she first went there.

I was in Minnie Mae's room. She was sitting in a big red chair when Elvis walked in. Minnie Mae said, 'Here's one of your cousins' and he hugged me and said, 'We hug our cousins.' He was a big star. He was thirty-two and I was just a sixteen-year-old girl. The [two elderly women] had aprons and dipped snuff. And I'd cut some black gum toothbrushes. They put them in the snuff and they were telling ghost stories.

Another episode of Elvis's life that few have ever heard of. No one imagined an Elvis Presley who took snuff.

He didn't know this hugging cousin well, but there was the usual generosity along with the hospitality.

We went back [to Graceland] nearer Christmas and there was this huge tree and loads of presents. Minnie Mae told me that he gave loads away. It was on the news that Elvis had given a wheelchair to a local lady. She didn't know that Elvis was going to be her angel that evening.

For his own family, he felt even closer.

Someone told Elvis that I had to get back to my family. He wasn't happy. He said, 'You mustn't leave, because I have a

present for you.' I waited patiently for my present and it was in
a little box. It was a crystal necklace – he'd bought it in Hawaii.
I still wear it.

There was also a scarf and earrings.

She didn't kid herself that he had her in mind when he
bought this and other presents. As nearly always happened,
he collected a stock of possible gifts.

The relationship between Edie and Elvis became the basis
of a book she wrote called *All Cooked Up*, how to prepare
Elvis recipes. When writing the book, she went round the
country's Elvis fan clubs 'and we got their favourite recipes of
Elvis's'. Which brought me to the question of Elvis's capacity
to eat – which, if you listen to some people, was his favourite
occupation next to singing. After the King's death, there was
a rush to try to prove that his eating habits killed him. Not
according to Edie. 'Are you kidding me?' a response intended
to bring the subject to a close. But you couldn't leave things
like that. She recalled not just Elvis talking about food but
eating it with her. 'We would think about what we would eat
late at night. I was close to Mary Jenkins, the cook. We did
buttermilk biscuits with chocolate gravy.' You have to admit
that that was not the sort of thing guaranteed to get into the
healthy eating books. But she doesn't believe his eating was to
kill him. 'He had high cholesterol. But he didn't have a normal
life. He ate late at night and at formal dinners. And Elvis loved
pot roast, down-home foods, you know?' And she admits she
didn't exactly help him to eat healthily – not that he would
have accepted it even if she had. 'I used to fix the fried peanut

butter and banana sandwiches,' she confessed, but it seemed there was nothing else to confess to.

The sorts of things she admitted were about all the food that his favourite maid, Nancy, denied he liked all that much.

And then there was a moment of concession – one that would harden anyone's arteries. 'But, then, something's got to kill you,' she said. which is perhaps not what the fans who contributed to her book would have wanted to hear, but was plainly the truth.

As Elvis sat, dressed, as usual, all in black – black trousers, black silk shirt, black shoes – he quite clearly ate what he wanted to eat. His workload, when he came back from a show, sweat dripping from his forehead, probably made him feel that, if he thought he had lost so many pounds why not put a few back on? Besides, he liked the taste – and liked Edie's and Mary Jenkins's cooking. 'He wanted his food, all cooked up.'

She loved being with him, she said, but she wondered about his hangers-on. She asked another of the Mafia, Charlie Hodge.

I asked Charlie what it was like at night with all the girls and he said to me, 'Do you know why you're always asked back? It's because you don't want anything. You know where to get a Cadillac, but you haven't asked for one.' Maybe that was it. He knew who was real and who wasn't.

But she wondered about a question I put to her, as I had to others. When he gave away his Cadillacs and other valuable presents, was he buying love? 'He was very insecure,' she told me. 'I don't think he was buying. I think he was giving love. He knew poverty. He had been taught Southern manners, giving love like his mom had told me.'

And he gave it in a certain identifiable way. Love equalled comfort as far as she was concerned.

All my three brothers died young. I can remember when my first brother was killed. I went to talk to Elvis about David's death. Minnie Mae said, 'Have Edie come up' and I went to talk to Elvis about David's death. He said, 'Edie, see that window. I want you to think about David's death. He's only a window away.' Now that is love, giving love.

She thinks he transferred that sort of love to his audiences. Yes, she agreed, he did make love to the people out front when he performed. 'Yes, he could sing to the balcony and make them feel special. You couldn't do that without passion, a zest for life, a rawness. He had edginess.'

It was a testament that could have been aimed at selling books, but there was an 'edginess' in her approach, too, that made her feelings convincing.

Of course, that could be said of so many of the people I spoke to about their friend Mr Presley. They talk about him as their friend, but sometimes it is as though they feel that he, if not his ghost, is still looking over their shoulder. That, too, was an indication of the man's presence. What struck me about it all was that whether he was playing or working – both of which he did hard – his influence was so strong that this essentially kind and sometimes insecure man had great power, a power that still lingers.

All that became clear in interview after interview. It was equally obvious outside his normal domain of Memphis. When his work centred on Nashville – and his love affairs, too – it was no different.

If Memphis was where it all was really born. Nashville was where he lived his dream – and that of his fans.

NASHVILLE

It was natural that Nashville would be Elvis territory. It was, after all, the home of the company that did so much for his career – RCA Records. What was at the time the most prestigious of all music labels (it used to boast the famous dog and gramophone logo) had other centres for its classical and popular music outputs but it was in Nashville that the country music catalogue was crafted. Once the deal had been completed with Sun, this seemed the obvious place for Elvis to work and where he would be creating most of his huge hits. It was where the Grand Ole Opry was the centre of country music and was for Presley something of a place of homage – yes, along with all the other shrines that commemorate his life.

To use a cliché – and, as we have seen, it is always difficult to avoid clichés with someone like Elvis, as if there *were* anyone 'like' him – the Opry and the city housing it was one of the milestones in his life and in the kind of music that he sang. Today, you can't walk around the streets of Nashville without seeing a photo of Elvis Presley in a shop window or in a restaurant. Walk into a record store and it is almost as if no one else sang country songs the Nashville way – yes, there are

all the other country singers but for every Johnny Cash or a
Carl Perkins there are a dozen by Elvis – thirty-five years after
his death.

It might have been different. As Elvis's old neighbour from
Lauderdale Jimmy Angel put into perspective and then went
back a bit:

[The 'Colonel'] Parker was a flim-flam cat. Without Parker,
Elvis would have been like Carl Perkins, Jerry Lee Lewis.
Parker was at the *Louisiana Hayride*. Jim Reeves was headliner
and Parker was managing Reeves and Eddie Arnold. Parker
went back to Nashville and went to see Hank Snow [who ran
the Hayride radio show] and told him he'd seen someone original. Snow went to see Elvis and said Presley was a joke. So he
didn't invest in him with Parker. But Steve Sholes at RCA did
want Elvis. Sam Phillips only had small hits because the thing
about consignment [is that] you have to press up the records
before you get the money. Hence Phillips sold out to RCA.

But, according to Angel, Sam Phillips had been one of the great
figures in his sort of music business. 'Sam Phillips was a brave
guy. The Ku Klux Klan tried to shut him down. So many times
– because he liked the blacks. He stuck in there.'

Today, the RCA studios form another one of those great
Elvis memorial museums. It is perhaps strange to explain to a
non-fanatic (surely the origin of the word 'fan'?) how a building with machines in it can be of such interest. But if your
enthusiasm does extend that far, it seems the most natural thing
in the world to want to share the experience – almost like the
way some people can remember going to railway stations and

collecting the numbers of the trains that speed by; or, indeed, the catalogue numbers of records.

There you see the piano where the rehearsal player would go through the routines he was to record. For technocrats, the actual recording equipment – the tape players and the decks where the voice and musical accompaniment were controlled – provides a fascinating look at what Presley experienced when he went into the studio.

Actually, Elvis was a new boy in a new studio. Owen Bradley had established a studio in what became known as Music Row in 1955. He went from the iconic Studio B to Studio A. He wasn't the first hit maker to work there. Don Gibson's 'Oh Lonesome Me' was recorded there before Elvis came along. And there was the Browns' 'Three Bells', based on a French folk tune. 'The Everlys [the Everly Brothers] recorded there,' said Luke Gilfeather, manager of Studio B at Nashville, who acted as my guide. 'That was one factor that made the man in charge, Steve Sholes, bring back Elvis Presley to Studio B, which had been opened in 1957.'

As he explained, before those studios were opened – Studio A came in 1964 and it was there that Elvis recorded most of those huge hits – the building was simply known as the RCA Studio and it was as such that Presley first went there.

Elvis recorded in Studio B in 1958 before going into the army. Between that time and the time he came back in 1960 there had been important hits. The studio had a reputation and Elvis was brought back because of that reputation – and he did 'It's Now or Never', 'Are You Lonesome Tonight?', 'Crying in the Chapel', 'Little Susan', 'Swing Down, Sweet Chariot', '(Marie's the Name) His Latest Flame' and 'Good Luck Charm' are all there.

Today, the studio is not primarily used for actual commercial recording (although it does do that, too), with all that wonderful equipment long ago declared obsolete. It is, in fact, yet another Elvis museum. As Luke Gilfeather told me: 'It has a dual purpose. Mike Curb owns it and Belmont University uses it for teaching recording and the Country Music Hall of Fame brings people here, too.'

The names of the different pieces of equipment would set enthusiasts aquiver. Ampex, EMT, Warner ... There's the microphone that Elvis used. 'The Ampex 300 allowed overdubs, multi-tracking – but there was not that much separation on those early recordings [so if things went wrong] you would have to do it all over again.'

It was in that studio that they invented the famous 'Nashville Sound'. 'The use of strings, marimba, vibes, celeste, piano organ. It was not like the traditional country music.'

Nashville was where Elvis crossed swords (not actually a weapon favoured by Presley) with Chet Atkins, an RCA executive who was also a 'great guitarist, with an original style who was very much a hands-on producer'. The problem came when, according to Elvis, Atkins messed up one of his recordings. Elvis was furious and Atkins became even more hands-on in future. Elvis also had difficulties with some of the equipment there – even a fairly common or garden record player. 'Elvis was having problems with it one night and he ended up kicking the cabinet in the studio.' The record player is still there – with a chunk of wood and veneer still missing.

The tour and the trail continued. 'Now we're in Studio B where Elvis's ghost walks.' Somehow, there had to be a momentous announcement at that point. 'Chip Young, a session guitarist, used to set up his guitars and Elvis came in with his bodyguard and said he could disarm any of the musicians with his karate chop – and he knocked a gun out of a guy's hand. And it spun into one of Chip's guitars.'

Elvis's own life in the army was not the only connection with the American services. In Nashville, I met Ronnie McDowell ('not to be confused with Roddy McDowall', as he emphasised). Ronnie is a songwriter and Elvis-type singer, although he stressed that he is not an impersonator. His LP of Elvis songs sold a million copies. 'Back in 1968, I was on the USS *Hancock* in Vietnam. I found out that Elvis had been on the ship with *The Milton Berle Show* in San Diego.'

To this self-confessed fan, that gave the very decks of the ship a kind of sanctity. He seems to be one of those people who thought of Elvis as a king who was there to rule. If so, his time in Nashville confirmed that the 'Colonel' was his prime minister. But one who listened. 'The Colonel said that whatever Elvis Presley wants, Elvis Presley gets. Because Elvis knew his limits and you dance with the one that brung [sic] you.'

It was in Nashville that I had first met 'Cowboy' Jack Clement.

'Elvis never talked that much about musicians,' he told me. But the groups were always something different. 'We know,' he said,

Elvis loved the Ink Spots. 'The Lord messed up on me in two ways,' he would say. 'I'm not black and I don't have a bass voice.' Elvis was never a racist and had no problems with ethnicity. When he bought that ranch in Memphis, he had a horse and a cowboy hat and he went out to 'walk the lines'. Next door, there were migrants working and he went out over to talk to them. One thing was always on his mind – religion. He asked them whether they could get to church. They said they couldn't and so Elvis ordered 150 Chevrolet El Caminos and gave them away.

I asked Ronnie McDowell if he had experienced Elvis's generosity himself.

Just by being his friend. Once, I met him on a TV show. There was one of the leading newscasters in New York City. She came over to do the interview – for 11 million viewers. It was a live show. She asked me about Elvis Presley. 'Does it not reek of dishonesty imitating a dead man?' she asked. I said, 'Oh no. Because Jesus said if you imitate me, you imitate my father.' At the end, I asked her about her specials on Elvis. 'Did you refuse your pay cheques that week?' I walked out.

Joe Esposito maintains that Elvis himself didn't care much for material things, but bought presents for people who couldn't have afforded to buy them themselves.

Elvis was very generous with all people. He loved to see the expression on their faces, the shock in their eyes when he would give them something that he knew they couldn't get. Friendship and loyalty were the most important things. He gave me so many cars, he gave me jewellery, a down payment for a house for my wife and my kids.

Sometimes, he would take pieces of jewellery off his fingers and give them to women he liked. Was money always from a bottomless pot? I asked. 'Well, money did run out in the last couple of years. He spent so much on cars, on planes. His dad said, "Elvis, you can't go on doing this." He said, "Dad, if I run out of money I'll just go out and work harder."'

Talking of jewels, one of the gems in the world of country music is still the Grand Ole Opry, which was originally a radio show on WSM (standing for 'We Shield Millions') Radio 650 AM. It started because the son of an insurance company boss was interested in radio and his father saw it as a good means to promote advertising. It was at the Ryman Auditorium, one of those huge old buildings that, externally, seem to look like a combination of old-fashioned office building and perhaps an ancient town hall or even a hospital, that I saw it at work. It was where the Opry began and where, in recent years, Dolly Parton, Hank Williams, Johnny Cash and the Carter Family had starred, reliving an old tradition and establishing a new one that declared that country was internationally 'hep'.

When the fans troop in, park their cars courtesy (actually a totally inappropriate word) of what seems to be a parking police force and go through inside, it is again reminiscent of one of those temples of the kind in which Elvis was always the god. But it is also the place that resonates with the same menu of hillbilly comedy and music. And, to be truthful, it is not renowned as the centre of a Presley triumph.

If country music was a religion, fans came with the object of worshipping. He was another who saw at first hand how audiences reacted to their idol, an oft-repeated story. But not at the Ole Opry.

That was where Elvis had to watch other people taking the limelight. He had what could be kindly described as a mixed reception at this place. Brian Wagner, marketing manager for the auditorium, explained the somewhat tortuous history for me.

He performed here in 1954 after he'd been on the *Louisiana Hayride* [another country music institution, the show on which the 'Colonel' tried vainly, in the old days, to get Elvis to appear]. Before he was here, Bill Monroe had had a hit with 'Blue Moon of Kentucky'. And on comes Elvis with a drummer and does a rocking version of the hit and the Opry crowd didn't like it at all. Legend has it that the Opry manager asked him if he had another way of making a living and Elvis said, 'Yes. Driving a truck.' [The manager] told him to stick to that because he wouldn't make a living as a singer. In later years, Bill Monroe changed his [interpretation] to be like Elvis's version, because of the amount of money he'd make from Elvis's cover. Elvis did come back here and hung out backstage – but he never performed here again. It is said that Tom Parker thought it would be a backward step.

Another example of the 'Colonel' laying down the law and changing elements of Elvis's career. On this occasion, he may have been right. Even Elvis's love life didn't blossom all the time in Nashville.

There were those in the city who walked out on romantic attachments with Presley. But not – at first, anyway – Anne Ellington Wagner, who is very big in the local music world. But when we spoke against the background of various acts doing their last-minute rehearsing for the Grand Ole Opry, it was her own love life we couldn't avoid talking about. For she and Elvis were very much an item. And when they were, it seemed as if Elvis was moving into very high circles indeed.

'When I first met him,' the still very attractive and elegant Anne told me,

my father was Governor of the State of Tennessee. Elvis was asked to come to the Capitol to receive accolades for the charity work he had done. People don't realise how much charity-wise he did. It was March of 1961. I skipped school and with the Jordanaires we waited for him to arrive.

Hoyt Hawkins, the clown of the Jordanaires, said, 'When Elvis Presley comes in, I'll open the door to the outer offices, packed with screaming fans and then, when I open the door, I want you to swoon.' My dad said, 'I don't think so ...' and when he arrived, here was this well-dressed handsome guy and the atmosphere went dead – as if he'd sucked all the life out of the room. Not much work being done that day in the council offices.

Elvis sat next to me and said, 'I thought you were supposed to be in school.' I said, 'I had an official excuse' and he said he was glad and that I should go upstairs with him and so I did – hand in hand. We went through the aisle. Elvis wasn't allowed to sing. The 'Colonel' said no. But Elvis still took over the Capitol.

He wasn't there to make a speech. 'It was more an acknowl-edgement that he had been honoured that he was there.'

As far as she was concerned, however, the important event was not the honour but the love that developed.

We dated for over a year. He was coming back to record here a week later and he asked me to join him here at the session. My dad and he had connections – two country boys who made good. My dad was fond of him. There was a kinship there. [Actually], my dad loved him.

It is often difficult to ask a former lover to explain what was so special about a partner. She didn't find it so. 'He made you feel like the only person in the world. He made you feel special, sensitive, caring. Just a feeling.'

That feeling first occurred on that evening at the executive mansion, she said. 'It was 10 p.m. He had been recording at the studio.' But that night the governor put his foot down. 'At 2 a.m. it was time to tell the "Hound Dog" to go home.'

I asked if she went everywhere with him.

No. I was the daughter of the governor. I was well protected. He understood that. Yet we were able to meet up here and there. One time in Memphis we had a date in the parking lot of the funeral home where his mom had lain in state. There was nowhere else we could go.

They also saw a Peter Falk movie. 'My cousin called to ask how I liked the movie. I couldn't escape being watched, seen. It put a hardship on the relationship. Elvis told Joe Esposito that

we were getting married. But he was clowning.' She wasn't
sure that he was.

'Well, I don't know. We laughed about our circumstances.
Don't know if we would ever have got married. I knew that he
would have helped me if I were to call.'

But it wasn't like other Elvis romances – if only for one thing:
they were chaperoned. 'Yes. All the time.' All the time? 'Well,
a patrolman was only fifteen feet away.' Plainly the daughter
of a state governor had to be protected and Mr Presley had
a reputation – and not just the one that said he was a pretty
good entertainer. In fact, I asked her if she were the only girlfriend he had at that time. 'Probably not,' she said. Did that
worry her? 'No. Not at all.'

Doubtless all the time there was the worry about what Daddy
might have said. Would he have approved? Again there was that
question of Elvis's reputation and, even in the 1950s, some people
viewed showbiz as less than respectable. And Anne herself was
less than sure. Yes, she said, her father would have approved.
'But ... having loved the life I'd been in up to that point, I realise
the limelight was not a lifestyle I would have liked.'

There was a lot to give up – including Elvis's legendary
thoughtfulness and generosity.

I got a call one day from the airport telling me, 'You've got
to go to the airport and pick up a dog.' Elvis had sent me a
miniature poodle, called Chadwick. He gave me a diamond
horseshoe ring. The newspaper picked up on it, but I sent it
back. Then he gave me a three-diamond ring. I was doing a
photo shoot for *Life* magazine. I lost the ring in the sea. He
gave me a lot of records. Many of them gospel.

She knew him so well – but did not experience all the facets of his life. Never once did he lose his temper either with her or in her company. 'Never. He could articulate his desires without raising his voice. He was very protective.'

It was a time that would obviously never be forgotten. Listening to that voice resonated with young women all over the world. For her, it is an experience that to this day runs deep into her psyche. She hears him sing and it is, as she told me, 'very difficult. It was and still is. There was a quality about his voice that I don't get with any other singer. Maybe because I knew him. The intensity, the depth, the glint in his eye, the smirk around his lips.'

Perhaps strangely, there was no bitterness about their break-up – on either side. 'No. I'd met someone. Elvis called me at that point and asked me to go to the studio and I said it wasn't fair [to the man she had met].'

Nashville was never going to have the appeal of Memphis for Elvis. It was a working environment, a place where they loved the sort of music he sang, the kind they had been listening to since they were wheeled round the streets of the town in their prams (or baby carriages as they knew them there).

Certainly, it had a part to play in Elvis's career and one not limited either to the concert appearances or his RCA productions.

Judy Nelon had a role that would tie her for ever more with one particular Presley triumph – his supposedly favourite gospel song, 'How Great Thou Art'. She was its publisher. 'It was the Jordanaires who suggested it to him,' she told me. He said, 'I don't know it.' But soon he would know it very well indeed. As she says: 'He soon recorded it and from then on he [almost] always did it on every show. He got three Grammys and two of them were for "How Great Thou Art". Gospel always inspired him.'

Judy told me how it really happened. 'Elvis was in the RCA Studio in Nashville. The song had come out of a Billy Graham crusade. He was taught the words and it became a big hit.'

But what did she, as a publisher, think was the secret of being able to do so well with a gospel song? 'It was his background,' she insisted. In his blood, in other words.

> He always had gospel singers with him. They would go to his suite to sing at the end of the day. He was moved by the message of gospel. He learnt to move his body and hips from the gospel singers who were very 'out there'. He went to the same church as the Blackwood Brothers.

Then she added something that the Blackwoods themselves did not say, but confirmed the thought among the Jordanaires. 'They loved him but they didn't think him good enough to be a gospel quartet singer. But they let him stand on the edge of the stage. He wasn't allowed to do so because of his contract, but he'd be there and take a bow.'

Was his love of gospel a means of him putting more heart into his work than he might have done singing other music? 'It was the beginning [for him]. But, well, he did love a lot different styles. But on tour, he always took gospel singers – J. D. Sumner, the Imperials, the Blackwood Brothers.'

The more I heard these stories, the more it became evident that Elvis, a man who seemed to have had everything, really had very little. His riches were beyond most people's imagination and yet there was always something about him that seemed to show he was a poor big rich man. I like to say that Frank Sinatra was not part of the Mafia (the real Mafia, that is); he had his own Mafia because no one would dare argue with him. Elvis's Mafia was a lot more benign. He would no more have wanted to have people rubbed out – which Sinatra undoubtedly did – than he would have said the time had come to go back to Tupelo.

He was proud of Tupelo, just as Tupelo was proud of him. And you could truthfully say that although he left the Mississippi town, the Mississippi town did not leave him.

He liked his peanut butter sandwiches, and probably even more, wanted to have them at whatever time of day or night the fancy took him. But that did not mean he was happy. A lot points to the possibility that he was insecure and perhaps he really was even buying friendship. It may go against whatever people say, but even what they say makes it seem more and more likely.

Elvis remained a Southerner for the rest of his life. He would never forget his origins or the audiences which were drawn to him like iron filings to a magnet. Yet it has to be faced there were two other places that would have a tremendous impact on him and on those audiences. The Southerners loved his gospel songs; they clung to the idea that he was all theirs. When they bought his records and, time and again, saw him in concert, they knew – and he knew – that he was among friends, that special kind of friendship that comes from being part of what Jews – some of whom to this day still claim him as one of them – called *landsleit*.

Hollywood could rightly say it was responsible for making Elvis Presley an international star. People all over the world heard his voice and recognised his picture in the papers while listening to him on the radio. But there was one place where the man they really did call the King could say he had his throne – that gaudy, dusty, horribly hot place called Las Vegas.

LAS VEGAS

Las Vegas – or simply Vegas to those in the business – is quite plainly a city like no other. It long ago took away the right of Monte Carlo to call itself the capital of the world of legal gambling. It – and the state of Nevada – does things its own way, to borrow and mangle a line from the signature song of Frank Sinatra, another entertainer who made the city virtually his own.

Gambling is so big that, as any one of the millions of tourists who flock there year after year will tell you, you won't find a clock in any of its hotels, for fear of interrupting the continual machinery of slot machines, blackjack tables and roulette wheels. At 5 p.m. you can walk into a dining room to be greeted by a waitress with a smile that might have been implanted by plastic surgery who then asks, 'Breakfast, sir?' Because of the need to get people as frequently and as quickly as possible to the tables and the machines, the hotels do something virtually unknown anywhere else in the world – they reduce the price of rooms to a low that anywhere else would be seen as inviting bankruptcy.

There is, of course, another way the hotels bring in the

customers. In the last sixty years they have created the kind
of show business that went out of fashion from Broadway to
the sticks – personal appearances that used to be restricted
to the now non-existent variety and vaudeville stages. The
moguls running the theatres inside the hotels call it cabaret.
Of course, some of them are exciting, colourful, extravagant
(find your own adjective and it fits) shows that are reminiscent
not just of Broadway or London's West End but of Paris, too.

What really makes this special, if not unique, is the way
that stars take over the stages in one-man shows the like of
which have not been seen for a long time outside of a television screen – and you don't see them there now either. Sinatra
took control at Vegas, but Elvis was the one whose face on
posters and in lights told people that it was his town. If you
were a Presley fan, you didn't need the backdrop of an Eiffel
Tower, a sphinx and a pyramid, a pirates' battle or a Statue of
Liberty outside the hotels in the main street to bring you in.

It is no coincidence that today it is here in Las Vegas that
they claim if not the biggest then certainly the country's most
active Elvis fan club and where a floor in one of the hotels
has been converted into a Presley museum. The man running
that museum at the Imperial Palace Hotel is Jimmy Velvet.
His exhibits show all the variety that summed up Elvis's life.
'We have got Elvis's clothes. We have pictures of Elvis with
Richard Nixon.'

There's a letter signed by Elvis on airline paper. Not good
writing.

Elvis Presley decided he wanted to meet the President and
wanted to get an anti-narcotics badge. He got on a plane

and flew to Washington. He wrote the letter, took a rental car and drove up to the White House and to the gate – totally unexpected by Nixon. The President called him and invited him in. We've got the letter on show here.

So does this mean that Nixon was an Elvis fan? 'Probably not. But you had to like Elvis after you'd met him.' Ray Walker remembers the occasion well. 'I got a call at 7 p.m. in Graceland, from Jerry Schilling. Elvis wanted me in Washington, DC. I went up there.'

They even have exhibits of clothes belonging to Johnny Cash – a coat – and Jerry Lee Lewis – a waistcoat and a white shirt. Why were they let into this Presley citadel? 'It's because we call this the "King's Ransom". It all adds up to the fact that Elvis had so many friends and valued them, so it's a whole thing about friendship. It's why we have dresses and gowns belonging to Elvis's lady friends.' Which, short of exhibiting the women themselves, is an important part of his life to put on show.

But most of the things there are pure Presley. 'There's his own pyjamas and his own bedspread on the bed. Linda Thompson got it for us.'

Velvet was an old friend of Presley and has the TCB badge to prove it. That's as vital to the Elvis story, too, as any song he sang.

Jimmy Angel, who also has a museum dedicated to Presley, became a regular at Graceland, but never considered himself a member of the Memphis Mafia. 'No, I wasn't, because you had to be an employee.' But he says he was part of the gang. 'Yes, I was. It was always great fun. There were guys who had problems with each other. But, overall, great guys.'

He went on tour with Elvis, which was quite an honour for someone outside the Mafia. 'Yes, the early tours. But I had my own career as a songwriter.' And also sang. 'I had national hits – like "Blue Velvet", "You're Mine", "We Belong Together" and "It's Almost Tomorrow".' He wrote some of the flipsides, too.

And once he was in competition with his old idol. 'I was at Vernon's house and I played my new record and Vernon looked at his [then] wife Dee in a funny way. He told me Elvis had just recorded "I Really Don't Want To Know".' That was also the choice for Velvet's own newly pressed disc. 'I had it shipped but I put it on an album instead.' No regrets? 'Not at all. But he would have done the same for me if he'd have known.'

And he says he learnt a lesson about Elvis and about the rest of the 'gang'. 'I didn't push my friendship by being there all the time.'

Nevertheless, the badge, of course, demonstrated a personal link with Presley. What the Vegas museum also proves is that the exhibits are there to show Elvis in various stages of life – from Tupelo to Graceland. Said Jimmy Velvet, 'We have his black trousers. Here's the jewellery, the Rolls-Royce grille belt. The black star sapphire ring he gave to his guitarist. Here's a ruby ring with diamonds. That came from Sonny West.'

There is also Elvis's pride and joy – his gold gun, demonstrated by Elvis before James Bond's gave the idea a certain amount of traction.

They even have the equipment used by the doctor who attended the birth of Elvis and his stillborn brother, Jesse, in Tupelo, a certain Dr Hunt. As I suggested to Mr Velvet, Dr Hunt was the first man ever to 'meet' Elvis Presley, certainly the first to see him. The written record of the births is there for all to see. All this can only justifiably be sited in a place where Elvis made the kind of impact that he alone did. And few others could command the sort of attention that he does – amazingly perhaps, because we are in a world of superlatives, in Las Vegas even more than in any other places. But that, too, is Elvis.

There was the advantage that people have of being so enthusiastic that they do almost a forensic research into the subject. Jimmy Velvet looked at the case of the doctor and the baby very closely. 'I have a lot of paperwork on Dr Hunt,' said the man who is, in effect, also the curator of the museum.

I had a chat with Dr Hunt's daughters and they said that when Jesse was born, the doctor filled out the paperwork for Jesse being stillborn and that, as he was leaving, they called him back. They told the doctor they saw the baby's head coming out. There was another baby.

Born thirty-five minutes later. A baby who was going to be called Elvis Aaron. Aaron was written as 'Garion'. Elvis was 'Evis' – 'because Vernon could not say Elvis'.

To add to the collection, there is a medicine case on view – with the compliments of what was called 'Glasgow's Drug Store'. 'Yes, and it's still there,' Velvet pointed out. Dr Hunt's surgery was above the store. 'There are his tax records – Hunt was also a teacher.'

Elvis, of course, made the film that contained the song which could be called the city's national anthem (and, since Vegas has so many people coming there and is so different from anywhere else, it could almost be called a nation). 'Viva Las Vegas', with its immutable opening lines 'Bright light city gonna set my soul/Gonna set my soul on fire', to many, says it all.

That was one of the contributions of Elvis Presley to the city. It's the best PR Vegas could offer – almost as important as the slot machines.

But what did he really do for what they like to call 'the town'? Sam Thompson has no doubt.

He had played here in the 1950s and had flopped. Las Vegas's effect on Elvis Presley relaunched him. He went out on tour again and he was a superstar again. He was back. But it also reinvigorated Las Vegas. I've been coming here since the 1970s. In the late 1960s, Vegas was becoming a bit tattered and worn. Artists played here on the way down, rather than on the way up. And then, suddenly you had a brand new showroom in this brand new hotel, the International – and Elvis Presley. He still holds the record for consecutive performances. It showed the business people, the number crunchers, you could make money by booking big stars. Thanks to Elvis, big shows came again. It was probably the most dynamic show that people had ever seen.

Elvis was great on the road. He was wonderful at mastering an audience. He could play and read an audience's emotions. He knew what songs to sing, what stories to tell, and he could reduce an audience to tears or laughter or wild applause. It was a dinner show. I think the tickets were about $25, a lot of money for then. It was dinner and a two-drink minimum and a show for Elvis. For fifty bucks you could get all that and

take your wife or your girlfriend and if you slipped the door-
man another fifty bucks, you'd get a front row seat – all for a
hundred bucks. In 1971, a lot of money. He did two shows
a day for nineteen days at a time. And the last show he did was
for the employees at the hotel to thank them for their efforts.
That was very unusual.

I asked Sam, as I had other interviewees, if Elvis was one of
those entertainers who seem to make love to his audiences.
'I don't think I've ever heard that said before. It's well put. I
think he did make love to his audiences.'

So Elvis was responsible for Vegas putting on a new face,
rather like a woman changing her make-up and attracting all
the male attention she could want? 'Well,' said Thompson,
more hesitant than I imagined, 'not solely – but he was in the
forefront and then the Wayne Newtons, U2s, Garth Brookses
and so on have followed on.'

Elvis was quite unusual in a world where stars smiled,
did their act, thanked audiences so profusely it was almost
patronising and then walked out of the stage door to their
cars, protected from fans who wanted nothing more demand-
ing from them than a signature in an autograph book. But it
fitted with the Elvis philosophy of recognising the people who
gave him his fame and fortune. As Thompson said: 'With the
modern people they wouldn't do that. But they have a block
of tickets to give away.'

Elvis was quite clearly unique, but he worked at his success,
perhaps more than most stars did.

And it was at Vegas that he used to ask his team, 'Did the
fans like it?' He cared that they did.

And he cared particularly that the young women liked being with him. Or more than that.

And, through him, some of those women who were lined up for his attention became friends, too. And none of them – at least as far as he knew – was married.

Naturally, he'd have to *know* who had a husband and who had not. He didn't go looking for wedding rings. They could so easily be removed – as easily as he himself would later remove more intimate parts of their clothing. But that was part of the job of the Mafia boys who lined the girls up in the first place. They were expected to find out – and, more important still, to know.

The girls, on the other hand, were, as usual, rewarded. And wonderfully. For that they had to thank not just Elvis, but a certain Mr Stuart Small. Small – not a big man so the name is more than appropriate – was Elvis's favourite jeweller, the by-appointment supplier of the most alluring and expensive sparklers in all Nevada. Elvis patronised him – or, rather, his business – for Elvis never patronised anyone in the usual sense of the word – because he could fulfil many of his requirements. He always needed to have a stock of diamonds and, occasionally, lesser gems ready to bestow on ladies who matched up to what he wanted. When he was in town and, perhaps running low on gems, Stuart Small, in his home in the desert, would be asked to deliver a small package for the star's attention.

'He was able to do this,' he told me, 'because he had a lot of money.' A simple, if not simplistic answer, but it said everything. Small experienced the beneficence resulting from that several times. And it started long before he went into the jewellery business.

'I had met him in the late 1950s when I managed a couple of

actors. I didn't even know who Elvis was.' It was a time when performers came and went in Vegas. He met him through a friend called Richard Gordon, who had a car-lease company specialising in Rolls-Royces and Bentleys. Elvis was a customer.

When Small switched to jewellery, they renewed their friendship. 'He started storing jewels to give to people who did him favours.'

The best example of just how he did favours for Small himself was the night the New York-born jeweller had a call from Joe Esposito.

He asked me to bring some rings down to the stage door. I took along two boxes from which he could make his choice. Each box had about fifteen pieces in it. He bought both boxes – all of them. He must have spent something in the nature of $40,000 on those boxes. Elvis was a giver. If he liked someone, he'd rush into my shop and he'd buy necklaces or other pieces of jewellery and so on and give it all away. He was going with a girl at this time and he bought her some very pretty necklaces. It's a long time ago. He bought a lot of jewellery from every jeweller he'd walk into. I was not the only jeweller but somehow if he wanted something, he'd ring me. We had a very good relationship with him. I was a shopkeeper but I kind of felt myself as a friend.

I wondered if that meant that Presley wasn't particularly choosy. 'Oh no,' he replied emphatically. 'He had great taste and everything I had was absolutely gorgeous.'

Elvis also bought some jewellery for himself. 'He bought jewels for lots of other people, too [not just the girls in his life]. Sometimes we'd just clean his own jewellery before a show.'

And the relationship was always more than just the handing over of a consignment of gems and a quick handshake. That was their professional relationship. Their friendship went beyond that, Small told me. 'We hung about for a day at a time. I wouldn't sell him anything. We'd just shoot the breeze.'

They hung about and they talked. But about what? I wanted to know. 'Oh, about wine, women and song.' In this case, the old adage or cliché could never have found a more appropriate subject. But their business arrangement was never far away. Elvis always got a discount, Small said.

Remarkably, a man like Presley with the showbiz world at his feet didn't change his own jewellery and there was, in truth, a lot of it. 'If he liked a piece, a bracelet, a watch, a jewelled accompaniment to his jumpsuit, or one of his varieties of TCB badges, he kept wearing it.' And there was the question of the TCB jewels which were, once given, the real statement of his affection for a person, man or woman.

When he was in Beverly Hills he bought them from Sol Schwartz. When he needed them or something else when he was in Las Vegas, he would ring me. Sometimes, he'd call me at midnight. I made twelve pieces of TCB badges [in one order] for him. I ended up making twenty-four of them. So I started stocking them. When he passed away, I had fifteen pieces left. When I needed some gold, I'd melt them down. Who would have guessed that this guy's stuff would be unbelievably priced? I ended up with four of them for myself. But I never wore one.

There's an old Jewish proverb about the shoemaker who is always going about with holes in his soles. Stuart Small put it

like this. 'There are butchers who are vegetarians. I don't wear
the jewellery I sell. He invited me to a do once when I would
have been given one. But I couldn't go.'

There are Elvis enthusiasts who can't understand that. Certainly,
the fans – the real fans – know everything they think they are
supposed to know about him. Susan Lorenz, who runs the Viva
Las Vegas Club and is the president of the fan club, has vicarious
memories of Elvis – through her father who was a sous chef at
the International Hotel, which became the Las Vegas Hilton. 'My
dad used to say he could make anything for Elvis Presley in the
kitchen and all he wants is hamburgers.' As for herself, it was
strictly an artist/audience reaction. She went to the Presley shows.
'At concerts I used to think, "My eyeballs are looking at Elvis
Presley in person, I'm breathing the same air as he."'

A lot of work is done in conjunction with Elvis Presley
Enterprises at Graceland. But Susan's main concern is Elvis's
relationship with Las Vegas.

'What we're doing is to remind people that Elvis Presley is
still well thought of here. We consider him as a local.'

She was responsible for raising $15,000 to provide a plaque
on the pavement of Las Vegas's Walk of Stars, running from
the Sahara Hotel to Russell Road. It's the town's answer to the
one on Hollywood Boulevard. For her and the other members
of the fan club that was worth every cent.

'I felt very emotional.'

Her father had been one of the Presley set. She herself says
he [Elvis] was a 'large part of my life. If I could have told him
personally, it would have been great. He showed me there was
a world out there that was much nicer than high school.'

She said something that was typical of the true Presley fan.

'I didn't know how to pray but I played the Elvis Presley songs instead. His music, his movies, added to my life. When I was in the navy, I wanted him to see me in my uniform.' She missed him on that occasion. But there were two evenings when they did get together – in a manner of speaking. 'I shouted out, "I love you, Elvis" and he yelled back, "I love you, too".' For a fan, that constituted a conversation. There was another time. 'I was with my dad. [Elvis] had on a jacket with multi-coloured fringes. He passed me by and I said, "Hi" and he said "Hi" to me. My two big conversations with Elvis Presley!'

And then she remembered an event that stuck out in her mind even more than allowing her eyeballs to look at him in his favourite Elvis outfit, his tiger suit. 'There was a karate demonstration in 1974 during the instrumental break of "If You Talk In Your Sleep". He had reached a high level in karate, a black belt, and he looked like he was killing someone all the way down the stage.'

Her members don't go in for that sort of thing.

We have candle ceremonies at the Hilton twice a year. Our other big focus is Elvis's history here in Las Vegas. We have a party for Elvis's first reappearance date here – 31 July 1969, called 'The Tigerman Returns'. He sang a song called 'The Tigerman' in the 1968 TV special. It was also his karate nickname.

Such details are the lifeblood of real fans and these people are certainly that. That – and the ever available repository of memories.

'He was at Vegas to go to the Liberace show.' Quite a combination, I thought. 'Many similarities. They had crossed paths.

Both were twinless twins. Both adored their mothers. Both were flashy. Both broke ground in entertainment. They were friends. I have seen Christmas cards from Elvis to Liberace.' Well, so that was something she had sorted out.

I asked Judy Nelon, the publisher of 'How Great Thou Art', about its association with Las Vegas. It fitted in perfectly, of course, with his feelings for gospel, which Priscilla Presley said was his greatest love.

> It came to Manna Music, the company I work for, and it was wonderful to get the remarks from Elvis and be invited to sing it. When you saw Elvis do that song you could hear a pin drop. It defined Elvis because it was the message he wanted to get across. Someone once said, 'Elvis, you're the king.' But he said, 'No. There's only one king. That's Christ.'

I'd heard that before – and I would hear it again.

The real *fans* privately don't like the word. To them, it tends to sully the kind, colourful but considerate image of their idol.

Vicky Sessler is one of those forty to fifty people who sign on and pay dues to the Las Vegas club. On a crowded Las Vegas Boulevard – it is always crowded – she denied that the membership was too small to be considered important in the Elvis story, which in her eyes would be a denial of the power that everything else points to. 'Small? Yes. But very strong. We need to learn about him, to pay tribute to him and to make friends.'

And then she said something that seems to sum him up. I asked the obvious question: had she ever seen Elvis? 'Oh yes,' she said, almost shocked that such a question needed to be asked. 'And that's the reason I live out here. My husband and I came here and we found out that Elvis Presley was going to be here and then from 1969 to 1970 we visited twice a year.'

Every time they saw Elvis perform 'fantastically'. 'The audience would go out of their minds.' And Elvis gave her a present – not a car, definitely not a TCB badge, but the traditional scarf. And that led to a solemn declaration of loyalty, although solemnity was probably not the emotion she had in mind.

> Elvis gave me the scarf – as he did to some women in the audience – and a drunk man stole it. I started to fight him, but the man got away with it. The next night, Elvis gave me another scarf. He hugged me and kissed me. It was the best miracle I could ever have had. He may have seen [the fight] happening.

As she told me the story, she burst into tears. That was another example of the posthumous effect Elvis Presley still has on people. So why still so emotional? She didn't have to look for an answer: 'I fell in love when I was twelve years old and I'm now sixty-five and I'm still in love.' With Elvis, of course.

When the scarf incident took place, it wasn't only Ms Sessler who was emotionally affected. 'Everyone there hollered and screamed,' she said.

The thought ran through my mind that if anyone deserved a TCB badge or brooch it was this woman who only wants to hear Elvis Presley's voice. As it is, she still wears a watch with Elvis's picture on it that she bought thirty years ago.

It was inevitable that I should put my courage where my mouth was and asked how she thought today's artists compared with the man she, given half the chance, would personally have crowned the king, if not the president, of the United States. She wasn't fazed by the question any more than I would have expected her to have been. 'Everyone claps them because it's expected. But when you saw Elvis Presley you did a whole lot more than you expected to do.'

To my surprise, this more than just dedicated fan has no objection to Elvis impersonators. Unlike Susan Lorenz, who had told me, 'We don't need these people.' Indeed, one would think that really dedicated purists would not usually appreciate the fact that these 'copycats' could match the original – and, therefore, risk spoiling his reputation and image. But Vicky Sessler doesn't feel that way.

One highly successful impersonator is Elvis's old former neighbour Jimmy Angel, who did well enough recording Elvis 'covers'. It was quite deliberate, he says. 'It was [columnist] Rhona Barrett's idea. She worked for Hedda Hopper. She was cute. Looking and sounding like Elvis was a serious operation.' But he claims no credit for it. 'I did what I was told,' he adds insouciantly. 'I'm seventy-four,' he says now. 'I write my little songs about Elvis. Elvis and Marilyn. I used to be mobbed. Nobody said no to me for eighteen years.'

Elvis never objected to his singing.

He loved music. Liked the chicks. He did what Parker said: 'You do the singing, I do the business' – which is why Elvis never said 'no' to him. Otis Blackwell was my producer for ten of my hits. He wrote 'Don't Be Cruel', 'Return to Sender' and 'All Shook Up'. [They say I] sounded just like Elvis Presley.

And, like everyone in the business, he likes to tell anecdotes about Elvis, even those he heard second-hand. True or not, they are like pieces in a jigsaw – they fit, like a straight edge in a puzzle can only fit in as a section of the sky or a bit of bark on part of a tree. One of his favourite tales is about Otis Blackwell.

It was at the Brill Building in New York [the successor music publishing centre which took on the old name of 'Tin Pan Alley']. Otis had a friend called Louis. He asked Otis to get a song to Elvis but Otis said Elvis would take part of the song – if you wrote a song for Elvis Presley his name was on the record as part-writer – so Louis said, 'No way. Give it to a man who shakes his leg and howls at the moon?' Otis got $585,000 for one song and Louis got … his song.

And then there is Ronnie McDowell, who recorded thirty-seven Elvis songs for the Kurt Russell film about Presley's life. Before that, he had recorded some of the numbers in his own voice. 'We were in the studio and I was singing like me but another songwriter said I should sing I like Elvis. I said, "No" but he said try it and so it came to be.'

Actually, he doesn't like to be thought of as purely an impersonator – he says he is equally keen on Al Jolson, because they have the same kind of magic and is impressed that Presley's 'Are You Lonesome Tonight?' has exactly the same arrangement as Jolson's version recorded more than a decade earlier. 'Impersonators have a bad press, but it's kinda neat that they carry on Elvis. But he's the most impersonated man – black Elvises, Chinese Elvises. Next door to me there's a man who runs a store and he's from Jordan.'

The fans, like Vicky Sessler, would have been happier to hear Elvis himself, but those interpreters are – if they are any good – at least acceptable substitutes. 'I always welcomed "Legends in Concert"' (an evening of celebration of rock singers). But, she said, 'Elvis is always the headliner.'

Impersonators are one thing. To the fans, they really do believe they are helping to perpetuate their own love. There are others, however, who go further. They proclaim that the stories that Elvis died that day in 1977 were untrue. As if he were some mythical god. McDowell is not convinced. 'It's so stupid,' he said.

> It was to sell newspapers and books. But Elvis Presley could never fake something like that. He was the happiest man on stage. And all that love ... he could never have retired. People say that it was not Elvis in the casket. Well, it was. I'm happy that he is still so popular.

Vicky Sessler did not need the sort of presents others received from Elvis. For her, even hearing impersonators is enough – because it proved that her hero somehow or other still lived and helped to foster the unique feeling that he gave when he was alive. As she told me, 'He saturates your whole body. With love.'

Anecdotes concerning Elvis say more about him than any critic's description of one of his sell-out mega shows. Edie Hood told me that only by being close to him – really close, although not in a sexual relationship of the kind that he had with most girls in his life – could you get any idea of the sort of man he really was. But the real personality did, she said, overlap into his performances. 'It was in the way he sang. He was anxious – even in his own rooms. He wanted attention. They [his entourage as well as his audiences] gave him that.' To study Elvis, she believes, you have to delve deep. 'The more I go into it, I want you to roll down a window, put on your blue suede shoes, let down your hair and go down memory lane.' I got the picture. The people interviewed in this book did a lot of all that.

Edie thought about what she herself had found out. 'One night I was with his aunt. [She told him] "You don't have to go on tour." But he knew he had to. He took care of people. He was driven. He had a desire to take care of people – his fans.'

HOLLYWOOD

For Elvis Presley, Hollywood was just another place on the map. His map. It was one of the towns, as they like to call their homesteads in America, where he built a house, two actually, if you lump Bel Air and Palm Springs into the Hollywood community. It was also one of those places that was so much a part of his life. You can logically add it to Tupelo, where he was born, to Memphis and Nashville, where he made his music, and to Las Vegas, where he performed to his biggest live audiences – and had a closer personal touch than anywhere else. But Hollywood was different.

Hollywood was where it all came together and from which, it seems, he couldn't get away quickly enough. And yet ... and yet it was from where he was able to demonstrate his talent to people who would never be able to go to Las Vegas or the other places where he wowed his public. It was also where he showed, to the surprise not just of his most fervent fans, but also his sometimes equally serious critics, that there was more to him than the jumpsuits, curled lips and long black hair. For the first time, thanks to Hollywood, he was able to demonstrate that he could be a pretty good actor.

In *King Creole*, for instance, he stunned people on the set by not only being able to take direction, but take it well. I remember Walter Matthau telling me (not for this project, which otherwise very deliberately is excluding star names) that he was amazed.

> I wasn't happy about having him star in this movie – apart, of course, from the fact that it meant it would make a lot of money. But this was a serious film. [Matthau played a nightclub owner.] I wasn't funny in it and I didn't really want anyone else to be either – be good, I mean. But he was.

The writer Michael Hoey – *King Creole* was not one of his films – got a similar reaction when he spoke to Matthau about Elvis. He told him that Presley looked up to him – 'absolutely'. 'I have heard Walter Matthau explain how much he admired Elvis in *King Creole*. He said he could have been a fine actor.'

The 'Colonel' saw to it that this would be a springboard to a new Elvis life. And every time his name appeared on billboards far away from Elvis's normal hunting grounds, it was more and more publicity for his records and those live contacts with audiences.

Hollywood is renowned for not just making stars out of actors and singers – and Elvis could now claim to be both – but also eating them alive. Presley wasn't sure when he first went there whether he was compromising his already huge star status or whether he was going to be on the menu for some big producer or studio. He himself turned what is still known as Tinseltown into a dish fit for a king.

If you wanted to know how Elvis – or any other star – really

coped with their film work, you could do worse than go to
the writer of the movie on which they were both working, like
Michael Hoey – his father was the actor who played the part
of Inspector Lestrade in the original Basil Rathbone Sherlock
Holmes films – who seemed, when we met, to be the perfect
witness. And so he is. We sat in one of those Los Angeles hotels
with palm trees in the gardens and not the most attractive
veneer on the furniture. We talked about Hollywood and Elvis's
part there. So there was the question to be answered – of what
in the pre-computer age could be summed up as carbon-copy
pictures. Elvis complained they were all the same. Strangely for
a writer, Hoey admitted that, yes, they were all the same – on
their producer's/director's instructions. Which was upsetting
because, he said, Elvis always 'wanted to be an actor, not a star'.

I wondered whether, since Elvis so much admired James
Dean and Marlon Brando, they represented the sort of actor
he would like to have been himself. You could almost imagine
him in some of those roles, I suggested. 'Yes,' he said,

> you could see him playing those kinds of roles. I am sure he
> would have liked to have been that sort of actor. You can't see
> that in the parts that he did, but he was an original. And, in
> *King Creole*, you could see James Dean in the character that
> he played because he was at that point just getting started and
> finding his way in that part to being an actor. It was taken away
> from him as time went on – as he was doing so much singing
> in films.

But his ambitions were certainly not given full rein. 'Norman
Taurog [who directed Hoey's Presley film, *Live a Little, Love*

a Little] used to say, "Jack up the hat and run another Elvis under it."' That was some confirmation.

Yes. We all knew that. The problem was, I ended up doing six pictures with Elvis, all but one with Taurog. And we made a strong effort to move him away from the usual Elvis Presley fare – *Tickle Me*, *Speedway*, *Spin Out* ... But *Double Trouble* was something a bit different. It was still a Presley movie. But the music was awful.

George Klein and the people cajoled into buying his records could tell him that.

There was, he reminded me, a take-off of an old French folk tune and 'Old MacDonald', but Elvis did what he was told. 'We came up with a football idea and we mentioned it to Elvis and he mentioned it to the "Colonel", who said, "Give me $1 million and you can shoot the phone book." He just didn't care.' Of all the indictments of Parker, this was one of the worst.

The big music companies were based in Hollywood and that, naturally enough, was no bad thing. Elvis got to meet not just film people, but composers of music far away from the 'Nashville Sound'. And he was feted by some of the most beautiful women in America. The other ladies in his life might not have appreciated the fact, but in that regard, if perhaps in no other, he was in his element. And a very big element it was.

Peculiarly, it was a time when he appeared to revive the interest he had always had in Judaism. The genealogist may have declared to me – and unequivocally at that – that Elvis had no Jewish roots at all. But he himself wondered. And so did members of the Mafia – and so did its fringe members.

Perhaps it is unfair merely to include Larry Geller in that

latter list. He was a man whose whole life was turned on its head thanks to Elvis – who, if you take Geller's word for it (and there is no reason not to do so) had a change or two himself as a result of knowing a man who started out as a hairdresser and turned into an adviser and sort of father confessor. To move into the Presley orbit, he says, involved a decision that 'changed my life and Elvis's life'.

Indeed, there were few people in Hollywood who were closer to Elvis than Geller, who became something of a guru for Presley. Or even a reverse guru – with each depending on the other for advice and innermost thoughts. But they got together in an exercise of pure idol worship.

'I grew up in Hollywood and I can remember so well the birth of rock'n'roll,' Geller told Neil Rosser.

> When I lived in Hollywood, a guy used to come to me and we played records of the time. It was Phil Spector. In 1957, Elvis came to town [for a rock concert]. We had duck tails, tight black jeans. We looked like extras in rock'n'roll films. We got there early and thousands of kids were streaming in from everywhere.
>
> We thought we'd get in to see Elvis, but we didn't have tickets. We walked around the building and there was Elvis. And I said, 'Come on, guys.' And I ran up to Elvis and I looked up to him and my jaw dropped. He said, 'I'm Elvis Presley' and I said, 'I'm Larry Geller.' And I was looking at him, the face, the sideburns. And I thought he was from another planet, glowing from within.

Later, he glowed both within and without, professionally. As he said, the idea of a men's hairdressing salon was unknown when he opened his own place and developed a star-studded clientele. Frank Sinatra, Rock Hudson, George Hamilton and Steve McQueen were among his customers. And then, one day, the name of Elvis Presley was added to the list.

'By 1964, most people couldn't get an appointment and one afternoon I had a call and it was one of Elvis Presley's people. Even though I knew all those celebrities, Elvis was the one to meet.' Elvis got on the phone himself.

It was the answer to Geller's dreams – and his problems. 'And I knew what I would do.' But he admitted to us that it was not a step to be taken lightly. Elvis told him: 'Come to the studio tomorrow and bring some books.'

'It was a humungous [decision]. I was about to open my own salon and another in Palm Springs. But I just felt it was right.' And Geller's making that 'right' decision revealed a much more self-confident Presley than we have grown to expect. Not exactly a modest man either. Take Geller's word for it, and this was a man who spoke about himself in the third person, like he was talking about some government member or a figure from history, like Abraham Lincoln or Winston Churchill. It was quite an apposite comparison.

As Geller said: 'He still touches millions of lives around the world. His music, the force of his personality, he is more than a legend.'

Elvis asked him: 'Do you want to be responsible for the hair of the biggest celebrity on planet earth and do you want to nurture Elvis Presley, guide his mind, be his friend?'

Some choice – for some people. And Larry Geller was now convinced he was one of those 'some'.

And Geller's conversations with Elvis made him something

of a thinker, too – in fact, it was a mutual admiration society story – which began with a phone call.

> I was styling someone's hair when the phone rang. It was a feller who worked with Elvis. He said he would like me to go up to his home to style [Presley's] hair. I was twenty-four years old. I thought, 'This is sensational. This is wonderful. Every day I'm hanging out [working] with Henry Fonda, Rod Serling of *The Twilight Zone*, Robert Wagner.' But Elvis was the celebrity of celebrities. I packed up my bag, drove into Bel Air [the most fashionable area of Los Angeles] and was met at the gate. I was taken up to Elvis's home. He holds out his hand and says, 'I'm Elvis Presley.'

They went into the bathroom.

> He explained to me he was making a picture called *Roustabout* with Barbara Stanwyck. For the next forty-five minutes, I restyled Elvis's hair. When I'm blow-drying his hair, Elvis is looking in the mirror. I ask if he liked it. He said, 'Oh great. Great.' He looked at me, pointed his finger at me and asked: 'Larry, who are you? What are you into?' I didn't expect that. During those forty minutes, I said nothing. I knew the routine. I knew how to behave and respect their privacy.

Geller told him that the most important thing in life is 'the meaning of existence ... is there really a God? Do we have a purpose to this life? I have to find out, Elvis.'

To which, Presley responded: 'You have no idea how I need to hear what you have to say. Please, Larry, keep on talking.'

Elvis told him about growing up in Tupelo, about the trials of his early days. The conversation lasted three hours. 'He told me about his mother and his father and the pain they had to endure and making it overnight. And I'll never forget Elvis telling me,' Larry recalled, 'telling me about spiritual things and why he was plucked out of the millions and millions of lives to be Elvis and [as he said] to be in the position I am in today and have what I have – and there has to be a reason.'

Hair was still going to be cut but it was the Presley mind that was going to be probed. Elvis's locks would be secondary, even though they were as vital to him as his jumpsuits and perhaps even his voice.

'A lot of others could have [looked after his hair]. I said, "I am looking after your hair as a front. We're probing the mysteries of life." He laughed.' But it doesn't appear as if laughter was the main subject on their agenda. The hairdresser had turned philosopher and so had the client. However, there was a wide assortment of topics. 'We talked about everything, books, girls [of course!], God [always]. Elvis was a voracious reader. He was an incessant speaker with a great sense of humour. He had an inquisitive mind.'

Geller says he gave Elvis books to read, including one called *The Impersonal Life*, which he then passed on to other people.

It was that time of change which other people in Hollywood had talked about. 'When I started working for him,' Geller recalled, 'both our lives took on a drastic change.' Plainly, that was what working with Elvis did to a person. 'We started making many, many movies.' And he started reading many, many books. They became part of his personality. That is not an exaggeration. It is an undisputed fact. He listed those films – *Roustabout* again.

And then, *Girl Happy*, *Double Trouble*, *Paradise*, *Hawaiian Style*, *Easy Come, Easy Go*, *Spinner* and *Clambake*. 'We'd chat all the time and he opened up and his library grew – hundreds of books. On tour two huge suitcases travelled with him. Suitcases with books. He read every day of his life.'

He maintains that his friend didn't do much in the way of reading before he himself came on the scene – although there are, as we have seen, others who recalled his voracious reading before.

When I met him, his potential was about to burst. He was the highest-paid actor in August 1965 and the Beatles wanted to meet him. I was doing his hair [when I heard this]. Elvis became stoic, silent, pensive. And he said, 'I know exactly what these guys are going through.'

Today, Geller gets very introspective about those days with Presley. The affection is obvious, as is the admiration.

'I have worked with beautiful people,' he recalled. 'People like Paul Newman, Warren Beatty, but no one was more beautiful than Elvis. Other celebrities would have their egos shrivelled meeting Elvis.'

The Beatles, he maintains, were among them. 'The Beatles came to meet him. We went into the Den [at Graceland], with the guys, their girlfriends. The door opened and we heard screaming. The four Beatles came in with Brian Epstein. Elvis stood up, shook hands. The Beatles sat down at the feet of Elvis.' They were in a semi-circle 'and they looked up at Elvis in silence. Fifteen seconds. He stood up and he said he was going to his bedroom – and they laughed and it broke the ice.

One of the Beatles said, "Look, a colour telly".' Which gives some idea how long ago that was.

Parker and Epstein went off together and the others played roulette. Later, Ringo and George left the room with the other Mafia guys, went off to play pool.

That left Elvis, John and Paul. John asked to play his guitar and Paul picked up a bass. Elvis picked up his Martin. At that moment in time and space, I was at the centre of the universe. It was magical. But nobody turned on the tape machine. Parker did not even allow a picture. Abhorrent!

When they went off together, were Epstein and the 'Colonel' cooking up some kind of deal for the Fab Four and Elvis to work together? We shall never know.

He does know that, that day, George was not part of the discussions. 'George was by himself under a tree, smoking a joint.'

If a deal ever had been arranged, Elvis, for one, would have been happy. 'I really liked those guys,' Geller says Presley told him. 'But there's one thing I don't understand: their teeth.' He was plainly impressed with British dentistry.

It was a notable day. 'That night, something happened. Parker had bought Elvis a sauna bath and we went up to see it – and we looked in the window and there was this fifteen-year-old girl in the sauna. We opened the door and she lunged at Elvis.' It was a mystery – because she was not one of Elvis's 'harem', not of the group who were lined up for his pleasure, and of all the things charged of Presley and his love life, underage sex was not one of them.

'We had no idea how she had got there.'

Geller is one of those people who finds it difficult still to think of Elvis Presley in the past tense. Certainly, he thinks their relationship is of today, very twenty-first century. 'I'm still working for Elvis Presley,' he says completely unabashed. 'He lived the American dream, rags to unprecedented wealth.'

So what did he think was the Elvis secret? 'He was brash, daring ...' Not, then, the shy man others had seen. But they were people who didn't have the advantage of the barber's chair, which many others have spoken of as being as revealing as that of any psychiatrist's couch.

Finally, as he talked there was that possibility of Elvis, like Geller himself, having Jewish blood. Or even that the star was secretly anti-Semitic.

Geller was having none of that. 'I've heard rumours that Elvis didn't like Jews, didn't like blacks, he didn't like this, didn't like that. That is such nonsense,' he says.

All nonsense. He embraced everybody. He had so many Jews around him. All nonsense – Alan Fortis, Marty Lacker, George Klein. When I started working for him, what is the first thing we do? We go to a cemetery, Forest Hill, where his mom was buried. We go there. There's a big statue of Jesus Christ, a cross, and he said, 'I wanted a Star of David [too] there and there it was – until his death.'

Despite the evidence presented to me in Tupelo, his friend is convinced that Elvis's great-grandmother really was Jewish and this could establish a Presley line in the faith. He told us that could be established by Halacha, Jewish religious law.

Elvis himself, Geller told us, wanted evidence of his ethnic identity. Not satisfied with a cross and his TCB badge, he wore the Jewish emblem of the Hebrew letter 'chai' – life. 'He always wore a chai around his neck. He did not have a prejudiced bone in his body. His backing group, the Sweet Inspirations, were beautiful black people. He was not prejudiced at all. He was the most universal thinker.'

Returning to the questions of his Jewish roots, Geller says that the question came up many times.

> One night we were in Baltimore. Every year, PBS would run a film about the Holocaust. Elvis was eating and this film came on. Elvis pounded his fist on the table and shouted, 'How did this happen!' He was deeply touched by pain, suffering. He was very tuned into the Jewish people.

Needless to say, the evidence points to his being tuned into almost everyone with whom he worked. Geller remembered being on a film set with him when 'Elvis would give gifts to all the crew, maybe over a hundred people.' We had heard that sort of thing before. But the man with the individual showbiz style proved while in the movie capital that those gifts would be pretty unusual, too. Not necessarily tasteful by some of the standards of those women who wore only the best diamonds Cartier could provide or the most pristine minks.

'One year, Elvis went to a jeweller and designed a watch.' And, by Geller's account, quite a watch it was, too. As he described it, this was a watch which might not have made the advertisements in the glossy society magazine pages but would have delighted a few million readers of the tabloids.

'Every twenty seconds, the face would fade out and you'd see a cross.' So not one for his Jewish friends – unless they were as ecumenical as Elvis himself.

Geller first came on the Presley scene in 1964. The fact that Elvis had started to change was, he says, noticed among the Mafia and those outside. The director Norman Taurog was among the first to recognise the change from rock singer to film actor – with the real emphasis on the word 'actor'. 'I've been watching you,' Geller recalled Taurog saying. It was at MGM when the two men, one the never totally self-assured young star, the other a man steeped in Hollywood lore, to say nothing of the big business aspects of the movie world, discussed the very noticeable differences in Elvis's work and personality. 'I've been watching you,' Taurog repeated. 'I don't know what's been going on in your life, but whatever it is, keep it up. I always said your potential would explode – and it will.'

Geller said he noted Elvis's reaction to that. His response to it all was not something that would normally have come from a big rock star. 'Elvis was so proud when he heard that. He wanted to do something about that change and he said he wanted to create a meditation garden in his life.' Which, of course, he ultimately did at Graceland.

Meditation was more part of Elvis's life than is usually recognised. In fact, it seems there were moments of the meta-physical in their relationship.

'I have read so many books over the years about Elvis, about the vision he had in the desert. The stories are a bit fuzzy, shall we say?' Geller believed that he himself was so close to that moment, he could say he was not in the least fuzzy about it. 'Six months after I joined him,' he recalled, 'he was reading a lot. We were driving because he didn't [want to] fly and we were in the Arizona desert and we were approaching the sacred mountains of the Hopi Indians. It was near sunset and the sky was iridescent blue and suddenly Elvis pointed.' What he pointed out was, to him, a clear indication of the way the Presley mind worked.

'Elvis pointed to the sky and there was a cloud in the perfect shape of Joseph Stalin. And then Elvis gasped. We ran into the desert.'

Elvis didn't always show his athletic prowess but on this occasion, walking would not have been enough. He was excited and so it seems was Geller who had no doubt that his friend was impatient and determined. 'Quick, follow me, Lawrence,' Elvis said and there was no alternative but to do as he said. 'Behind us were Jerry Schilling, Red West and Billy Smith [another Mafia member] and they had no idea what was happening. He said, "You're right. All those books are right. You saw that face?" I said, "Yes".'

From time to time all of us have seen images in the sky that prompt the imagination to come to conclusions that are not always the same as other people's. On this occasion, not much room was left for doubt, at least in Geller's mind. Elvis would have convinced him, even had it not been so obvious. To the Presley mind, this was an extreme religious moment. 'That was a sign from God,' Geller says Elvis told him. 'When I saw that face in the cloud a bolt of light shot out and filled my body with love. And I don't have to believe in God any more.' What, the prophet of gospel, the kid who went to church in Tupelo and never stopped showing how pious he was, saying he didn't believe in the ultimate spirit? No. Not quite. 'Now I know. I'm not a believer. I'm a knower.' Well, that made it clear. But why Stalin, the total anti-God? How did that explain it was the Soviet dictator who came as a messenger from God? He didn't explain and apparently Geller didn't ask.

What he did ask, for there is no doubt that this friend-cum-guru was very much in Elvis's confidence, was something that none of the other interviewees revealed: the star's ultimate ambitions. The answer was a shock, if not a surprise. 'He wanted to become a monk. [He said:] "I want to show people there's more to me than you see on the screen."'

Geller himself knew about Elvis's relationship with his wife, Priscilla.

> I first met her when she was nineteen. She was a positive influ-
> ence in terms of his health. She'd push him to get up early.
> She pushed him to eat better. He ate terrible food. He was a
> phenomenal individual. But when it came to his body he put in
> the worst food, sugar, carbs.

But if she knew how to feed his body, he believes she was a lot less careful about feeding his mind. 'She didn't like him read-ing books,' he alleges. And that was a serious fault to Elvis, who, despite what his image seemed to declare, was already the avid reader whom Geller knew.

But even more important, Geller believes she was jealous, notably of the relationship he himself had with his friend. 'She [herself] wanted quality time with him. There was resentment. She was young. But after they broke up, she blossomed. She was the force behind Graceland. She is very spiritual. I've always liked her very much.'

Elvis was, of course, very spiritual himself, clouds or no clouds. A spiritual man who was never alone.

Geller makes no bones about his relationship with Elvis. 'He was surrounded by a dozen people who travelled with him. But they weren't privy to his private life. They had no idea of his plans. Two of us knew his future plans. His father [and I]. Elvis knew exactly what was going on around him. He was a genius.'

But a flawed genius. We had reached the point in the Elvis Presley story when the real devil in his life was being spoken of openly. George Klein talked to me about it first.

> I saw a lot of prescription drugs. He thought if he were taking those, they wouldn't hurt him. But there were two bad doctors. A guy in Las Vegas [who called himself 'Doctor to the Stars'] and a Jewish dentist in Los Angeles. But back in Memphis Dr Nick was my doctor. He was taking care of Elvis. But we didn't know he was taking drugs from the bad doctors.

All that gives the impression that he was a hypochondriac. Not so, says Klein. As Larry Geller had said, that was not the principal difficulty. 'Food was the problem. And there was no question of [non-prescription] drugs.'

Sam Thompson saw it differently – although he agrees about the food, even though he repeated that he had never seen him consume the banana and peanut butter sandwiches. He thinks Elvis's prescription habit was partly responsible for the break-up between his sister Linda and his employer. He himself was almost seen to overstep the mark. 'Yes, I saw it [the taking of prescription drugs]. I raised it with him and he threatened to fire me because he said the pills were more important than me. But they were prescription, not drugs as such. There is a clear bifurcation between drug abuse and prescription drugs.'

Ironically, he says Elvis was 'hard on drug-taking'. He had a badge to prove it, Thompson says.

Did that mean, then, that he was kidding himself that he wasn't taking anything dangerous? 'Yes,' he said, 'he was.'

The real drug was the stage and the way Elvis worked on it. Geller summed it up: 'Most people are interested in his music.'

But, strangely, as the 1970s dawned, there were problems with that music – for the people who listened to it in their homes rather than at his concerts. Record sales were dropping, sometimes alarmingly. And it was in that branch of his business that Hollywood, it was hoped, would come to his rescue. George Klein says he knows what the problem was – and was there when the solution looked as if it could be solved.

[The fall in sales] was because he was recording B-sides from his movies. We were having dinner at Graceland. He hasn't been number one for ages and he's about to do Las Vegas. His producer stood up and said, 'We're going to Hollywood. We can't get Hal Blaine [Elvis's favourite drummer and the man he considered essential to his best recordings]. We can't get the studios.' His songwriters were saying they had some pretty good songs. I was angry. But I needed to get him on my own. I saw my opening. I said, 'Elvis, can I please say something?' It got real quiet. 'You're a superstar and these guys are saying they can't get a studio or a drummer and these songwriters are bringing you crap because they want the song writing publishing [rights]. You should have the best.' Normally, he'd say, 'Let's have a meeting later.' But he said, 'George is right. I want to cut hit songs.' Another guy said, 'I got one from Barry Manilow.' And he said, 'Bring it to me.' He cut 'Suspicious Minds' and then 'In the Ghetto'.

Now it was really clear that he needed to extend his work in the film capital from the screen to sheet music, but there was one really lost opportunity. *A Star Is Born* could have been the best thing he did. We can only imagine what might have been. Barbra Streisand wanted him as her co-star in the film. She not only asked for him, she argued for him, she cajoled for him. But the 'Colonel' kept saying no.

There is no doubt that in almost everything she touched Barbra Streisand called the shots. She thought she did just that in this film project, as she did in everything else. From her side of the argument, that is, but it was her side which lost. Would the combination of Streisand and Parker have proved difficult? It could have been fatal, but perhaps not as fatal as things turned out, with the twinning of the then most power-ful woman in American music (and, she would have liked to have said, American show business) with the country singer Kris Kristofferson. If Klein and others had had their way, they could have put their foot down to make sure that the songs in that film were a lot better than the ones that actually made it to the screen with the final pairing.

There are scores of theories as to why that happened and always the 'Colonel' is the villain of the piece. Ask any of the interviewees how this actually came about and you'll get an equal number of suggestions. But what if the film had been as big a flop with Presley as it was with the S and K combination, as they were known? It could have plunged Elvis into a morass at a time when, more than ever, he needed another triumph.

The 'Colonel' was not one of the boys. He was above that – or so he believed. But George Klein says of him: 'He was a great manager. I have to give the devil his due. He got Elvis Presley on television, publishing and so on. He made mistakes in Elvis Presley's career.' And, to his mind, *A Star Is Born* was the biggest error of all.

> She was big, the real deal. Elvis asked for a script. Members of the Memphis Mafia and others read it and they all said, 'This is great, Elvis. It will relaunch you in films.' But Parker made too many demands. He wanted top billing. You don't get top billing over Streisand. Streisand wanted to renegotiate. Parker said they'd get another deal. They never did.

The general feeling is that if it hadn't been for the 'Colonel' it would have gone ahead. Sonny West sees it differently. It wasn't Parker's fault at all, he told me. 'It was all Elvis who did it. He wanted to get out of *A Star Is Born*. He made impossible demands.' And Sonny West is sympathetic about the manager's role.

'He was the most maligned person. He was accused of everything that went wrong, overworking Elvis Presley, all the movies, stepping down from *A Star Is Born*.'

The fact remains that to many people it was a lost opportunity, an opportunity that could have lifted Elvis into becoming one of the big movie actors of his generation. Of course, it could also just as easily have turned into an indifferent movie, or worse. On the other hand, it might just as easily become one

of those films that could be filed under the word 'iconic'. The first version in 1937, starring Janet Gaynor and Fredric March, and, even more so, the 1954 remake with Judy Garland and James Mason, have both gone down in cinema history. With all the usual hindsight, a Presley–Streisand partnership could have made the picture truly memorable – and not for its awfulness.

Certainly, as Geller and the others have noted, this was a different Elvis who went to Hollywood. That, of course, was the intention of the studios that employed him. In truth, they did not know what to do with a Presley on their books. Once again, there is a parallel with Al Jolson, quite clearly the Elvis of his time. Here was a magnetic stage performer who found it impossible to be confined to what was, in the late 1920s, a very primitive camera lens and microphone. The man who called himself 'the World's Greatest Entertainer' was a terrible movie actor but sold millions of cinema tickets on the strength of his stage and singing reputation.

Elvis had it easier. The technology of the 1950s and 1960s was a lot kinder to him. After a somewhat shaky start – when, as we have seen, he was helped by mature actors like Walter Matthau – he began taking the work in his stride and, indeed, had changed.

He endeared himself to the people with whom he worked in ways in which others had only hinted. The musical director of *King Creole*, *Tickle Me* and *Lovin' You*, Walter Scharf, told me:

I was amazed at how cooperative he was. Elvis and I had an education together. He taught me a great deal about the rock business and how it worked. And I like to think I taught him something about music.

He never played the big star. He was so respectful – I was old enough to be his grandfather – that I was almost embarrassed. It was always 'Yes, Mr Scharf' here, 'If you think I should sing it that way, Mr Scharf' there. Sometimes, I had to pinch myself that he was who he was.

And then Scharf emphasised: 'He was the most respectful man I have ever known. I saw that Elvis worked harder than many a supposedly more accomplished singer. He took my advice when I told him songs needed to be rerecorded and just picked up his guitar and did them again.' But things were always different when the 'Colonel' was there with him.

It was as though Parker put some kind of hypnotic spell on him. If he wasn't fully concentrating on Presley's eyes as he was recording – which was rare – the songs were poor, the voice with what I regarded as no quality at all. I had never seen anything like it before. It was extraordinary. But Elvis, whom I got to know quite well, was a great deal more intelligent than people were prepared to credit.

Despite what he had said about Parker, he says that the 'Colonel' was 'very kind to me. He was a straightforward man and appreciated that I could do something for his "boy".' Apparently, both Parker and Elvis appreciated that relationship. 'He would say, "Thank you, Mr Scharf" when I suggested something. If I thought something needed changing he would say, "I'm really sorry, Mr Scharf."' It seems that at the time *Tickle Me* was made, Elvis really was sorry. He told Scharf:

I can't go to a restaurant because I'd be mobbed. I can't go to a
theatre. So if I want to see a movie, I have to hire the theatre for
the night after hours. I sit there with the Jordanaires or maybe
some girlfriends and we watch the latest movies.

It was before the age of the DVD. Perhaps he wouldn't have
liked those quite so much as sitting with another girl (to say
nothing of the gospel group) in a cinema.

Ronnie McDowell, who wrote a tribute song, 'The King
Is Gone', summed up Elvis in Hollywood for me like this: 'I
always tell people that the mystery of Elvis Presley will never
be solved. The camera bares your soul and I think people [the
audiences of his movies] saw his soul and his heart. Everyone
who knew him, all, say he was a great human being.' I had
heard that before, but it fitted with the Presley story.

It fitted in, most of all, with the people with whom he
worked, particularly the women. It's not too big a stretch of the
imagination to say they fell in love with him – any more than
it is to confirm that he got pretty friendly with them himself.

In one of those smaller Hollywood residences which would
still make some largish homes elsewhere look like garden
sheds, Celeste Yarnall recalled among other things the kiss of
a lifetime. But that was after talking about the books she had
written, her paintings and her beloved cats. For a mere man to
dominate that sort of conversation, one gets the idea just how
important working with Elvis Presley was for her.

It was while making *Live a Little, Love a Little* in 1968 that
she was given, she said, the 'the consolation prize' of a supporting role. She had been passed over for the lead. Nevertheless,
that role made the title of the film come true for her.

I was being considered for the lead role, but I got the role of Ellen, a capricious model type. [One day] the producer asked me if I wanted to meet Elvis. I was wearing jeans and a T-shirt. I said I would love to meet him. I said I can't wait to meet Elvis. I turned round and there's Elvis, who folds me in his arms and gives me a giant hug and immediately put me at ease. I could have died there and then of a heart attack. It was so amazing because I didn't expect it.

And the relationship, as they are wont to say, blossomed. 'Yes. I won't tell you just how it blossomed. He was a lovely man and we became very good friends. We had a strong spiritual connection. He loved women, yet he was a man's man.' Joe Esposito told me he related more to women than to men, which shows that beauty was in the eye of the beholder's beholder. Celeste explained:

He loved women with personalities. He loved women who were funny, who were outgoing. He had two personalities. One was with women – he adored women, and in another aspect of his life he was very much a man's man. With women he could play that sensitive, more gentle side. I absolutely adored that. You know, we girls are suckers for the little boy in our men.

She added,

He was perfectly at ease with his 'little boy' side. He was a bit of a prankster and loved to tease. You know, we barely knew the word 'charisma' in those days. He truly was charismatic, bigger than life with those gorgeous sapphire eyes and

magnificent skin. His hair was not really black. That was a tint.
You could see the little light brown in his roots.

By her account, there were plenty of opportunities to see those
light brown roots.

> We were having lunch one day in his dressing room and I noticed
> the wonderful aquiline patrician profile and I said, 'You look
> exactly like [the face on] a Greek coin. You have one of those
> profiles.' He just kind of blushed and said, 'Oh, little lady ...'
>   He was interested in you rather than being 'interesting'. You
> felt like you were the only person in the world. He was so beau-
> tiful and kind and intelligent.

If you took her word for it, his intelligence was highly important, perhaps even with an aphrodisiacal quality about it. 'I
have a memory like an elephant,' said this most unelephant-
like woman. 'Because of his curiosity – and he loved to read
– he could relate and talk to me. He had a deep spiritual side.'
Again, confirmation of his reading and his spirituality.

According to Celeste and the stories she had heard, his deep
spiritual side 'upset the "Colonel", who had his books confis-
cated. But he loved to explore that side with people he could
relate to and, indeed, he could relate to me.' He talked about
his personal life, too. 'In April 1968, Lisa Marie had just been
born and he was in a whole new league. Fatherhood.' She says
that he was 'quite overwhelmed by it' to the extent that he

> felt a stranger in his own home. He said, 'I'm afraid to sing in
> case it might wake the baby and I have to sing. What'll I do?'

He said, 'There's so many women in the house. It's so feminine. Gee, it's so quiet in the house and I'm so loud!'

She said that he would have wanted to be more 'hands on' as a father but his schedule wouldn't allow it.

Then there was that 'spiritual connection', which, of course, she has not been the first person to mention in this project. 'He was quite esoteric. He was reading Erich von Daniken's *Chariot of the Gods*.' That was a book title and name not known well among the Elvis Presley fan clubs of this world.

He frequently talked about 'spiritual things', she said. They were 'experiences that were told to him in adulthood – such as a blue light over his house when he was born. "Why me?" he would say to me. But there were no answers. He did not try to answer it "verbally",' she said. 'But he could not understand why this glorious kingdom was granted to him.' She thought it came to him 'through his explorations, his love of people, love of animals. Elvis had a wonderful memory.'

I asked if all these things – none of which were in the public domain – surprised her. Astonished, more likely.

It's very like being in a family on a movie set. He was very comfortable on a film set. You start opening up, a depth of friendship.

He managed the set and the crew very well. Like – I've never seen it before – he would jam on the set. When he sang [Mario] Lanza songs, you could swear you were listening to Lanza. He would then segue into country, rock, light opera – and he was able to pick up so many different instruments and be able to play them.

The amazing thing to her was that when he sang operatic arias, he didn't even sound like himself. 'No, he didn't. He sounded like one of the great tenors.' And he did it there and then, while electricians and technicians were going about their work, surrounded by all the equipment of their business.

> The crew on the set treated him like royalty, but those who knew him well treated him like a member of the family. When I was on the set he would get up on a makeshift bandstand and do a performance, play an instrument. He could sing bass baritone, a three and a half octave range.

The set crews seem to have been as enamoured – well, almost – of the man they were told was the King as she was herself. 'They admired him. You wouldn't have been retained to work on an Elvis Presley set if you couldn't get on with Elvis.'

But then ... none of them had experienced the, or rather THE, kissing scene. 'The kissing scene is the first scene in the picture for me. I am lit for this kiss. It was quite nice [the scene, that is] I must tell you. [The film] was from a book called *Kiss My Firm But Pliant Lips*.' Surely not a title to be taken lightly, I suggested, and to which she could only agree.

> The very first thing I thought was I am indeed kissing firm but pliant lips, a beautiful set of lips, topped up by beautiful sapphire eyes, gentle sparks flying. We would rehearse and rehearse, do one take. He is wearing dark make-up, I am very fair. The make-up artists were constantly taking my fair make-up off of him, and his dark make-up off of me. So, poor me, I spent the whole morning kissing Elvis. It's coming up to time

for lunch and we are in the middle of this madly passionate kiss and I hear the director through one ear say, 'OK. Cut. Let's break for lunch. Cast one hour, crew half-hour' and Elvis won't stop kissing me. I hear the arc lights going 'boom, boom, boom'. The camera is up on the crane. I can feel the set getting dark and Elvis is still kissing me.

Norman Taurog is calling, 'OK, Elvis. Lunchtime! OK, Elvis. Stop kissing.' And finally, he shouts, 'For God's sake, we have to feed her.' I don't want to insult this beautiful man, but I am starting to break and eventually he lets me go. Off we went to lunch. It was only a rehearsal. There was more kissing after lunch.

I asked if the kissing had to stop after the cameras were shut down. She replied, somewhat enigmatically: 'Our friendship lasted during the filming – and there was a later attempt to get back together. But our lives had some complexities which precluded it happening. But I carry with me today the profound feeling of having been a friend of Elvis.'

She then told me that Elvis had perfect pitch and 'an incredible memory for the script'. Plainly, it wasn't the script of their future life to which she was referring.

Elvis's work didn't help, she maintains. 'His schedules were too hectic. He was preparing for the comeback special [which was being planned] and he was very nervous about that. I put him at his ease, saying they'd love him.' Which is what, she says, she also said when he asked her: 'Do you think they will remember me? Will they like my music?' He could not have known how it would be when we spoke, all those years after his death.

He was, she says, very concerned with things that were happening to America and the world at that time.

> During the funeral of Martin Luther King he asked me to join
> him in his dressing room – and he said that if he couldn't be
> there [at the ceremony] in person, he was going to sing – and
> he did. In his dressing room in front of me and the powers that
> be, he sang 'Amazing Grace'. He was very worried about what
> had happened and what was happening to our country. It was
> a very powerful experience.

So there was now the ever-present Hollywood question to answer: I wanted to know how she herself saw his attitude to film making. Did he love it or did he hate it? In fact, was it a love–hate relationship? 'Love–hate, yes,' she said. 'He was a brilliant actor. But it was a talent that remained untapped.'

Like almost everyone I met in Hollywood and the surrounding suburbs which have given Los Angeles the slightly less than flattering soubriquet of the city in search of a centre, Celeste, almost inevitably, had to mention *A Star Is Born*. In fact, in her case it was more than just a mention. It was a declamation. 'Had he done *A Star Is Born*,' she said, 'there was an Academy Award on the horizon for him.' The film they themselves made together was, shall we say, a little less ambitious.

> I felt he enjoyed making *Live a Little, Love a Little*. There were
> only a few songs in it. It was a romantic comedy to show another
> side of himself that he hadn't shown in the other movies. He
> expressed to me that he really enjoyed this film-making experi-
> ence and I really think he did enjoy it.

As I told her, with that big kissing scene it was not exactly surprising.

But if he had won an Oscar ... You can only imagine the reaction around the world to the sight of Elvis cuddling the iconic award, the way he had caressed hundreds of women. If only ... she says. After all, Elvis 'brought himself to different situations; acting is not about wigs and copying people'.

The British-born Suzanna Leigh, who co-starred with him in *Paradise, Hawaiian Style* and replaced Shirley MacLaine who had thought better of it, saw Elvis both before the cameras and off. He could be petulant, she remembered, not necessarily the nice easy-going, polite star. 'Elvis had never heard anyone say no to him and I once said no to him when Richard Harris came down to see me. Elvis that night went mad.'

On the set, he was much as others had said, which meant he was a thoroughly nice guy. 'Oh yes, he loved making movies. His films that were bad he worked to make them OK – movies that were watchable.' That is a clever actor. And she, too, came to the big event that never was. She said: 'Elvis should have done *A Star Is Born*.' Then she added another ingredient to the pot of missed opportunities. He should, she said, have starred in *West Side Story*, too. What Leonard Bernstein and Stephen Sondheim would have made of a very different kind of music star performing their work is another one of those 'if onlys'. But Suzanna is certain.

She recalled working with Elvis and the producer Hal Wallis, who had spent his earlier years at Warner Bros, with little things like *Casablanca* under his belt. He was a father figure to all those on the set, she says. 'He had the knack of looking at someone and seeing a star. He did the same with Elvis. He was very clever.'

To Wallis, she told me, Elvis was 'guaranteed money. And there was no other star like him. He respected Elvis. He was an underestimated actor and Hal wanted him to make better films.'

Wallis, she said, knew how to deal with the 'Colonel'. 'Hal said he just HAD to deal with it. Like my mother. My mum and the "Colonel" were a perfect match! It was very ching, ching. Money. No one knew the "Colonel" was a gambler.'

The arrival of Parker on to the set of any film was a danger signal to his client. Suzanna remembered: 'When the "Colonel" walked on the set, he said I looked "dreadful".' That was not what a young lady wanted to hear. It was also not what Elvis wanted to hear. 'Elvis said, "I'll have him off the set." Whether or not it actually happened as a result of his protests is not now sure, but it seems that the message did get through.' It got through sufficiently for Wallis to want to make one Presley film after the other. Not surprisingly, as the co-star told me: 'Hal would make $3 million from every Elvis film.'

As for Elvis himself, he seems to have wanted Suzanna to make all those films with him. His generosity decreed that he would give her a present. But not, she said, one he would buy from a jewellery store of his choice. That would not have been precise enough for him. 'I went into his trailer,' she recalled 'and I saw he was sketching a design for a sapphire and diamond brooch for me.'

I suppose that if Stuart Small wasn't able to make the trip from Las Vegas there was no choice but for Elvis to exercise this rather unique form of do-it-yourself.

Any Presley study proves that point. Similarly, it doesn't take much imagination to realise that the fan base was pretty wide. Very wide indeed. Suzanna Leigh is convinced that it

stretched further than most people would have imagined. She
recalled meeting Queen Elizabeth II at the premiere of the *Born
Free* movie.

> She asked me all about Elvis Presley. I said Elvis would love to
> come to England. Later on, I told him that he was going to get
> an invitation to the Palace. But he didn't get one. So I contacted
> St James's Palace. The invitation was sent, apparently. It had
> gone to the 'Colonel'. But he couldn't travel. Hence Elvis didn't
> get to the Palace.

Music was an essential part of an Elvis Presley film and the
screenplay writers had to grin and bear that, but they were not
responsible for the placing of the music. 'We never did that,'
Michael Hoey told me. 'We wrote the script and then went
back to look for places to put songs. We tried to cut down on
the songs – there were only a few in *Live a Little, Love a Little*.'
I wondered whether he should have just made the films and
ditched the music. 'Well, he did – towards the end of his career.
But they weren't successful movies.'
For a writer to be satisfied with a screenplay was one thing.
Seeing an actor's performance and reciting those lines he
produced is another. But he says he was always satisfied with
the way Elvis performed. 'Taurog thought he was a terrific light
comedian. He had problems with sub-text. But given time, he
could have got there.' And then he said what everybody seems
to have felt. 'He could have been good in *A Star Is Born*.' There
it was again.
I wondered whether Elvis had discussed the famous film
that never was (as far as Presley was concerned, that is),

particularly if he felt that the star who was already very much born, and had become such a huge success, 'smarted' at losing the opportunity to play in a film whose title could once have applied so much to himself.

'There must have been fights with the "Colonel" but we never discussed him. In fact, we never discussed his personal life. Although on *Live a Little* he showed me pictures of Lisa Marie, just after she had been born.'

There was no doubt in his mind that he was manipulated by Parker, he told me. 'Yes, there were two Elvises ... Elvis Presley the performer and Elvis Presley the person. Every business decision was taken by the "Colonel". When he left films and went to Vegas to perform again, he was taking back his life.'

He would have been sure of doing that had Svengali been given his marching orders by Trilby. Larry Geller said: 'I was all in favour of Elvis leaving Parker.' The story was that the 'Colonel' was going to sack Geller. 'I left. But he wanted to sack me. We were arch enemies. He thought I wanted to be Elvis's manager; that I was whispering that the "Colonel" was no good. I was saying that Elvis could do more with his career.'

Nevertheless, he remembers now that Elvis really was going to make a radical change to the way he operated his business and, indeed, his life. 'Elvis was going to get rid of the Memphis Mafia, go to Hawaii, get healthy. He was going to get rid of 90 per cent of the people around him. He only wanted three or four people around him. We had picked out a house in Hawaii.' Above all, he wanted to end the association with Parker.

That was not something that Parker would have wanted to hear.

One night in 1977, Elvis had been very ill. Pathetic. One afternoon, I was sitting in Elvis's suite. When he woke up I was there and all of a sudden there was a pounding on the door. It was Parker and he demanded to see him. They had a very tense relationship. I saw the doctor dunking Elvis's head into a bucket of ice water and Elvis was moaning. [Parker] had no idea what was going on in Elvis's life. He should have said, 'This man should get rest, not be on tour. He should be in hospital.' But he said, 'Nothing else matters but this man must be on stage tonight. Nothing else matters.' Elvis called me in and said, 'Why did you leave me alone with that man? I need someone new, new blood ... No more touring. We're going to that house in Hawaii. We're going to read, get more books, meditate, start a charity, produce movies.'

The Mafia members couldn't understand any of that. Said Geller:

When people are presented with something new, people get frightened. Here's this Hollywood hairdresser. They couldn't understand how we spent so much time together. Elvis reading books, we don't understand. So much jealousy. But if I'd been in their shoes, I'd have felt the same, I'm sure. But to this day a lot of those guys still don't understand the relationship we had. Once he told me: 'I've outgrown most of these people I've been with almost all my life.'

But always there were the health problems.

He had hypertension, a spastic colon, he had a bad throat, his nightstand was like a drugstore. He was spraying his throat.

He was taking pills every day, four or five doctors who weren't even in touch with one another, prescribing poison. In those days you couldn't admit it. Today, it's a boost to your career!

Dr Nick was with him on most of the tours. Geller says he knows why: 'It was because of [Elvis's] upbringing, being born in a two-room shack. No running water. Couldn't afford a hospital.' 'Colonel' Parker didn't think about that. 'Well, of course he didn't.'

The 'Colonel' was not the only influence in Elvis's life at this time. In a way, an equally important behind-the-scenes figure, but a much more benign one, was Norman Taurog. Ask Michael Hoey and there is not the slightest doubt that Taurog was good for both Elvis and for he himself. 'I learnt a lot from him. I loved him,' the writer revealed. 'His one problem was sight gags. He'd come from silent movies. Elvis loved him.' And, of course, showed his appreciation in his usual way. 'He gave him a Cadillac.' But not one he could drive. 'Taurog was blind by then.' But not unseeing of Elvis's affection. Hoey himself was not quite so lucky. 'I didn't get cars, but I got televisions, belt buckles ...'

The first time he met the 'Colonel' was in Palm Springs.

I was invited to a dinner party. The 'Colonel' was trying to impress me. He tells me of how he first went to talk to Hal Wallis, how he would sew cheap labels in expensive suits so as to wrong-foot people, make people think he was a hick. And so he did this and Wallis offered too little. So the 'Colonel' said he left, saying Wallis would have to pay more. Every minute he was out the door the price would go up $10,000. He was trying to impress me [by telling the story]. I didn't like him.

There seems little doubt that Wallis took the Presley pictures very seriously. They were not, as I suggested, retirement projects for the veteran producer. 'No,' said Hoey, 'while he was making an Elvis Presley movie he could have been making a John Wayne [picture]. Also, he made *Becket*.' But that was not to say he put Elvis Presley movies in the same class. It was, indeed, a question of money. 'He made Elvis films so that he could make higher-brow movies of the Tennessee Williams books.'

How, though, did Elvis himself fit into the time that he made those Hoey films? 'Elvis fitted right in. The interpretations vary. In some of the Fox movies, he was trying to act. Yes, he was of his time.'

On the other hand, this admirer of Brando and James Dean had no ambitions to be regarded alongside them. 'He *was* a star and I think he wanted to be a good actor. But I don't think he wanted to be a major movie star per se.'

All the time, though, talking about Elvis in Hollywood is also talking about Elvis and the 'Colonel'. Presley, if he ever thought of writing his memoirs, could have taken a little-remembered Danny Kaye movie as its title, *Me and the Colonel*.

As Hoey sees it, Parker had no interest in the Presley films for their own sake. He was indifferent to them. 'Yes, absolutely. His participation in the films was just promotion. He was there for merchandise. Elvis Presley was a product for him.'

This was one of the occasions to talk about the two Elvises. 'Elvis Presley as a person didn't let the 'Colonel' control him. They never left the country because the 'Colonel' didn't have a passport. They went to Hawaii. But *Fun in Acapulco* was shot on the Paramount lot.'

For others in the cast of Presley films, things were a lot more pleasant than they were for the star himself – perhaps because he didn't have himself to work with.

Paradise, Hawaiian Style was 'a dream come true' for Suzanna Leigh, who confessed to me to being an Elvis fan since childhood. Hal Wallis spotted her when she was in the film *Boeing Boeing*. 'Hal said, "I'm sending you to Hawaii for a few weeks." He asked me, "Are you an Elvis fan?" I said, "Yes." "Oh dear," he said. We got on so well. The film length was doubled, so much fun it was.'

It would have been much more fun if it hadn't been for the 'Colonel'. At which point she joined the queue of the Presley people for whom Parker wasn't among their favourite people. 'He was not a nice man,' she told me. 'He would come on the set. He was SO rude and Elvis got him removed from the set.'

That was something we had not heard before, an amazing example of Elvis exerting a power that few knew he had. 'Yes. He had lots of power. I'll tell you a story,' said Suzanna:

There was this girl who was going to sing a song in the movie – 'You Scratch My Back'. She was sucking up to Elvis. I saw her and I said out loud, 'And she's another blonde.' Elvis popped up and said, 'Tomorrow, I'll have her in a black wig.' And then he ordered the wigs.

She was one of the people to whom I spoke who talked of Elvis being shy.

He was so different. He never abused his massive power. I said, 'I've got to change now' and he said, 'Sit down' and he told the director he was going to be late on set to listen to my stories. The director asked how long and he replied, 'Four or five weeks'. That was the sort of thing that would drive people on a film set mad. Had he meant it he would have had no choice but to get the next plane to Las Vegas.

The film and its star made a huge impression on this still attractive blonde actress. 'I did twenty-odd movies, but people always remember the Elvis Presley film.'

The problem was to discover if Elvis actually liked the films he made. Larry Geller was among those who heard just how unhappy he was with his output. 'Look,' he told his hairdresser, 'look at these movies I'm making. What do they mean? They're teeny-bopper movies. They have no meaning to them.' And to underline his comments:

> I have to do something with meaning in my life. The studios are making millions of dollars off me, 'Colonel' Parker is making millions of dollars. They package me into these stupid, idiotic movies. Don't get me wrong, I'm also making money like everyone else. But I'm not here just for the money. I have to get back to a live audience – that's where the energy is.

'I have one regret,' he told Geller on another occasion. 'My one regret is the world doesn't know I'm an actor. I'll always be a singer but my greatest desire is to be an actor.'

Again, there is contrary evidence – although there are those who really did think he was happy with his output. But not his old friend George Klein. 'No. He did not like those films, though he did like *Blue Hawaii*. He liked about ten of the thirty-one that he made. He didn't like the scripts and songs in the later films.'

And those songs were the ones that Klein says he had been made to record, with comparatively derisory sales figures. 'He wanted to be an actor. But [in those later movies] he'd say, "It's the same story. I beat up the guy, win the girl. It's a winning formula, so should I change it?"'

Elvis, said Klein, would have wanted to change things with Priscilla, the girl whom he himself liked so much. Rumours abounded that Presley 'put a hit' on one man. There was talk of her being involved in a love affair after the marriage was over. Klein skates over the matter with the ease of a man saying that Elvis liked singing. 'If you've been through a divorce, you hate the guy who's with your wife. No, it wasn't serious to put a hit on a man.'

There were others whose only contact with Elvis in Hollywood was through his work. Michael Hoey told me:

> He got ill for seven months. When he came back he was doing a movie called *Tickle Me*, the only Elvis Presley Allied Artists film, which was made at Paramount. It was the first time I had met him, although I'd seen him on the set of *It Happened at the World's Fair*. He was kidding around and he seemed nice, a good sense of humour. He seemed stand-offish at first but he was shy. Hence, he had the Memphis Mafia to sort of hide behind.

I asked if it was difficult to take him seriously. 'I thought he was rather lightweight as an actor, but I came to respect him more.'

Studios were normally very jealous of their rights and their roles, but as far as Elvis was concerned the 'Colonel' was the puppet master and Presley his doll. Again, a story to contradict the idea of that 'doll' really being the one with all the power to pull the strings. 'The "Colonel" had that control,' Hoey told me. 'When the script was at a semi-final stage, we indicated the placing of the songs. *Live a Little, Love a Little* had the best music. "A Little Less Conversation" was a hit much later. "Almost in Love" proved he could still sing ballads.'

Working it all out was like a military operation. Hardly surprising, perhaps, with a 'Colonel' in charge. 'The process [was] you send in the script and you do demos – many by Glenn Campbell – then you'd have a meeting with Taurog, Elvis, the "Colonel" and I and then we'd play a song and discuss it. Elvis would make comments, but afterwards at the recording studio he would piss and moan that he didn't like the songs – but he didn't fight it then. The "Colonel" decided.'

Coming to Hollywood did, in fact, improve the songs Elvis sang, although generally not those that were connected with his films. His friend Don Robertson wrote a number of them – including 'Anything That's Part of You' and 'There's Always Me'.

'He liked to make up lyrics which were sometimes on the naughty side and this was one,' Robertson told me. 'Like "When evening shadows fall", to which he added: "Now it's time to ball".' There were also 'I'm Yours', 'They Remind Me Too Much of You' and 'I'm Counting on You', all of which hit the charts. Altogether, he wrote fourteen Presley numbers. His influences were, like Elvis's, gospel. But unlike Presley, there was nothing in his background to show it. 'I sang in a church choir, but my parents were atheists and never came to the church to listen to me.' Which was a reversal of the conventional story

– here was the notion of a circus boy running away from the big top to become a lawyer. 'Yes. I used to sneak out [to go to church].' All of which would bring him and Elvis together as natural friends, perhaps. 'He was a delight,' Robertson told me. 'He wanted to please songwriters.' Songwriters, if not the 'Colonel'.

Robertson and Elvis first met in 1961. 'There was a phone call from one of his entourage,' he told me, sitting at the piano in what appears to be a very English-style house – complete with log fire – and ready to pound the keys to illustrate his work and, of course, Elvis's, too.

His wife, Irene, a former air hostess, remembers meeting him after he had 'the worst divorce' – all he had left was his grand piano – on a plane. 'People thought he was Rock Hudson.'

It was a good opening for the couple. And so was his first actual get-together with Elvis.

Their professional relationship blossomed after Elvis had recorded his first Robertson song, 'I'm Counting on You'. He said it took no time at all for him to get used to the idea of Elvis singing his music and his lyrics – 'which particularly interested him'. 'It seemed a natural process,' he said. 'I'm Counting on You' was written and recorded before he ever met Elvis.

I got a call from one of the primary music publishers in Los Angeles, Jean Aberbach. He liked 'I'm Counting on You' a lot, he said, and could get a big artist to record it. And then he called back and said he couldn't but he'd got this new chap, Elvis Presley.

Which was OK with Elvis himself.

'He said he wanted to meet me. He'd already recorded a few of my songs by that point. I went to the studio, Radio Recorders, with him and he had a captain's hat on. Very handsome. Very impressive man. Unusual.'

As he said, Elvis by then was already a huge star. 'He came in between takes and we chatted for a few minutes. He reiterated that if it weren't for [his first lucky break] he'd have been driving a truck now.'

He gave me some insight into how he sought the inspiration for Elvis songs. Like one of the singer's own favourites, 'Marguerita'. 'I wanted to get the flavour of flamenco, so I went to a little club called the Purple Onion. It was research. I spent the whole evening listening, getting into the right frame of mind.'

Not all the songs became hits. His number 'I'm Gonna Like It Here' was written for the film *Fun in Acapulco*. But, in one of the vagaries of the movie business, not for the scene in which it appeared. 'We were given a script and [like always] they move it so that it doesn't really fit. In the movie, Elvis was fired from his job and he's adopted by a youngster in Acapulco. But it didn't happen in the [final] film.'

One of his songs that Elvis sang had originally been written for Johnny Cash. 'What Next, Where To?' was based on a poem by Carl Sandburg. Cash 'didn't see it that way, never recorded it. He was showing me his collection of pistols, but he didn't like the song. But Elvis did. It was a very easy [tune] to work on.'

If playwrights worry about how actors will interpret their work, it is all the more concerning for songwriters. A mere note out of place can change the whole concept of a piece.

There were never those worries with Elvis. Robertson told me he 'couldn't have been happier' with the way Presley sang his work. 'Once he got his arms around a song, his interpretations were wonderful.'

It has to be admitted that some songwriters do get unpleasant surprises when they hear their work performed for the first time (writers hearing their scripts read by other people sometimes have the same reaction). Elvis, however, had the gift of switching on to the minds of the people who supplied him with his material. But that mindset was helped, as far as Robertson was concerned, when he himself performed the numbers and Presley listened. 'We had a similar voice quality,' said the man who frequently recorded his own work on albums. 'That's why he recorded quite a few of my songs.' Even so, he rarely wrote songs that were specifically Elvis numbers. 'Only for a few movies,' he told me. 'But as time went on, I started imitating him in my demos.' With him in mind? 'Yeh.'

But, then, Elvis was a romantic singer and Robertson says that songwriters have to be romantic, too, when they write for artists like him. Which was a perfect arrangement when his wife first came on the scene. It seems to have been romance all the way. As he told me: 'Yes, I was head over heels in love with Irene Simpson [the current Mrs Robertson].' Irene herself told me that they spent their wedding day with Elvis. 'We all sat in a coffee shop and I was praying someone would come by with a camera.'

These are mostly testimonials to the goodness and talent of Elvis Presley, but it has to be said that this was not quite – not *quite* – the view of all the people to whom I spoke. Notably Sonny West, who contributed to the book about the star in

which he talks about Elvis's drugs problems and how difficult
he was to work with, Memphis Mafia or not.

He wrote about Elvis punching him. 'He never said he was
sorry. I never heard him apologise.' Except on one occasion.

Apologies or not, the indictment grew. 'I stood up to him
and he admired that, but it [also] annoyed him, ticked him off.'
He was using the term in the American sense, not quite as
benignly as it might have been used in a British context. Before
long, Elvis fired his former buddy.

He says that his dispute with Elvis was really all down to
the star's bad temper. And that was nothing new. In fact, it had
blown up long before.

One time in his anger, he hit me – over a situation in which
he thought I said something bad about him. I had been sitting
with a girl and with [the film actress] Tuesday Weld. Elvis didn't
drink, but he drank a little bit when Tuesday was there because
she was young and giggled. So he would drink so that he could
handle it. All of a sudden, he came over in between my girl Kay
and me. He looked at her with his back to me and said, 'Damn
yer, you're cute.' And he kissed her on the cheek and then he
left. She flushed. I grinned and said, 'What was all that about?'
We started talking again and he came back and started kissing
her, I saw her arms come across him and I thought, 'That's it.'
I came off the stool and Alan Fortis said, 'Smooth as silk, ain't
he?' I said, 'Yes, he is.'

He himself was with another of the crowd, Elvis's cousin,
Gene. I said, 'Gene, given the choice, what one [of the two girls]
would you choose?' He said, 'Tuesday, man.' I said, 'Me, too.'

Elvis hollered from across the room, 'What did you just say about me, Sonny?' I said, 'Nothing.'

He insisted West was talking about him and that he wasn't going to like what he thought he heard.

Well, he picked up a soft-drink bottle and started walking towards me with it and said: 'You're going to tell me or I'll break your head open with this.' That was enough for me. I said, 'You're not going to touch me with any bottle or anything else. You've changed so much, I don't want to be around you. I quit.' He said – the bottle had gone – 'You can't quit, you're fired.' I said, 'I'm out of here.' He drew back and hit me in the jaw. Tears came to my eyes and I said, 'I never thought you could do something like that.'

It was smoothed over. 'Elvis never should have hit you,' said Gene. 'I'm sorry,' he later said. It was the only time he ever apologised to anyone. He admired that I had stood up to him.

Drugs, he is certain, were behind all the later problems. 'He got jealous after Cathy [Westmoreland, his current girlfriend] started seeing other men.' West knew that it was only a matter of time before he would be fired. 'Before he got sick he warned us we would have to look for other jobs if we didn't stop saying things. But he meant more to us than the jobs, so we didn't stop being on to him about the drugs.' That was why he and his co-authors wrote a book. 'We couldn't get to him any more. We had to smack him down,' he said – and then asked me an obviously rhetorical question: 'Were *we* the bad guys?'

'We discovered that not only was he using those [prescribed] drugs, he was also taking cortisone spray for his throat because he had lost his voice one night in Vegas and it panicked him.' By then, they were no longer on the same old terms. 'He became paranoid and he kept taking it. It's a steroid and steroids make you mean. It just made him a different person. If someone had done that when Elvis was in his right way, he would have hit him himself.'

Matters came to a head, he said, when Elvis was, West believed, offensive to his backing group, the Sweet Inspirations.

We couldn't say to him, 'You're a rude SOB [to the Sweet Inspirations]; the stuff is just getting to you.' But we did say, 'You just don't care about people. I don't know what it is.' He replied: 'Oh, hell I'm just kidding around. If they don't like it, don't get the ass out. Hire the Blossoms.'

He warned us. And he fired us. Red and I knew he was killing himself, that he was going to die. It was just a matter of time. So when he said, 'If you guys don't stop this, you're going to be looking for other jobs', we didn't stop. It was June 1976 and we were just getting ready to start a new tour.

Someone at a show I was doing asked why I wrote that book. I said I did it to save Elvis's life because we had no more access to him. He said, 'You didn't have to write that book.' I said, 'We had to smack him down, to hit him right in the face. He went places where he had security and we couldn't get to him.'

West told me: 'We were offered an amount not to do the book. Elvis's private detective [one of them, that is] John O'Grady called me and said he had a business proposition. Money not to write it. I said it wasn't about the money.' It would mean, he said, they were being bought off. Had he accepted the money, 'we wouldn't accomplish what we wanted to do'. This book, he said,

> is just for Elvis – it's a message to Elvis. I had discussed with John in the past about what Elvis was on. Elvis was on Demerol, Percodan and when I began to remind John about this, he cut me off – as presumably Elvis was in the room with him and John wouldn't have wanted him to know that he had discussed this with me. He was taking cough syrup, sleeping pills, Valium. I took them, too. You would literally fall asleep as you're talking. Elvis fell asleep in his food.

The question was, how did he know what his boss was taking?

> I took in a parcel once in the name of my six-month-old son (Demerol was in there) from Max Shapiro, the dentist. I called Shapiro and told him that if he ever did that again, I would get him arrested. Shapiro got married in Elvis's home in 1977. He got Percodan for Dean Martin.

As we have seen, Dr Nick has always denied he had anything to do with Elvis's drug intake. Nevertheless, in 1980 the Tennessee Board of Medical Examiners brought charges against him. They claimed he overprescribed drugs to people, Elvis among them. After a month-long trial, the doctor was acquitted. 'Elvis took pills for certain situations,' he told me. 'If he had a strep throat, he would take what was necessary. He had blood pressure and diabetes. He wasn't taking off-the-street drugs. He hated drugs.'

But did he take too many prescription drugs? 'Not from me,' said Dr Nick. 'He got pills from other doctors. I controlled his pills. I never left him with pills. A nurse had pills in a little brown envelope, but he never had pills in his hand.'

He then repeated something he had said before. The jump-suits didn't help his health condition. 'His clothes were too heavy. They were made from synthetic fibres. He couldn't breathe through them. His clothes could weigh ten pounds.'

The pills were just one cause of friction between the doctor and the 'Colonel'. 'We didn't see eye to eye. Elvis could get pills from loads of doctors. The "Colonel" thought I was one of the ones who wanted to make money from Elvis.'

Larry Geller said he had a similar reaction from the manager – who one day, towards the end, 'shook his cane at me' when Geller said Elvis was not well enough to perform and go on tour, but should be in hospital.

Elvis's plans to pack everything in and go to Hawaii was just whistling in a stormy wind. Everyone around knew time was a-wasting. Dr Nick told me he knew in his heart what was about to happen. And yet the more obvious outward signs of impending disaster were not there.

Elvis and his Mafia entourage were about to go on tour. 'Five days before this tour, I'd given him a complete physical and found nothing wrong with him. And weeks before, he'd passed a multi-million-dollar health insurance.' But then, insurance medicals and even men like Dr Nick, who have good reason to think they know their patients, can sometimes be wrong.

THE END

Some members of the Mafia were convinced that Elvis couldn't go on. Not only were there the drugs and the food, there was the work. The man whose first audiences called him Elvis the Pelvis, the young performer who stood up on stage, legs akimbo when they weren't kicking out to screaming audiences, and with his guitar strapped round a shoulder, had matured into a superstar of stupendous proportions – stupendous *physical* proportions, that is. His face was bloated almost out of all recognition. His girth, like his face, bore no resemblance to the attractive young man he had been so very recently.

Yet still the fans lined up to buy tickets, to make arrangements for going to the various venues, boyfriends making plans with their girls, parents organising babysitters, older people putting it in their diaries, friends ensuring that nothing would prevent them going to the shows and RCA making certain that the record shops had enough discs to cope with the expected demand. But his friends knew better.

One Mafia member put it like this: 'Most of us have people in our lives who glue us together. He had his mom, Linda

Thompson, friends on the inside. But he'd come apart. He'd become tired. His eyes were twinkleless.'

But did those friends tell him about their fears? 'No,' he said, 'who wants to hear negative things? I wasn't around much then. I didn't tell him what to do.' It is easy to say that it would have been better if his watchdogs had done so. However, as the man said, there was little that Elvis had to do or to prove. 'He'd packed so much in, was there anything left to do? I'd thought of that.'

Linda had little doubt that there was trouble on the way. 'He had two hospital stays and he insisted I had a hospital bed next to him. If his bed was raised, so was mine. He didn't like the hospital food, so we had the housekeeper at Graceland bring us peas and meatloaf and mashed potatoes and gravy into the hospital. I stayed with him the whole time. I was this young, healthy, vibrant girl who never drank, never did drugs. There I was in the hospital with him, the entire time.

There were others, including people in his business, who also saw what was coming. Ray Walker of the Jordanaires told me: 'Brenda Lee saw him in 1975 and she said that if he didn't do something soon, he would go.' That was the man Walker said had been like a man caught up in a tsunami.

There was, he said, a kind of reconciliation with Priscilla. 'Priscilla told me that towards the end, he would phone three to seven times a day and they would always talk for twenty minutes.'

And then, on 16 August 1977, it happened. Nancy Rooks, the ever-faithful Nancy, maid, sandwich and hamburger maker and confidante, was there in the Graceland mansion when she realised that all was not well. Elvis was not answering any of their calls, the ones that before long had turned into shouts.

Graceland was in a panic. No one really wanting to go and
see what had happened. But, then, they knew: in a bathroom
upstairs Elvis had breathed his last – after completing an altogether different body function, with a book on his lap.

Nancy recalled for me:

Elvis had played racquet by 6.30 when he came in the house.
Ginger was already upstairs. I asked him if he wanted to eat
breakfast. 'Just bring me some water,' he said. Another girl took
up the water and he grabbed [it]. I said that maybe he was hot
and tired. I heard a rumour that Ginger did not want to leave
that day. She wanted to leave the next day. And he said that if
she didn't leave, someone else would be there with him. She
said she [was going] to bed and he went to the bathroom.

She got up and down several times, but she didn't check on
him because they'd had a row. At 2 a.m. she went into the bathroom to check on him. She asked me who was down there and
she began to cry. I knew there was something wrong. I could
tell from the position he was in.

Nancy saw the employer whom she realised she loved. He
was plainly dead. No one was needed to confirm the fact.
Nevertheless, she asked Al Strada, another of the Graceland
set, to go upstairs. 'When he came down, I said, "Don't you
look at me. Go and do something."'

The one they called was Joe Esposito. She asked him to go
upstairs.

He was there a little while and then he called for an ambulance.
I led the ambulance men into the house and they asked me

what happened. I told them I didn't exactly know. I showed them how to get the stretcher upstairs – and when they brought him down, he was blue. He had been passed [sic] since 8.30 p.m.

That was more than six hours earlier – six hours dead without anyone knowing about it.

I asked Nancy how she felt. Her silence provided the answer. Did she, I wondered, cry that day in 1977? I thought the answer was obvious. But it wasn't. 'I hurt too much to cry,' she told me. What happened next was no more predictable. 'I knocked on Lisa Marie's door because I didn't want her to see him in that position. I beat and knocked on the door.' Elvis's daughter didn't want to open up. It was, after all, in the middle of the night. But that wasn't the reason. 'I shouted, "Open the door!" She said, "I won't open the door because I know something's happened. I'm not opening." But she did open the door and she came downstairs and everybody was crying and she started crying. It was a sad day that I'll never forget.'

So many others came to the same conclusion.

Joe Esposito has had all these years to reflect on what happened that night. It is still vivid, still with him as a sort of feeling of responsibility – that he himself was the closest and the first member of the Mafia to have experienced the trauma of Elvis's death.

He was amazed when it happened. 'We were about to go on tour to Portland, Maine. The uniforms were all being packed up. Ginger Alden called on the intercom from upstairs and asked Al Strada to go upstairs because Elvis had fainted. Al said he needed me.' They both realised it was more than just a faint.

> I could see that he had been reading a book on the toilet. He had fallen face down on the carpet. I turned him over and I could see that things weren't doing too well. I couldn't give him mouth to mouth because his mouth was clamped shut. I called an ambulance. I tried to massage his heart but I realised he had been dead for a while. Dr Nick jumped out of his car and we went to the hospital in the ambulance. I did not like to accept that he was gone.

Dr Nick himself told me about those first hours after Elvis's death. 'I was at the hospital and I went to Graceland. I had a red light on my car.' He said that he rushed into the bathroom.

> Looking back, I knew that he was dead. But one of the guys said he'd breathed. I had so much trouble with him – because I was told he had breathed. I wondered if [by any chance he could still be] alive. But he had rigor mortis. I was hanging on to the thought that perhaps he had breathed. I got into the ambulance and went with [Elvis's body] to the hospital.

Esposito was certain then (and still is) that there was no evidence of Elvis still breathing. 'No, when I turned him over, air came out of him. We got him in the ambulance and Dr Nick had turned up and jumped in. We gave Elvis oxygen. He went to the emergency room and then, half an hour later, Dr Nick told us he'd gone.' Esposito told Priscilla.

He wasn't surprised that Elvis had been reading while on the toilet. 'He liked to read all the time,' he said – and then gave me rather more information than I would have expected. 'He had two feet longer intestines than other people, so they would take longer and he got constipated.' But Elvis's complaint was more serious than mere constipation.

Marian Cocke, the personal nurse who was on hand for a damaged finger or a headache, had gone home for a few days and was not there when it happened. 'But he knew all he had to do was call and I would go,' she told me.

> Then, one morning, a few days before he died, he said he couldn't sleep and I went out there. I sat on the side of his bed. Elvis was a toucher and I reached out and put my hand on his arm and we hardly spoke. And finally, he said, 'I'm OK now.' And I left and he said, 'Miss Cocke, the doors of this house will always be open to you.' It was the last time I saw him.

When she heard he had died, she told me, 'it was like someone had pulled the rug from under me. You could tell he'd been dead for hours. I talked to Vernon.'

But this woman who had seen Elvis Presley so closely and so differently from the other females in his life was brought in at the moment of crisis. As she told me: 'It was a nightmare. He was going to Maine and he asked me to go and stay with him till it was time to leave. I left a seminar and I left early to terminate an employee. I then got the call – to go to the emergency room.' She saw him lying in that hospital room, blue. 'I asked them to stop working on him. He was obviously dead.'

Sam Thompson told me:

The day Elvis was leaving for the tour [in Maine] was the day Lisa Marie was leaving. On that day I was supposed to join Elvis in Maine. My role was to collect Lisa, deliver her, get back to Graceland and then go on tour after the first show at Portland.

But, as we know, he didn't go there. Instead, Thompson went to Graceland.

I went there to get Lisa. When I got there, they had already found Elvis's body, they'd already transported him to the hospital, pronounced him dead. I followed the ambulance from Graceland which contained the paramedics who worked on Elvis as well as Dr Nick. Dr Nick had come back to Graceland to talk to Vernon and tell him the bad news – because Vernon had a bad heart. When I walked in the back door, I actually saw Nick tell Vernon that Elvis had passed away. Vernon fell apart and began moaning. Chaos evolved after that. I was stunned. I actually thought the ambulance was for Vernon. Nick was crying. We were in the Jungle Room. I took him by the arm and was saying, 'Nick, what happened?' and he said he didn't know. Things began to kind of deteriorate around me.

He immediately set about, in his words, 'securing Graceland'.

I suddenly worried about Lisa Marie and I found her in the Dodger's [Elvis's grandmother's] room and she was phoning Linda. She hadn't believed Lisa Marie and when I took the phone Linda began to cry – because she realised something had happened. It's amazing that, under those circumstances, Lisa

Marie at nine years old had phoned Linda. I heard her say, 'No, Linda, he's dead.' Linda said at the other end: 'No, Gubernical, [her name for Lisa Marie] he can't be. You just made it up.'

At that point, Sam took over the phone and tried to explain the situation to his sister. 'I said, "No, Linda, he's dead." She began to cry. I told her it was real.'

Linda herself has, understandably enough, never forgotten her 'conversation' with Lisa Marie. 'She sounded excited,' Linda remembered. '"Linda," she said. "My daddy's dead." She told me everything. I threw the phone in the air. I picked it up again.' Linda now recalls: 'I'll always remember her for thinking to call me right away. She's always in my heart and I wish her well.'

Of course the thoughts came. Could she have done more?

We have to monitor our own actions. In the final analysis, it wasn't my responsibility to keep someone else alive for the rest of my life. I was a saint at the time – to be that attuned to someone else's needs I couldn't be again. Vernon thanked me for keeping him as long as I did.

George Klein to this day says he was not expecting Elvis to die when he did. 'He'd been in hospital a few times. He wasn't taking care of himself, not eating the right foods. We'd seen all that, but it was a shock when he died. He was expecting to go on tour.' He says he wasn't even worried about the expanding Presley body. 'No – because he lost weight for the comeback special and then the Hawaii special. He could lose weight. I didn't know he had a colon and intestinal problem.'

The Graceland police director Buddy Chapman said he heard about Elvis's death from Dr Nick.

When he told us, there were a lot of things I had to do. I had to call Priscilla, the 'Colonel'. Dr Nick said, 'Hang on until I get back to Graceland to tell Vernon, the grandmother' and then I told the doctor to tell the press. We sat around talking and I said, 'We have to get this organised. Do it right for Elvis. It's his last show on earth.' I asked Vernon what he wanted to do and Vernon went for a white limousine [and] an open-casket job – to let the fans say goodbye.

There was, in fact, a whole fleet of limousines. 'We had to go out of the state to get them,' said Joe Esposito. 'There weren't that many in Memphis at the time.'

It was a 'miserable night', Chapman remembered – the weather perfectly mirroring the atmosphere at Graceland. 'There was cold rain.' He said that he first heard the news when he and the local fire chief were called out of a meeting. Bad news travels fast. Very bad news gathers with the speed of a hurricane. By the time Chapman reached the mansion, a crowd had already started gathering.

I knew there would be problems. I went down there and I started 'combing the crowd', splitting up the people, which makes crowds angry. But people did not get mad, maybe because of the special nature of Elvis. [There was] a press conference. Late night, I went out to the gates. The media had tents. I looked through the gate and the crowds were pressing again the gates. There was a young lady I recognised. It was [the assassinated

President's daughter] Caroline Kennedy, who was a reporter for *Rolling Stone*. She couldn't get in.

One of those who also tried to get in was Marian Cocke. She didn't find it easy. 'I stayed at Graceland and the crowds were huge. The police pulled me over, but they [heard] I was expected. [Elvis's aunt] Delta told me they'd just brought him home. Priscilla embraced me. She said Elvis cared about me and I told her he loved her.'

The crowds said it all. They all loved Elvis.

FINALE

The outpouring of sadness was mirrored throughout the world. Ordinary people found they were unable to contain their emotions. Senior Hollywood and music figures admitted they had burst into tears. Business executives stopped meetings in the middle of discussing minor matters like the price of shares or the inevitability of bankruptcy. Teachers allowed children to go home because they couldn't summon the energy to chalk the names of the presidents of the United States or the kings of England on their blackboards.

The Presley family were determined that Elvis should be buried at Graceland. Everything about it pointed to it being the ideal site and if Presley had thought that far ahead – and there was no evidence to show that he had – it was where he himself would have wanted to lie for eternity. At first there were problems. The idea was not viewed kindly by the Memphis municipality. Eventually – and something for which millions of fans have since been eternally grateful – the idea was approved. 'Vernon went to see the mayor of the city and, because it was Elvis, they allowed him to do it,' said Joe Esposito.

It would have been difficult to say no to Elvis Presley, even in death. But until the plot in the mansion gardens could be readied, the body was taken to a mausoleum at Forest Hill, where his mother was buried – after a funeral service to which millions came to pay their respects from far and near. As Buddy Chapman told me: 'The crowds expanded on both sides of the highway to the cemetery – that's a couple of miles.' Many people would have said that their affection for Elvis could be measured in miles, too – like the Blackwood Brothers who, with J. D. Sumner and the Imperials, sang at the funeral. Joe Esposito told me he believed there were 70,000 people lining the route taken by the white limousines. 'Fans were out there, fainting in the hot, humid atmosphere.'

Elvis's cousin Charlene Presley was there. 'I have never experienced anything like it,' she told me.

And I grew up in Memphis and had been by many times, but I had never seen so many people in front of Graceland. I was in total shock. I thought Vernon was so kind to allow so many people to view the body. But it was a typical Southern funeral. The trees were what fascinated me. They were full of people climbing them to see the funeral. I was by one tree and a lady said, 'You can't have my limb [the branch of the tree].' I said, 'I don't want your limb.' I asked how she had got up into the tree. She said she had climbed up there yesterday – into the branch of the tree. 'I brought,' she said, 'a blanket and a pillow and a stack of food.' She said, 'I'm staying there till they take him to the cemetery.' All the trees up to the stone wall were full of people.

Elvis was made to look good on this last engagement. The Lanskys were asked to make him the new suit in which he could be buried. The ever ebullient 'Mr B' took to the task with all the enthusiasm and artistry he had used for so many years before. 'It didn't come cheap,' he told me. 'But I knew his measurements. I knew his size. I'm like a broken drum.' It was just another job, or, as he put it, using his favourite Yiddish expression for the only time talking about that typical Southern funeral, 'noch a mol'.

The idea was that Elvis would rest peacefully, if temporarily, in the mausoleum into which his coffin was carried – a sort of Graceland for the dead.

So, plainly, the intention was to treat the body of the man who had been *the* superstar of his age with all the respect his followers and family expected. But then there was a message from the police that seemed ready to shatter all the plans that had been made. Buddy Chapman told me the story: 'It was a bizarre incident. We got information from the organised crime unit. There was a plan to steal Elvis's body. A power company truck with a cable and winch were planning to unreel the cable, hook it on to the truck and drag it out of the mausoleum.'

To say that was a shock was one thing, to explain it another. How do you claim a ransom for a dead body that could never be hidden? Much more difficult would have been to get it out of the building. As Chapman said: 'I had confirmed that Elvis was dead. I saw his body and it was huge and very heavy. We arrested them before they could do it. They were small-time crooks. They were locked up but not for a big charge. They hadn't actually done much.' But it convinced the municipality that Elvis's body had to be kept in a safe place and there was nowhere safer than Graceland.

The death of Elvis had a tremendous effect on the Memphis

Mafia, people who seemingly – unless they did anything to upset their master – had jobs for life and were now left to join the ranks of the unemployed. Perhaps the most successful was Sam Thompson, the policeman who became a bodyguard. With no Presley job, he went to law school and, after he graduated, the 'Colonel' gave him 'a letter of recommendation' to the state bar. He became a fully fledged lawyer.

Joe Esposito recalled that a few weeks after the death, 'a lot of guys got a few weeks' pay. Vernon asked me to inventory all of the stuff in his houses, to go to the studio in Hollywood. So that's what I did for nine months. It was tough. After that, Vernon let me go.'

The West cousins, who in any case were out of Graceland, became stuntmen in films. Jerry Schilling became a road manager for Billy Joel. Joe Esposito did similar work for other stars, using his invaluable experience with Elvis.

Elvis's friend Larry Geller says: 'One of the great ironies is that he once said, "I wonder if I will be remembered" and he is the most loved celeb in the world. He has sold more records than any other artist. The Elvis Presley stamp is the largest selling stamp ever.'

He added:

Elvis left us more than thirty years ago and I'm still working for Elvis, so to speak. Elvis lived the American dream. He rose from desperate poverty to unprecedented fame and fortune and also embodied the American spirit. Elvis was optimistic, he was brash, he was pioneering. And just like America he embraced everyone. It could be a president, a gardener, a janitor. He treated them all the same. The force of his personality continues as a living, vibrant presence. He is more than a historical presence. He is an icon.

The people who were around Elvis in his earlier lives couldn't forget him. Like Azalia Smith Moore who gave me so many graphic accounts of the early days in Tupelo and thinks of him still. Well, of course she does. 'I met Vernon – about two years before his death – at Memphis airport and we talked about their lives. I have a profound regret that I didn't see Elvis in later years. I gather he was a virtual prisoner.' This was another example of how people who really did know Elvis came to different conclusions about him. A prisoner? Of his fans? Of the Memphis Mafia? Or of that mysterious man, the so-called 'Colonel', who was to die in 1997, twenty years after Elvis? Who really knows?

Azalia is convinced her old school chum came back to religion in a big way. 'He gravitated away from the Assembly of God church. But two weeks prior to his death, he reclaimed his faith when he met up with an Assembly of God preacher.'

Elvis's faith in motorcycles was perhaps less complicated. Fred Frederick, the ex-Lauderdale Courts resident who became a cop and then an investment banker, as we have seen, went to Graceland soon after the death to work out a list of how much equipment was there – his cars, his beloved Harley-Davidsons. There were his cars – a lot more than five – to look after. And also to find guardians for Elvis's horses.

All these thoughts are now filed in their minds under 'M' for 'Memories'. They have all told their stories and many of them have come to different conclusions. But like the pieces in a giant jigsaw puzzle, one thing is sure. They all fit.

Ray Walker put it perfectly. 'Elvis is Elvis. I've never felt him gone. He has an everlasting existence in the memory of anyone who met him.'

Joe Esposito certainly thinks so. He had never believed that Elvis would die when he did.

> I loved that man. I believed that one of these days, he would get out of bed and say, 'What am I doing to myself?' Once he had made up his mind to do something, he usually would do it. Previously there were occasions when he would take off a month or so and he would be fine.

Jimmy Angel, the singer who once modelled himself on Elvis, talked about his contribution to rock'n'roll which, he says, before Elvis

> didn't have a face. The most important thing that Elvis did was that he knocked down the door for all those black cats who couldn't walk across the street into a white station and say, 'Play my music.' Elvis could. So could Pat Boone. So could Ricky Nelson. They are the reason you got all those cats, anyone who's black doing music, every time they hear the name Elvis Presley should salute and say, 'Thanks', for that's the reason they are bopping.

And then there was Sonny West:

'I was devastated. I had done an interview that morning for the *Chicago Tribune*.' They talked about Elvis and his health. 'I told them I was scared it was going to happen. We didn't know that Elvis was already dead.' And when it did happen

... 'The sun went out for me. I said to God, "Why didn't you stop this?"'

Only the fans could stop the power of Elvis Presley. And they refused. How else would that one name 'Elvis' still mean so much, so long afterwards?

ACKNOWLEDGEMENTS

Every biography is by way of a collaborative endeavour, particularly one depending exclusively on original research. This is essentially an assembly of memories. So my thanks essentially are to those who shared those reminiscences with me – and many of them with the listeners to my BBC radio series, *The Elvis Trail*, although very few of the events recalled here actually made it into shows that were essentially opportunities to play Presley's music. So most of the material here is published for the first time.

That it all came together owes a great deal to two people – my producer Neil Rosser and the best researcher in the business, Barbra Paskin. She made the interviews I conducted all over the United States so much smoother. But it was the interviewees who make up this unique story. Names most people would not know, but who have proved themselves essential to this tale: Jimmy Angel, James Ausborn, Sam Bell, Jack Berelson, Ken Black, Jimmy Blackwood, Gene Bradbury, Buddy Chapman, 'Cowboy' Jack Clement, Marion Cocke, Susie Dent, Linda Eliff, Joe Esposito, Buzzy Forbess, Fred Frederick, Mike Freeman, Jimmy Gault, Larry Geller, Shirley Gilentine, Dick

Guyton, Bill Halton, Guy Thomas Harris, Lois Hathaway, Shirley Hathaway, Michael Hoey, Steve Holland, Kevin Kern, Stan Kesler, George Klein, Howard Hite, Bill Kynard, Linda Kynard, the late Bernard Lansky, Hal Lansky, Suzanna Leigh, Susan Lorenz, the late Walter Matthau, Judy Nelon, Dr George Nichopoulos ('Dr Nick'), Neil Niker, Robert Norris, Charlene Presley, Sybil Presley, Julian Riley, Ronnie McDowell, Don Robertson, Irene Robertson, Nancy Rooks, John Rumbole, the late Walter Scharf, Blanche Gordon Scott, Vicky Sessler, T. G. Sheppard, Stuart Small, Azalia Smith Moore, Matt Ross-Spang, Linda Thompson, Sam Thompson, Roy Turner, Jimmy Velvet, Anne Ellington Wagner, Brian Wagner, Ray Walker, Charlie Watts, Billy Welch, Sonny West, Don Winders, Becky Yancey and Celeste Yarnall.

The book also owes a great deal to my publisher, Jeremy Robson, whose guidance, help and, above all, patience, is so appreciated.

Finally, and sadly, this is the last time I shall be able to thank my wife, Sara, for her fortitude while one of my books was being prepared. Sarala you will always be missed and loved.

Michael Freedland
Bournemouth, 2013

INDEX

Also available from The Robson Press

WALK LIKE A MAN
Coming of Age with the Music of Bruce Springsteen

ROBERT J. WIERSEMA

Walk Like a Man is liner notes for a mix-tape, a frank and
funny blend of biography, music appreciation and memoir.
Bestselling novelist Robert J. Wiersema grew up with
Springsteen's songs, from his own working-class youth,
through dreams of escape, falling in love and becoming a
father. His book tells the story of a boy becoming a man
(despite getting a little lost along the way), and of the man
and the music that have accompanied him on his journey.

208pp paperback, £12.99
Available from all good bookshops or order from
www.therobsonpress.com

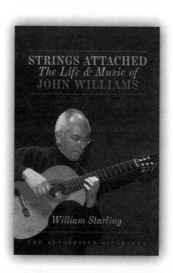

Also available from The Robson Press

MICK
The Wild Life and Mad Genius of Jagger

CHRISTOPHER ANDERSEN

Based on interviews with friends, family members, fellow music
legends and industry insiders – as well as wives and legions
of lovers – *Mick* sheds new light on a man whose very name
defines an era. With never-before-revealed accounts of his often
turbulent relationships – from his bandmates, groupies and
rabid fans to such intimates as Andy Warhol, John Lennon,
Jackie Onassis and Bill Clinton – this book is as explosive and
riveting as its subject. The definitive biography of a living legend.

384pp hardback, £25
Available from all good bookshops or order from
www.therobsonpress.com